Using Human Learning Strategies in the Classroom

George R. Taylor

A SCARECROWEDUCATION BOOK

The Scarecrow Press, Inc.
Lanham, Maryland, and London
2002

A SCARECROWEDUCATION BOOK

Published in the United States of America
by Scarecrow Press, Inc.
A Member of the Rowman & Littlefield Publishing Group
4720 Boston Way, Lanham, Maryland 20706
www.scarecroweducation.com

4 Pleydell Gardens, Folkestone
Kent CT20 2DN, England

British Library Cataloguing in Publication Information Available

Library of Congress Cataloging-in-Publication Data

Taylor, George R.
    Using human learning strategies in the classroom / George R. Taylor.
        p.   cm.
    Includes bibliographical references and index.
    ISBN 0-8108-4210-6 (pbk.: alk. paper)
    1. Learning.   2. Educational psychology.   I. Title.
  LB1060 .T29   2002
  370.15'23—dc21   2001049503

♾ ™ The paper used in this publication meets the minimum requirements
of American National Standard for Information Sciences—Permanence of
Paper for Printed Library Materials, ANSI/NISO Z39.48-1992.
Manufactured in the United States of America.

Contents

Preface

This textbook provides a functional and realistic approach to making practical application of human learning to the classroom. Additionally, it is for classroom teachers who have limited background and experience in psychology. Frequently, classroom teachers may be aware of the many theories of learning, but are unable to transpose these theories to practical classroom application. This textbook is designed to accomplish such a purpose.

It contains seventeen chapters. Chapter 1 covers the psychology of human learning; chapter 2 overviews the impact of behaviorism on learning theories; chapter 3 summarizes the work of Ivan P. Pavlov; chapter 4 highlights the contributions of Burrhus F. Skinner to the field of human learning; the impact of Bandura's social learning theories are reported in chapters 5 and 6; chapter 7 provides strategies for teaching direct instruction strategies; the field of cognitive psychology is discussed in chapter 8; chapter 9 covers the major cognitive theories of learning; chapter 10 contains information on theory of multiple intelligences; chapter 11 lists the major components of concept learning; chapters 12, 13, and 14 discuss some commonly used cognitive strategies for promoting learning; chapter 15 summarizes the most recent research on brain-based learning; chapter 16 discusses strategies for improving memory; and chapter 17 provides some concluding remarks.

Acknowledgments

Many individuals are responsible for the final version of this textbook. First, I wish to acknowledge the contributions of students in my learning theory classes who constantly reminded me to associate principles of learning with practical classroom applications.

I also wish to thank my colleagues who reviewed chapters. Sincere gratitude is extended to Dr. Thomas Terrell. The staff at Scarecrow Education was instrumental in bringing this textbook to its conclusion. The professionalism shown was beyond the call of duty.

It would be a remiss if I did not thank Emma Patterson-Crosby and Karen Chewning for their secretarial competencies and assistance in typing, retyping, and formatting the manuscript until the final draft was accepted.

CHAPTER 1

The Psychology of Human Learning

Even though learning has been defined in many ways, there are similarities in these definitions, with most of them indicating changes in behavior that result from experience. Two common definitions of learning are a potential change in behavior; and the acquisition of information, or psychological, learning is an invisible, internal neurological process. Generally, changes in behavior as a result of learning usually constitute learning, providing that these changes are not the result of drugs, physical fatigue, biological or physical growth, or a physical injury. Psychologically speaking, learning may be defined as a relatively permanent change in potential for behavior that results from experience, but changes are not the result of fatigue, maturation, drugs, disease, or physical injury (Lefrançois, 2000).

With these and many other considerations (Ormrod, 1999), we can conclude that learning is a change in performance through conditions of activity, practice, and experience. This is an operational definition that is derived in part from scientific investigations. In the classroom, the activities and experiences that lead to change in performance involve telling and listening, judging, reading, reciting, observation of demonstrations, experimenting, pupils interacting, and individual learning quests and activities. It is hoped that both sporadic practice and formal drill in reading, writing, computing, and speaking will carry over to performance in daily life. Living and working with others, and supplementing the feedback that comes from reflecting and discussing while engulfed in classroom learning will, I hope, lead to continued learning beyond the school years.

Learning begins with the organism. It is the means through which we acquire not only skills and knowledge, but values, attitudes, and emotional reactions as well. Our learning may be conditioned by our sensory acuity. If our vision or hearing is impaired because of a bad cold, our learning may be influenced. Hearing may also be influenced by the physiology of one's emotions. There can be no doubt that pupils' learning abilities are affected by the speed with which nerve messages move and are sorted and combined and by the degree of permanence of the impression they make. Whether this physical base is hereditary, congenital, or developmental in origin, it influences the natural speed of learning. Learning depends on the inclination and ability to receive and respond to stimulation.

PHYSICAL ASPECTS OF LEARNING

There are physical aspects of learning that cannot be ignored by the teacher, such as vision and hearing. Biochemical factors affect the comfort and satisfaction that an individual derives from learning. Such influences bear heavily on personality, orientation, and on the teaching–learning processes (Taylor, 1999). Learning includes not only the acquisition of subject matter, but also that of habits, attitudes, perceptions, preferences, interests, social adjustments, skills of many types, and ideals. Even such seemingly simple things as learning to spell and add involve varied forms of learning.

It is quite likely that researchers are coming closer to knowing what chemical, electrical, biological, and neurological changes occur during the learning process (Goleman, 1995; LeDoux, 1996). I do not know so much about those changes as is desirable, but much is known about the conditions under which learning takes place most effectively. Some conditions affecting learning and the ways in which they may be improved are, at least in part, subject to the control of teachers, while other conditions, such as cultural deprivation and physical and physiological handicaps, are beyond teachers' control. Even so, these factors are part of the psychological field with which teachers must be concerned.

Learning also involves the modification of perception and behavior. Not all behavior change is learning. A child may eat more because his/her stomach has enlarged and because his/her energy needs have increased, but the changed behavior is not learning. He/she may, however, learn to eat more because of parental example or because of psychological needs that appear to be satisfied through food. The loss of a hand modifies behavior, but the loss itself is not learning. The person may, however, learn to compensate for the loss of his/her hand by learning new skills. Modification does not necessarily result in improved learning.

The permanent effects of learning may not be immediately apparent. Sometimes, the results of learning are latent due to the capacity or condition of the individual performing the behavior.

EARLY CONTRIBUTORS TO LEARNING THEORIES

Experimentations with learning theories can be traced to William James and Edward Bradford Tichener. They attempted to explain behavior based on instinct and emotions. These researchers instructed individuals to examine their own feelings and motives to discover information relevant to their learning and behavior. Results of their research could not be scientifically verified, and therefore it received negative feedback.

Wilhelm Wundt is considered by many psychologists to be the father of psychology. He established the first psychological laboratory in Leipzig, Germany, in 1879. Wundt and his associates experimented with mental attributes, such as consciousness, sensations, feelings, imagining, and perceiving. They attempted to use the scientific method to study these mental attributes (Lefrançois, 2000).

These early contributors to the field of psychology laid the groundwork for our present understanding of learning theories by attempting to systematically observe and experiment with human behavior. Early experimentation was mainly based on a method called introspection. William James is frequently called the father of psychology because of his work in introspection. Individuals are simply asked to look inside their mind and describe what they are thinking. It would take the works of Ivan P. Pavlov and Edward L. Thorndike to develop a more objective approach to the study of learning, one that was based on observable behaviors rather than on having an individual describe mental events. The contributions of Pavlov will be discussed in greater detail in chapter 3. Thorndike's contributions to learning theory have had a significant impact on learning and are reviewed in chapter 2.

THEORY DEFINED

In attempting to explain phenomena, scientists constructed hypotheses to test theories. A hypothesis attempts to explain a limited set of facts, whereas a theory attempts to involve a broad range of facts. To be useful, a hypothesis must be testable. It must lead to predictions that may be validated as true or false. A single experiment may disprove but rarely disclaim a hypothesis. Several disapproved hypotheses are needed to disclaim a theory. A new theory with few hypotheses or facts to support it is soon abandoned.

THEORIES OF LEARNING

Ormrod believes that theories of learning provide explanations about the process involved in learning (Ormrod, 1999). They permit investigators to summarize research findings from several research studies and extrapolate and classify them according to principles of learning. Theories provide incentive for conducting new research. They suggest possible approaches that may be employed to conduct the study, as well as interpret research findings in light of the theoretical framework. Additionally, theories can assist us in understanding how humans learn, which we must agree that no one learning theory can completely cover all aspects of human learning and behavior. Educators should draw from various theories and formulate their own theories relevant to the learning process.

CLASSIFICATION OF LEARNING THEORIES

The first systematic study of learning according to Lefrançois is behaviorism (Lefrançois, 2000). Behavioristic theories of Pavlov, John B. Watson, and Thorndike will be addressed in greater detail later in the text.

Cognitivism theories include those of Robert Rescorla, Allen Wagner, Wilson, Donald Hebb, Edward C. Tolman, Kurt Koffka, and Wolfgang Köhler. The theoretical framework of these theories has led to evolutionary psychology, sociology, stimuli, responses, reinforcement, and mediation behavioral orientations. Unlike a behaviorist psychologist, a cognitive psychologist places values on perception, decision making, processing, and understanding information. Gestalt psychology was one of the first cognitive theories to indicate the importance of the organizational process in perception, learning, and problem solving (Ormrod, 1999). The work of Jean Piaget concerning developmental and information processing will be expanded in chapter 9.

Behaviorism and cognitivism approaches differ in that behaviorism's focus on external behavior can be shaped and modified (the blank state concept), and learning principles may be applied to all species. Cognitivism emphasizes the mental process and maintains that global learning principles cannot be applied to all species. It maintains that many types of learning are reserved for the human species only. Both approaches support the premise that the study of learning should be studied objectively and based on scientific research.

SCIENTIFIC THEORY

A scientific theory is a set of related principles and laws and explains a broad spectrum of learning behaviors. Hergenhahn and Olson add additional clarity to scientific theories by stating that a theory has a formal aspect, which includes the words and symbols the theory contains, as well as an empirical aspect, which consists of the physical events that the theory is attempting to explain (Hergenhahn and Olson, 1997).

Regardless of the complexity of theories, they all begin and end with observations. To support assumptions based on observations, hypotheses may be formulated to test the validity of the observations. If hypotheses are supported, they aid in strengthening the theory; thus, generalizations may be made concerning the theory. If generalizations are strong, they may help with forming principles and laws. Theories provide starting points for summarizing, conducting, and making sense of research findings, as well as assisting us in designing learning environments that facilitate human learning.

Principles of learning identify specific factors that consistently influence learning and describe the particular effects of these factors. Principles are most useful when they can be applied to a wide variety of situations. When a principle is observed countless times, and results are repeated, principles may eventually become laws (Ormrod, 1999).

In support of this view, Lefrançois states that laws are statements whose validity and accuracy have been well established (Lefrançois, 2000). They are conclusions that are based on what appears to be undeniable observations and irrefutable logic. Unlike principles, laws are not ordinarily open to exceptions and doubt.

CHARACTERISTICS OF SCIENTIFIC THEORY

Hergenhahn and Olson summarize characteristics of scientific theory as follows:

1. A theory synthesizes a number of observations.
2. A good theory must generate hypotheses that can be empirically verified. If such hypotheses are confirmed, the theory gains strength; if not, the theory is weakened and must be revised or abandoned.
3. A good theory is heuristic, that is, it generates new research.
4. A theory is a tool and as such cannot be right or wrong; it is either useful or not useful.
5. Theories are chosen in accordance with the law of parsimony of two equally effective theories, with the simpler of the two being chosen.
6. Theories contain abstractions, such as numbers of words, which constitute the formal aspect of a theory.
7. The formal aspect of a theory must be correlated with observable events, which constitutes the empirical aspect of a theory.
8. All theories are attempts to explain empirical events and they must, therefore, start and end with empirical observations (Hergenhahn and Olson, 1997).

THE SCIENTIFIC METHOD

The scientific method is used to solve problems. According to Leedy, there are six steps to this method:

1. Definition of the problem
2. Statement of the hypothesis
3. Design the experiment survey
4. Deductive reasoning
5. Collection and analysis of data
6. Confirmation or rejection of the hypothesis (Leedy, 1997).

The scientific method is objective, reliable, and replicable. It considers only those results that have been replicated by others in a basic format and under similar conditions. It is an objective way for developing and testing a learning experiment.

LEARNING EXPERIMENT

The learning experiment begins with observations. Observations provide the initial approach to begin scientific inquiry in both quantitative and qualitative research methods. Observations may be supported by reviewing the professional literature. Review of the literature in qualitative research is usually conducted after the study; the reverse is usually true for quantitative research.

REVIEW OF THE LITERATURE

Reviewing the literature is important when learning experiments using quantitative and qualitative research methods. The use of the review of literature has different purposes when using the two methods. In quantitative research, the review is conducted after the study has been completed. The researcher using the qualitative method may find minimal use of the review since he/she will be constructing a theory that may not have current research on the topic. The quantitative researcher may use the review liberally, since he/she will be testing theory based on current models and research findings. In quantitative research, the review of literature will enable the researcher to use it inductively, so that the review will not have a significant impact on the question being posed.

In quantitative research, the review of literature is used deductively, where the researcher is drawing from general principles and theories in the field while developing and conducting his/her research.

IDENTIFICATION, SELECTION, AND THE STATEMENT OF THE PROBLEM

The identification, selection, and statement of the problem are frequently minimized by the research in both quantitative and qualitative research. These areas must be carefully considered and weighed against such factors as:

1. Values and needs of the study
2. Prospects of making a contribution to the field
3. Training and experience of the researcher

4. Availability of human and physical resources to conduct the study
5. Interest and motivation in the study
6. Use of expert advice in identifying and selecting the problem
7. The intended audience for the study

A systematic and detailed investigation of these factors will assist the researcher in determining the feasibility of pursuing the problem in greater depth or to change and modify procedures.

DEVELOPMENT OF TESTABLE HYPOTHESES AND RESEARCH QUESTIONS

Once the research has been selected and the problem formulated, the next step is to develop testable research questions or hypotheses to scientifically guide the study. In quantitative research, questions or hypotheses are developed to test theory, where as in qualitative research they are designed to test theory. Researchers may employ a variety of techniques in developing research questions or hypotheses for the two paradigms. In quantitative methods, various types of hypotheses may be used. The null and alternative hypotheses are frequently used. In qualitative methods, research questions are most frequently used.

VALIDATING AND ESTABLISHING THE RELIABILITY OF INSTRUMENTS

The use of validated instruments is required and necessary in conducting quantitative research, but is not a prerequisite for conducting qualitative research. In conducting quantitative research, many researchers choose standardized instruments in which validity and reliability have already been established. When a researcher constructs his/her own instrument, validity and reliability will need to be established. Creswell provides an excellent approach to validating and establishing reliability for instruments (Creswell, 1994).

EXPERIMENTAL CONDITIONS

An essential part of quantitative research is the experimental condition, sometimes referred to as the intervention or treatment. This aspect closely follows the scientific method. Variables are systematically identified and controlled. Subjects are randomly selected and matched in the experimental and control groups and performances of the two groups are compared at the end of the experiment. In qualitative research, experimental conditions are not employed since they are not required. By deleting the experimental conditions, researchers may readily use the research design to conduct qualitative research.

STATISTICAL ANALYSIS

Various statistical tools to test data quantitatively may be explored. Both parametric and nonparametric statistics may be used to test hypotheses. Various methods and procedures for testing different types of experimental designs may be selected based on sampling, instruments, and experimental conditions. Statistical analysis is limited in qualitative research. Some descriptive statistics may be used, such as graphs, charts, percentages, and measures of control tendency. Descriptive analysis is the most frequently used technique.

DESCRIPTIVE ANALYSIS

Descriptive analysis may be used in both designs, such as graphs, mean scores, percentiles, and correlations. Generally, researchers categorize and develop themes when using qualitative methods. These themes provide narrative descriptions of the behaviors. The process can be completely voided of numerical data. Numerical data may add to the understanding and the interpretation of the research questions or hypothesis under study. Quantitative research has more structure and narrative interpretations are limited. Observations and interviews are used in both designs. In quantitative research, descriptive and inferential statistics are used to analyze data. In qualitative research, analysis is continuous and infrequently employs the use of statistics.

CONSTRUCTING THEORY

Qualitative research attempts to construct theory using observational and interviewing techniques to define human behavior. Experiences are documented, identified, and described. Patterns and categories are developed in an attempt to provide theoretical explanations to human behavior. Theory is used inductively and is developed at the end of the study. Data are collected and analyzed before the theory is developed.

TESTING THEORY

Quantitative research attempts to test theory deductively. The theory provides the framework for conducting the study and is usually placed before the experimental conditions. In essence, the theory guides the type of research conducted. The major emphasis is to test or verify a theory. Instruments are developed or selected, and data are analyzed to test the hypotheses. Hypotheses accept or reject the variables in the study.

FINDINGS/RESULTS

Data are analyzed in both quantitative and qualitative research. In quantitative research, statistics are employed to determine to what degree the hypotheses have been accepted or rejected. Some degree of objectivity is inherited in the process. Findings in qualitative research are usually reported in narrative form. Data must be coded and classified and categories formed in order to appropriately analyze data. Findings are subjective and are frequently not considered obsolete.

TRIANGULATION

Today, attempts are underway to combine the two paradigms in the collection and analysis of data. The process is referred to as triangulation. The trend is to objectify techniques by combining the two approaches in research activities. Computer programs have been developed to assist in the interpretation of the massive amount of data generated through the qualitative method. Computer programs can assist greatly in using the two paradigms in evaluating research. Using maps is another technique that may be employed by making diagrams of the relationships among data through the use of computerized hypertext techniques. Descriptive types of statistics may be employed to assist in analyzing data from the two methods. Data sources such as interviews and demographic information may yield qualitative data, which may be analyzed through descriptive statistics. These data can enhance quantitative data reported by the researcher.

The learning experiment outline can assist the researcher in either qualitative or quantitative research. The research design provides a mechanism by which both qualitative and quantitative approaches can be used when employing the scientific method. In both approaches, the scientific method begins with observations and proceeds to the analysis and reporting of results. Ethical issues must be considered in conducting any type of research.

ETHICAL ISSUES IN CONDUCTING RESEARCH

Historically, issues related to subjects have constituted the greatest concern to society in the violation of human rights during the early part of the twentieth century. Specific guidelines have been developed for researchers to follow under the following areas:

1. Consent
2. Harm
3. Privacy
4. Deception

Consent

Subjects must be given a choice to determine whether or not they wish to participate in the study. They must be both mentally and physically able to make the choice or someone must be designated to act on their behalf. Assessment should also be made of the legal qualifications of the subjects. Subjects under the age of eighteen years old should not be permitted to participate in the study unless a parent or guardian gives written permission (Kimmel, 1996).

Guidelines

1. Type of intervention or treatment to be conducted. Specific procedures for conducting the research should be clearly articulated, and the

length of time as well as human and physical resources needed to conduct the research should be addressed.

2. Impact on the normal activities of the subjects. The researcher should address to what extent the research will affect the normal activities of the subjects. There should be strategies to restore subjects to the normal routines of the inclusion of the research.

3. Informed consent. It is incumbent upon the researcher to inform the subjects what is expected of them and what they will be expected to do. This is usually accomplished by a consent form.

4. Right of withdrawal. Subjects should be told and given the right to withdraw from the research at any time. A statement should be developed outlining the procedure.

Harm

Subjects participating in the research should be assured that no harm will come to them as a result of their participation. Harm covers physical and psychological factors, which may adversely affect the functioning or the well-being of the subjects. The extent and possible harm that subjects may experience should be clearly articulated in the questionnaire or survey completed by the subjects. Treatment should not leave the subjects more psychologically depressed or physically incapacitated than they were before the treatment began (Robinson, 1992).

Guidelines

1. Safeguarding subjects from harm. The researcher should assure the subjects that no physical or psychological harm will come to them as a result of participating in the research. The researcher should inform subjects concerning any possible risks associated with the research.

2. High-risk subjects. Researchers should consider the characteristics of the subjects involved in the experiment such as age and physical or mental disabilities. These subjects may be unable to make realistic decisions on their own, thus placing them "in harm's way" for certain types of experiments.

3. Assurance to subjects. It is incumbent upon the researcher that subjects are returned to their original physical and psychological conditions when they are no longer needed in the experiment.

4. Results of other experiments. The researcher should provide subjects

with how other studies safeguarded subjects or how the lack of safe-guards brought harm to subjects, and relate how his/her study will avoid some of the pitfalls.

Privacy

Our privacy in this country is considered to be a valued right as reflected in local, state, and federal mandates. Subjects participating in the research should be guaranteed the right that sensitive data collected through the research process will be made confidential. Researchers should assure subjects that sensitive data will be held in the strictest confidence in order to protect their anonymity (Kurtines, 1992).

Guidelines

1. Selection of the site. The rationale for choosing the site should be outlined and clearly articulated. The researcher should consider the setting in which the study is to be conducted. Settings in public places are not generally considered conducive for assuring privacy. Other factors that should be considered are:
   - The reputation and competencies of the staff
   - Safeguarding information
   - Protecting information from individuals not involved in the research
2. Making results of the research available. Subjects should have an opportunity to review a draft copy of the report in order to determine invasion of privacy. This is especially true when some of the data may be damaging to the institution or subject. Feedback should be incorporated into the final report providing that the hypotheses or findings are not altered.
3. Feedback. The researcher should assure subjects that he/she will provide an opportunity for them to obtain accurate information relevant to the research and that he/she will respond to all participants' concerns.
4. Confidentiality. Confidentiality should be maintained at all times. The proposal should indicate that names will not be used or revealed with the data.

Deception

Misleading subjects and under- or overrepresenting facts are forms of deception. There should be no hidden agenda relevant to the treatment process. Any deception that is an integral part of the research must be explained to the subjects as soon as feasible (Jensen, 1992).

Guidelines

1. Limitations. Factors such as finances, time, resources, and data sources should not be a standard for using deception.
2. Consent. Subjects should be given an accurate description of what tasks they will be required to perform.
3. Justification. Any deception employed should be clearly justified by the researcher and clearly explained to the subjects at an appropriate time.

The researcher should indicate what the subjects will gain from the research in the areas of improved treatment, innovative methods, in-service training needs, and the need for additional physical or human resources (Marshall and Rossman, 1989; Bogdan and Biklen, 1992).

It should be incumbent upon the researcher to safeguard all subjects involved in experiments. Certain ethical concerns should be considered. These considerations may involve submitting a research proposal to an ethics committee for approval. In some cases, an oral presentation may be required.

SUMMARY

The many branches of psychology all have one basic principle: the study of human behavior. Objective measures are employed in studying human behavior. Learning theories have greatly aided researchers in study learning by organizing and systematizing what is known about human learning. These theories provide information needed for predicting and controlling human behavior. Learning experiments provide researchers with an outlet for testing theories and determining to what degree hypotheses are supported. Factors such as defining the problem, statement of hypothesis, instrument construction, testing or developing theory, data analysis, and reporting the findings must all be clearly articulated in the design. Learning experiments should follow the scientific method by starting with observations and proceeding to the analysis and reporting of results. The issues of using humans and animals in research should be conducted with published guidelines as articulated earlier in the chapter.

The two major divisions of learning theories are behaviorism and cognitivism. Behaviorism is an approach that deals with observable behaviors, whereas cognitivism is concerned with mental traits such as perception, information processing, concept formation, and understanding. Each division provides information into how individuals learn and how educators can modify the learning environment so that all individuals can reach their optimum level of functioning (Epstein, 1991; Reynolds, Sinatra, and Jetton, 1996; Gilovich, 1991).

This textbook is designed to serve as a blueprint for educators to use when instructing individuals. Although various approaches to learning are summarized, I emphasize that no one theory can cover completely the gamut of human learning and behavior. Educators must draw from the various theories those attributes that they consider important for improving the learning process.

BIBLIOGRAPHY

Bogdan, R. C., and S. K. Biklen. 1992. *Qualitative Research for Education: An Introduction to Theory and Methods*. Boston: Allyn and Bacon.

Creswell, J. W. 1994. *Research Design: Qualitative and Quantitative Approaches*. Thousand Oaks, Calif.: Sage.

Epstein, R. 1991. "Skinner, Creativity, and the Problem of Spontaneous Behavior." *Psychological Science* 2:362–370.

Gilovich, T. 1991. *How I Know What Isn't So: The Fallibility of Human Reason in Everyday Life*. New York: The Free Press.

Goleman, D. 1995. *Emotional Intelligence*. New York: Bantam.

Hergenhahn, B. R., and M. H. Olson. 1997. *An Introduction to Theories of Learning*. 5th ed. Upper Saddle River, N.J.: Prentice Hall.

Jensen, R. E. 1992. *Standards and Ethics in Clinical Psychology*. Lanham, Md.: University Press of America.

Kimmel, A. J. 1996. *Ethical Issues in Behavioral Research*. Cambridge, Mass.: Blackwell.

Kurtines, M. 1992. *The Role of Values in Psychology and Human Development*. New York: Wiley.

LeDoux, J. 1996. *The Emotional Brain: The Mysterious Underlining of Emotional Life*. New York: Simon and Schuster.

Leedy, P. D. 1997. *Practical Research: Planning and Design*. 6th ed. New York: Macmillan.

Lefrançois, G. R. 2000. *Theories of Human Learning: What the Old Man Said.* 4th ed. Belmont, Calif.: Wadsworth.

Marshall, C., and G. B. Rossman. 1989. *Designing Qualitative.* Newbury Park, Calif.: Sage

Ormrod, J. E. 1999. *Human Learning.* 3rd ed. Upper Saddle River, N.J.: Prentice Hall.

Reynolds, R. E., G. M. Sinatra, and T. L. Jetton. 1996. "Views of Knowledge Acquisition and Representation: A Continuum from Experience Centered." *Educational Psychologist* 31:93–104.

Robinson, D. N. 1992. *Social Discourse and Moral Judgment.* San Diego, Calif.: Academic.

Taylor, G. R. 1999. Curriculum Models and Strategies for Educating Individuals with Disabilities in Inclusive Classroom. Springfield, Ill.: Thomas.

CHAPTER 2

The Impact of Behaviorism on Learning Theories

The first systematic study of human behavior may be traced to behaviorism. Prior to behaviorism, there was no systematic study of human behavior. Ivan P. Pavlov and Edward L. Thorndike were the first theorists to objectively study human learning. Major contributions of these theorists will be discussed in a greater detail later in the text. Behaviorism advocates that principles of learning apply equally to humans and animals. Research findings from animals have been applied to humans premised on the belief that animals and humans principally learn in the same way.

To the behaviorists, learning can be studied objectively by measuring and observing behavior by the research observing stimuli in the environment and responses that organisms make to those stimuli, frequently referred to them as stimulus–response (S–R) psychology (Ormrod, 1999). The role of cognitive and internal processes in learning are not considered necessary or important in observing and measuring human behavior and learning by behaviorists. Additionally, they maintain (1) if there has been no change in behavior, then no learning has occurred, and (2) the mind is a blank tablet at birth for humans, and environmental factors shape behaviors, other than some instincts, of all organisms (humans and animals).

CONTRIBUTIONS OF EARLY THEORISTS

Several theorists have made major contributions to behaviorism. The work of those who have influenced education and classroom practice in this country include Pavlov, Thorndike, John B. Watson, Edwin R. Guthrie, and Burrhus F. Skinner (Herrnstein, 1997). I will address the contributions of these theorists later in the chapter.

There are two excellent texts concerning the contributions of Guthrie and Watson to the field of human learning. Therefore, I will not attempt to repeat their findings, rather, I refer the reader to Hergenhahn and Olson and Ormrod (Hergenhahn and Olson, 1997; Ormrod, 1999).

Ivan P. Pavlov

Pavlov is noted in the professional literature for his work in conditioning. He conditioned dogs to salivate not only to food, but also to environmental stimuli. Pavlovian conditioning of dogs is known today as classical conditioning. The major features of Pavlov's classical conditioning procedure with the dogs included: (1) unconditioned stimulus (meat power); (2) conditioned stimulus (the bell); (3) unconditioned response (salivation); and (4) conditioned response. During the experiments, Pavlov noted that if meat power was placed in or near the dog's mouth, the dog would salivate. The meat power provoked this response automatically without prior training. A more detailed description of his work will be summarized in chapter 3. Pavlov's experiments were based on stimulus–response involving the pairing of the neutral stimulus with the unconditioned stimulus until the former comes to substitute for the latter in eliciting a response.

Edward L. Thorndike

Thorndike believed that the major components of learning are stimulus and response connections. He called this connection "connectionism." Thorndike conducted several experiments with humans and animals. He concluded that animals who completed tasks took several trials, which he called trial-and-error learning. Based on his experimentation with animals, he formulated several laws of learning: the Law of Effect, the Law of Exercise, the Law of Readiness, and Subsidiary Laws. Refer to the glossary for definitions of the laws. Thorndike transferred his trial-and-error learning to humans by inferring that they learn the same way as animals.

Thorndike's theories, principles, research, and findings represented his views of learning theories. His experimentation and research supported the notion that learning consisted of the formation of physiological connections between stimuli and responses. Thorndike also made significant contributions to the field of education and teaching by applying psycho-

logical principles of learning to develop, teach, and evaluate the effectiveness of teaching.

John B. Watson

Watson is frequently called the father of behaviorism. He introduced
the term early in the twentieth century. It was Watson who first called for
the scientific study of the psychological process by focusing on observable rather than unobservable behaviors. Watson's work was greatly
influenced by early behaviorists such as Pavlov and Thorndike. He
employed their classical conditioned process as well as a model to conduct his experiments in human learning.

He proposed two laws: the Law of Frequency, where the importance of
repetition was stressed in learning, and the Law of Recency, where the
importance of timing was stressed. He believed that past experiences were
essential for almost all behaviors. He refuted the role of heredity factors
in behavior and learning. He defended his view with the following quote:
"Give me a dozen healthy infants, well-formed, and my own specified
world to bring them up in and I'll guarantee to take any one at random
and train him to become any type of specialist. I might select—doctor,
lawyer, artist, merchant, chief, and yes, even begger-man and thief,
regardless of his talents, penchants, tendencies, abilities, vocations, and
race of his ancestors" (Watson, 1925).

Edwin R. Guthrie

Guthrie's work was based on Watson's theory in that it emphasized the
S–R connections. He did not support the role of rewards in modifying
behaviors. Guthrie supported the view that only observable behaviors
could be employed to understand learning. Unlike some behaviorists, He
produced only one significant publication, rather than several: *The Psychology of Learning*, published in 1935 and revised in 1952. He com-
pounded one theory of learning, one-trial learning, where he explained all
behaviors based on the following principle: A stimulus that is followed
by a particular response will, after its recurrence, tend to be followed by
the same response again. This S–R connection gains its full strength on
one trial. Guthrie conducted little research to support his premise, however.

Burrhus F. Skinner

Several researchers in psychology have concluded that Skinner was the major contributor to psychology in the twentieth century (Hall, 1972; Lahey, 1998; Neef, Mace, and Shade, 1993; Wolfgang, 1995). He is considered to be the leading individual of experimentation and research based on principles of operant conditioning. His research has shown that it is not necessary to reinforce every satisfactory response in order to get results.

His work in behaviorism and behavioral engineering is well known. He brought experimentation in animal behavior to a quantitative scientific level. His principles of operant conditioning have been extensively used in research and clinical and therapeutic settings. Refer to chapter 4 for additional information on operant conditioning. Skinner's theory is based mostly on the use of reinforcers. He experimented with the use of positive and negative reinforcers in shaping behavior (Skinner and Epstein, 1982). His operant condition principles have stimulated research in several fields of learning and psychology, mostly with animal research. He has used principles of operant conditioning to explain a variety of complex human behaviors (Skinner, 1954, 1958, 1968, and 1973). Chapter 4 explains the major contributions that Skinner made to the fields of psychology and human learning.

IMPACT OF BEHAVIORISM

Today, behaviorism owes much of its survival to theorists such as Pavlov, Watson, Skinner, and Guthrie. Principles of behaviorism are currently being used by researchers to evaluate human and animal learning. Historically, behaviorists placed little to no emphasis on intrinsic traits. Today, behaviorists recognize the value of intrinsic traits such as motivation and interests in affecting learning or punishment have changed from early theorists' views. Early theorists maintained that punishment had little to no effect on behavior. Present-day theorists support the notion that punishment may affect learning (Rachlin, 1991). Historically, behaviorists divorced themselves from the role of cognitive factors in learning. Present-day behaviorists recognize the role of cognitive traits and environment in understanding learning (Church, 1993; Hulse, 1993; Rachlin, 1991; Wasserman, 1993).

Early behaviorists were not concerned with the role of mental traits in the learning process. They inferred that evaluation of learning could not be achieved through observation, but rather through introspection. This view lasted until the late nineteenth century, when the study of learning was scientifically studied. The works of Pavlov, Thorndike, and Skinner added significantly to the movement. Pavlov's experiments assisted in making the study of learning a scientific process. Thorndike developed several laws of learning using scientific procedures. The Law of Effect still has implications for classroom instruction.

Skinner was concerned with the relationship between behavior and its consequences. He articulated that if an individual's behavior is immediately followed by pleasurable consequences, the individual will engage in that behavior more frequently. The use of pleasant and unpleasant consequences to change behavior is often referred to as operant conditioning (Slavin, 1999). Principles of operant conditioning and Skinner's experiments and their scientific relevance are discussed in chapter 4.

The impact of behaviorism on classroom practices emphasizes the role of drill and practice, rewards, and breaking negative behaviors in the classroom. In order to fully realize the impact of behaviorism in the classroom, the learning must be actively in the process. Strategies must be introduced that will enable the teacher to assess the learner's behavior and learning by objectively noting changes in behavior. According to behaviorists, implications of behavioral strategies in the classroom by teachers should involve drill, practice, behavioral intervention strategies, and appropriate rewards and reinforcement for changing negative behaviors.

BEHAVIORAL STRATEGIES

Behaviorism continues to influence educational practices. According to Kohn, education cannot avoid behaviorism entirely (Kohn, 1993). Reinforcement will always be an important tool for shaping behavior. Principles of conditioning are reflected in many aspects of learning. The following is a summary of the strategies that I believe have relevancy for education.

Mastery Learning

According to Slavin, mastery learning is one of the most well-researched instructional models of the twentieth century (Slavin, 2000). The model had its inception in the works of Camenius, Pestalozz, and

Herbert. Research conducted by Guskey and Gates indicates that mastery learning significantly improves achievement of children engaged in the process (Guskey and Gates, 1986).

Mastery learning is based on the behaviorist's approach, in that it supports the belief that gives appropriate environmental conditions, such as reinforcing appropriate behaviors, to people because they are capable of acquiring many complex behaviors. Mastery learning requires that students learn one lesson well before proceeding to the next lesson. It is based on the operant conditioning concept of shaping. Refer to chapter 5 for ways to develop shaping techniques (Ormrod, 1999).

Mastery Learning Defined

Mastery learning is an educational theory developed by Benjamin S. Bloom, with the basic principle being that all children can learn when provided with conditions that are appropriate for their learning (Chance, 1987). Mastery learning is defined in various ways. In its simplest form, it means a learner must be able to demonstrate mastery or attainment of specific criteria in three areas—cognitive, affective, and psychomotor domains—that encompass all phases of education from the preschooler to the graduate (Palardy, 1987). In essence, mastery learning is a theory about teaching and learning that is closely tied to a set of instructional strategies (Guskey, 1987a).

Hunter's model is based on the mastery learning model (Hunter, 1995). Referring to that model as mastery teaching, she reflected that it is [a] way of thinking about and organizing the decisions that all teachers must make before, during, and after teaching. These decisions are based on research but should be implemented with artistry.

Components of Mastery Learning

Mastery learning is premised on the fact that most students can learn curricula skills providing that they are broken down into small sequential steps. In addition, Slavin maintains that teachers must state objectives clearly, determine the type of instruction to employ, assess abilities and disabilities of children, and provide individualized and enrichment activities for the varying needs and abilities presented by children (Slavin, 2000). Each of the points advanced by Slavin require detailed planning and assessment of children.

In support of Slavin's beliefs relevant to mastery learning, Ormrod reflects that in order for mastery learning to be effective instruction must be broken down into small management and discrete units (Ormrod, 1999).

Units are sequenced such that basic concepts and procedures are learned first so as to build a foundation for more complex concepts. Instruction should move from the simple to the complex (task analysis), from the known to the unknown, and from the concrete to the abstract.

Tests or other objective measures determined by the teacher are used for students to demonstrate their mastery at the conclusion of each unit. A concrete, observable criteria for mastery of each unit must be clearly articulated to students. Additional remedial and/or enrichment activities should be provided for students who need them in order to master the units.

What is and is not mastery learning has caused a great deal of controversy. The label "mastery learning" has been applied to a broad range of education materials and curricula that bears no resemblance to the ideas described by its founder and refined by its advocates. In the mastery learning framework, students are given a pretest. The items of the pretest are correlated to a set of learning objectives. The pretest gives the teacher a clear picture of what the students know or lack for the purpose of devising instructional strategies to enrich their knowledge or to improve their weaknesses. Students are constantly given feedback and correctives as they move through the learning objectives.

Feedback and correctives are means of monitoring students' progress and providing activities to remediate their deficits. At the end of the unit, the students are given a posttest to determine the extent to which they have mastered a unit's objectives. In essence, all mastery learning programs must have feedback and corrective activities. If teaching strategies are not congruent with feedback and corrective activities, then there is no mastery learning. For example, suppose an English teacher provides students feedback relating to grammar and punctuation, while evaluating the content and organization of their composition. In the mastery learning framework, the feedback students receive should always be congruent with specific learning criteria and the procedures used to evaluate their learning (Guskey, 1987b). Mastery learning is equal to a set of behavioral objectives, plus feedback and corrective activities, tied together by effective instruction to produce the competent learner.

Proponents of Mastery Learning

There have been a variety of approaches used by educational systems around the country and world to improve the quality of education received by our young people. However, mastery learning has attracted a great deal of attention and controversy within the last decade. Many studies have shown that the quality of instruction and highly effective schools consistently point to the components of mastery learning as an integral part of successful teaching and learning. According to Guskey, many school systems believe that the implementation of mastery learning can indeed lead to striking improvements in a wide range of student learning outcomes (Guskey, 1987b). Research findings have shown that mastery learning can improve students' achievements and promote positive self-esteem (Kulik, Kulik, and Bangert-Drowns, 1990; Semb, Ellis, and Araujo, 1993).

Several studies have found mastery learning to be of significant benefit for low-achieving children (Bloom, 1984; Kulik, Kulik, and Bangert-Drowns, 1990; Slavin, 1987). The research indicated that when mastery learning strategies were used in conjunction with corrective techniques, achievement gains were noted.

Classroom Implications

According to Kulik, Kulik, and Bangert-Drowns, students engaged in mastery learning clearly do better than other students on tests developed to fit local curricula and do slightly better than others on standardized tests that sample objectives from many school systems and many grade levels (Kulik, Kulik, and Bangert-Drowns, 1990). Many researchers have found evidence that standardized tests do not always cover what they are assumed to cover, such as the basic skills curriculum contained in textbooks (Anderson and Burns, 1987). Standardized tests are better measures of the long-term effects of schooling rather than the short-term effects of instruction because their broad, stable knowledge structures are more indicative of ability than recently acquired curricular knowledge.

Contrary to many critics, mastery learning places no restrictions on the scope, depth, or level of the objectives that are to be taught or that the students should learn (Guskey, 1987a). In essence, mastery learning is neutral in regard to curricular issues. Feedback and correctives are essential elements of mastery learning. Students who are having problems with a particular objective are allotted additional time to address their weaknesses. However, feedback and correctives serve as obstacles for high-achieving students. Mastery learning should be highly individualized, with a great deal of focus placed on the extent of achievement, rate, and style of learning (Palardy, 1987). The learner should not wait for others to master the material. Guskey states the following rebuttal against the critics who believe that mastery learning does nothing else but teach test taking:

> The element of congruence has led to the criticism of mastery learning being nothing more than teaching a test. This is not the case. If a test serves as the basis of the teaching, and if what is taught is determined primarily by the test, one is teaching the test. Under these conditions, the content and format of the test guide and direct what is taught and how. With mastery learning, however, the learning objectives, which are generally determined by individual teachers, are the basis of the teaching and the primary determiner of what is taught. In using mastery learning, teachers simply ensure their instructional procedures and test match what they have determined to be important for their students to learn. Instead of teaching to the test, these teachers are more accurately testing what is taught. After all, if it is important enough to test, it ought to be important enough to teach. And if it is not important enough to teach, why should if be tested? (Guskey, 1987a)

Critics of Mastery Learning

Several authors voice their opposition to mastery learning (Arlin, 1984; Berliner, 1989; Prawat, 1992; Sussman, 1981; Slavin, 1987, 2000). These authors claim that students who learn quickly receive less instruction than their classmates and sometimes must wait for their slower classmates; thus, they learn less than they normally would. Some students have greater difficulty passing mastery tests, despite repeated testing. As such, mastery learning does not permit interaction among students as other strategies.

There are four main disadvantages of mastery learning:

1. The effect of mastery learning is far greater on teacher-made tests than on standardized tests
2. Mastery learning restricts the teacher's ability to cover other areas or objectives that are not part of the unit objectives

3. High-achieving students are held back in group mastery learning programs until the majority has reached mastery
4. Mastery learning only teaches a test

Some researchers feel that standardized tests are more appropriate than criterion reference tests in measuring students' achievements in coverage (the amount of content learned) as well as mastery. Other critics of mastery learning feel that standardized tests tap a broad, stable knowledge structure more indicative of ability than recently acquired curricular knowledge (Guskey, 1987a).

Behavior Analysis

The entire premise of the Behavior Analysis Model as it applies to the classroom, which is based on the previously described work of Skinner, is based on the analyzing of one's behavior. It includes gathering baseline data and clearly defining the behavior in measurable and observable terms that is undesirable, the target behavior. In order for the shaping to occur, behavioral objectives must be chosen, defined, and committed to in writing. Graphing random samples, observing students in several areas, and keeping daily anecdotals will aid in the overall effectiveness as well. Clearly defining the steps necessary in shaping the target behavior in writing before the behavior is modified helps in noting and showing progress being made toward the ultimate behavioral goal. Similar to Skinner's animals, students' behaviors must be shaped in gradual successive approximations, with timely, effective reinforcements consistently being awarded. This technique can be time consuming and intrusive in the classroom setting, but it ultimately helps students gain self-control of their own behaviors. Effective reinforcers must be identified and followed by a specific intervention plan based on the target behavior to be changed. Both baseline data and data yielded from treatment are compared and measured.

The Application of Behavior through a Token Economy System

A token economy system is based on behavior modification principles. As in a behavior modification system, positive and negative reinforcers are part of the system. A token system may be employed to assist students in identifying and improving their target behaviors.

Several researchers have summarized what they consider to be important components of a token economy system.

- A set of rules, developed with input from students, delineates specific behaviors that will be reinforced
- Immediate reinforcement of tokens when appropriate behaviors are demonstrated
- Have in hand alternative reinforcers for backup or for special events
- A place where tokens can be used or exchanged for reinforcers (Osborne, 1969; McKenzi, Clark, Wolf, Kothera, and Benson, 1968).

School-Wide Token Economy System

Each student in the program should be individually evaluated by all staff and goals assigned to each student. The majority of the students participate in the development of behavioral goals with their therapist and/or homeroom teacher guiding them through this process. The students are split in two groups: returning students and new students. New students to the program should be evaluated at the end of each forty-five-minute period by a staff member. If the goal was accomplished for the majority of the period, the student receives a reward. If the student achieves the goal for at least half of the period, the student receives a partial reward. Points are tallied at the end of every period, day, and week. The student receives a paycheck every Friday for the amount of points earned in the week. Returning students follow a similar system, but rather than staff evaluating their behaviors, students evaluate themselves at the end of every period. Staff then has the opportunity to agree or disagree with the evaluation. These students use the traditional A, B, C, and D system to grade themselves rather than the 0, 1, and 2 system. This system empowers students to become reflective and self-monitoring. It also rewards those students who can accurately self-evaluate rather than just those who can achieve their goals.

The students keep a working checkbook using the "money" they are making on their point sheets. The money can be used to buy items from the school store (candy, microwavable lunches and breakfasts, hair products, chips, and so on) and privileges (getting lunch out in the community, music listening privileges, applying for "credit," and so on). Students must pay monthly rent of $600.00 in order to make use of both the school store and other privileges.

Contingency Contracting

Hergenhahn articulates that contingency contracting comes from the fact that while an agreement is made between a teacher and student, certain activities will be reinforced that otherwise may not have been (Hergenhahn and Olson, 1997). In essence, the contract rearranges the reinforcement contingencies in the environment, causing students to be responsive to behavior patterns that one hopes to modify in some way. The teacher and student specify the conditions in the contract. When the conditions are approved, both teacher and student sign and date the contract.

Contracts may be designed to serve a variety of purposes, such as modifying classroom behavior, completing homework assignments, and improving social behaviors, attendance rates, and academic performances. Specific rewards are identified with each contract, and the amount and frequency of the rewards are also specified in the contract.

Computer Technology/Technological Services

Today, computers are widely used in educating individuals (Frazier, 1995). Many computer software programs teach children a variety of skills. Other programs are used to develop social and emotional skills. The instructional units developed in this text can be facilitated through the use of computer software. Benefits from the use of microcomputers in improving the performance of children in the content areas have been well documented (Hughes, 1996; Frazier, 1995; Walters, 1998; Fodi, 1991; Bader, 1998; Lester, 1996; Polloway and Patton, 1993; Peha, 1995).

One of the major reasons why computers and other technological devices are not in great supply in many classrooms is due to expense. Many school districts simply do not have funds to equip their classrooms. To assist school districts, the Clinton administration proposed increased spending for computer technology (Hughes, 1996). Subsequently, the passage of the 1996 Telecommunications Act included goals and provisions to network classrooms to the Internet by 2000. On January 1, 1998, approximately $2.3 billion of annual, additional funding was made available to schools to offset connectivity costs. This law enabled school districts to use technology to enhance their instruction program by having access to the World Wide Web. The North Carolina Department of Public Instruction appears to be in the forefront by profiting from the new federal regulation. The department has advanced a plan to have computers in every classroom by the next decade.

Advantages of Using Computers and Other Technological Devices

Computers are based on principles of operant conditioning. Instruction is programmed in small sequential steps by computers and reinforcement is applied immediately after the student supplies the correct response.

Generally, in computer technology the drill-and-practice type programs lend themselves nicely to developing fluency on a skill. Currently, the best research suggests that when a student is in the fluency stage of learning, his/her use of drill-and-practice software will result in very positive student gains. Perhaps the best example of why these features are necessary can be seen in the area of mathematics (Polloway and Patton, 1993). Students who have difficulty in any area can spend time looking at the creative artwork on the introductory screen while they gather their thoughts and this is considered to be a constructive use of learning time.

Prior to starting to use the computer, the teacher may wish to introduce computer-based vocabulary words to the students. Words such as "information highway," "on board," "user-friendly," or "e-mail" help students become familiar with some computer terminology. A vocabulary list that is user-friendly to the student can be a source on which the teacher can motivate students' interests.

The impact of computers and other technological devices have been well entrenched into the American culture. Computers have impacted all aspects of society, and their effect on education is too numerous to be adequately covered in this chapter in any great detail. There are adequate texts that comprehensively address this issue. My intention is simply to summarize what I consider to be major advantages of using computers and technological devices in the classroom.

- Computer laboratory teachers are better able to teach classes of students with divergent abilities, and individual needs of children with disabilities can be successfully met through the use of integrated media systems (Cornish, 1996)

- While at one sitting, students can literally visit a Web site in virtually any country or research a topic anywhere in the city, state, country, or world (Lester, 1996)
- Students choose computers to complete assignments when they are functional and real (Bolger, 1996)
- Since classrooms are information-rich environments, computers offer a slow student an opportunity to sit down and repeat the right answer as many times as possible (Polloway and Patton, 1993)
- Video conferencing can be offered in one class via camera and computer screen with a class in another wing of the school (Choate, 1997)
- Cyberism, the creed of information, will become a practicable solution to some of the problems faced by disabled students (Fodi, 1991)
- The integration of integrated technologies, such as combining computers and telephones, and other assistive devices can open a source of information to children with disabilities, which have historically been denied to them (Lester, 1996)
- Digital technology has the potential for making polished presentations of research findings and publications
- Computer software has the potential for remediating skills in any content area (Choate, 1997)
- Modifications and adaptations in Web site designs and computer software packages are needed for many children to use effectively (Necessary and Parish, 1996; Bigge, 1991; Ryba, Shelby, and Nolan, 1995)
- Computers have the ability of presenting information in a multisensory mode (Goldstein, 1998)

Lester contends that computers and high technologies offer children the ability to access databases (Lester, 1996). Ryba, Shelby, and Nolan remark that adaptations of computers enable many children full access to them (Ryba, Shelby, and Nolan, 1995). Adaptations of other technological devices such as laser scanners, alternative keyboards, and voice recognition allow children to achieve their optimal level of growth.

Cornish predicts by 2025 teachers will be better able to handle classes of students with widely different abilities (Cornish, 1996). Children will be the beneficiaries of infotech-based education by having state-of-the-art equipment. The assistance computers offer special education children is little short of miraculous. Many children with disabilities who may possess writing or math blocks and are unable to produce even one neat page of handwritten text often discover the labor-saving faculty of word processing programs. Computers can give independence, employment, knowledge, and accessibility to the outside world for children. Additionally, they promote individualization of instruction and have high interest values for children.

The Internet

The Internet can serve as a lure or a magnet to attract children to the computer and make them work. The attraction of the Internet for children has been widely discussed on television and radio and while all the material obtained via the Internet can be validated, the informational and research use of the Internet cannot be denied.

Technology is a tool that can assist the teacher by providing children with a multisensory environment. The Internet can provide information so children can make associations between information and transfer information to solve problems. The Internet arranges information hierarchically. Broad topics are presented first, and information is narrowed down by requesting more specific facts. This process enables children to employ critical thinking skills to solve problems. Additionally, working on the Internet can give children the opportunity to work at their own pace. By the school providing early Internet training to children, it is equipping them to be prepared for the challenges they will face in competing for employment in the job market of the future (Goldstein, 1998).

According to Andrew and Jordan, multimedia technology allows one to develop stories in two or more languages, or to present information in different formats (Andrew and Jordan, 1998). This technology has many benefits for instructing children because video dictionaries of sign language can be built right into the stories. The technology allows a child to explore information at his/her own pace. It combines printed text, narration, words, sound, music, graphics, photos, movies, and animation on one computer page.

Many children have difficulties accessing information over the Internet due to poor Web site designs (Walters, 1998). Many of the Web sites create barriers for some children. Children who have vision problems have difficulty accessing the Web because it requires a degree of vision acuity. Students who have reading problems are not be able to access the Web appropriately because information is in a text format. Children with attention deficit disorders have problems accessing the Web due to their short attention span and inability to stay focused for an extended time. However, other children with disabilities without the aforementioned disabilities can easily access the Web. Specific modifications and adaptations have been recommended by authors for Web designers to implement so that the Web can be accessible for all children. The reader is referred to the references section of this chapter for additional information modification and adaptation of Web site designs for children with disabilities.

SUMMARY

Waal states that several decades ago thoughts about animal and human behavior had opposite views (Waal, 1999). One view dictated that animal behavior was characterized as instinctive and human behavior as learning. Another view stated that differences among species were irrelevant and that learning, instinctive or otherwise, applied to all animals, including humans. Currently, behaviorists view all behavior as the product of trial-and-error learning.

These views began to change with scientific studies involving learning. Behaviorists began to realize that learning is not the same for all conditions, situations, and species. For example, animals are specialized learners, being best at those conditions that are most important for survival, which include strategies for adaptation to the environment.

Klein states that behaviorism is a school of thought that emphasizes the role of experience in governing behavior (Klein, 1996). He further alludes that according to this principle, the important processes governing behavior are learned. Both the drives that initiate behavior and the specific behaviors motivated by these drives are learned through our interactions with the environment. The behaviorist's major goal is to determine the laws governing learning. The impact of early theorists such as Pavlov, Thorndike, Watson, Guthrie, and Skinner all contributed to shaping today's concepts of behaviorism; even though these theorists had separate views, each made a major contribution to the field of psychology. Conditioning and behaviorism have significantly impacted learning with techniques such as mastery learning and behavior analysis.

Results reported in this chapter show that when the basic elements of mastery learning (feedback and correctives) are congruent, students' test scores on criterion reference tests are extremely high. Even though students who are exposed to a mastery learning program only perform slightly better than other students on standardized tests, mastery learning students continue to perform better. Results also show that when cooperative learning strategies are paired with mastery learning strategies, students' test scores are even higher (Guskey, 1990). Both mastery learning and cooperative learning strategies compliment each other, promote positive self-esteem, and increase student involvement. Other studies show that the use of computer-based instruction and high technology has helped learning disabled students learn more complex content such as earth science, chemistry, fractions, health promotion, reasoning skills, and vocabulary (Carnine, 1989). Mastery learning is not a panacea for all of our educational woes, but if used correctly it can improve students' achievements and self-esteem.

Computer technology is here to stay. The values of computers in increasing achievement and ability to solve problems are well documented in this chapter. Computer technology is a valuable tool that when used appropriately can augment instructional programs and enable children to become self-sufficient and more independent.

BIBLIOGRAPHY

Anderson, L. W., and R. B. Burns. 1987. "Values Evidence and Mastery Learning." *Review of Education Research* 57 (2): 215–223.

Andrew, J. E., and D. L. Jordon. 1998. "Multimedia Stories for Deaf Children." *Teaching Exceptional Children* 30 (6): 28–33.

Arlin, M. 1984. "Time, Equality, and Mastery Learning." *Review of Educational Research* 54:65–68.

Bader, B. 1998. "Measuring Progress of Disabled Students." *American Teacher* 82:15.

Berliner, D. C. 1989. "The Place of Process-Products Research in Developing the Agenda for Research on Teacher Thinking." *Educational Psychologist* 24:325–344.

Bigge, J. L. 1991. *Teaching Individuals with Physical and Multiple Disabilities.* New York: Macmillan.

Bloom, B. S. 1976. *Human Characteristics and School Learning.* New York: McGraw-Hill.

———. 1984. "The 2 Sigma Problem: The Research for Methods of Instruction As Effective As One-to-One Tutoring." *Educational Research* 13:4–16.

Bolger, R. 1996. "Learning with Technology." *Teamwork* 1.

Carnine, D. 1989. "Teaching Complex Content to Learning Disabled Students: The Role of Technology." *Exceptional Children* 55 (6): 524–533.

Chance, P. 1987. "Master of Mastery." *Psychology Today* 21 (4): 42–46.

Choate, J. S. 1997. *Successful Inclusion Teaching.* Boston: Allyn and Bacon.

Church, R. M. 1993. "Human Models of Animal Behavior." *Psychological Science* 4:170–173.

Cornish, E. 1996. "The Cyberspace Out by 2025." *Education Digest* 46:4–9.

Fodi, J. 1991. "Kids Communicate through Adaptive Technology." *Exceptional Parent* 21:36.

Frazier, M. K. 1995. "Caution: Students on Board the Internet." *Educational Leadership* 53 (2): 26–27.

Goldstein, C. 1998. "Learning at Cyber Camp." *Teaching Exceptional Children* 30 (52): 16–26.

Guskey, T. R. 1987a. "The Essential Elements of Mastery Learning." *Journal of Classroom Interaction* 22 (2): 19–22.

———. 1987b. "Rethinking Mastery Learning Reconsidered." *Review of Educational Research* 57 (2): 225–229.

———. 1990. "Cooperative Mastery Strategies." *Elementary School Journal* 91 (1): 33–42.

———. 1995. "Mastery Learning." In *School Improvement Programs*, ed. J. H. Block, S. T. Everson, and T. R. Guskey. New York: Scholastic.

Guskey, T. R., and S. L. Gates. 1986. "Synthesis of Research on the Effects of Mastery Learning in Elementary and Secondary Classrooms." *Educational Leadership* 43 (8): 73–80.

Hall, M. H. 1972. "An Interview with 'Mr. Behaviorist,' B. F. Skinner." In *Readings in Psychology Today*. Delmar, Calif.: Communications Research Machines.

Hergenhahn, B. R., and M. H. Olson. 1997. *An Introduction to Theories of Learning.* Upper Saddle River, N.J.: Prentice Hall.

Herrnstein, R. J. 1997. "The Evolution of Behaviorism." *American Psychologist* 32:593–603.

Hughes, R. T. 1996. "Computers in the Classroom." *The Clearing House* 70:4.

Hulse, S. H. C. 1993. "The Present Status of Animal Cognition: An Introduction." *Psychological Science* 4:154–155.

Hunter, M. 1995. "Mastery Teaching." In *School Improvement Programs*, ed. J. H. Block, S. T. Everson, and T. R. Guskey. New York: Scholastic.

Klein, S. B. 1996. *Learning: Principles and Applications.* New York: McGraw-Hill.

Kohn, A. 1993. *Punished by Rewards: The Trouble with Gold Stars, Incentive Plans, A's, Praise, and Other Bribes.* Boston: Houghton Mifflin.

Kulik, C. L., J. A. Kulik, and R. L. Bangert-Drowns. 1990. "Effectiveness of Mastery Learning Programs: A Meta-Analysis." *Review of Educational Research* 60 (2): 265–299.

Lahey, B. B. 1998. *Psychology: An Introduction.* New York: McGraw-Hill.

Lester, M. P. 1996. "Connecting to the World." *Exceptional Parent* 26 (11): 36–37.

McKenzie, H. S., M. Clark, M. M. Wolf, R. Kothera, and C. Benson. 1968. "Behavior Modification of Children with Learning Disabilities: Using Grades As Tokens and Allowances As Back-up Reinforcers." *Exceptional Children* 34:745–752.

Necessary, J. R., and T. S. Parish. 1996. "The Relationship between Computer Usage and Computer Related Attitudes and Behaviors." *Education* 116:384–386.

Neef, N. A., F. C. Mace, and D. Shade. 1993. "Impulsivity in Students with Serious Emotional Disturbance: The Interactive Effects of Reinforcer Rate, Delay, and Quality." *Journal of Applied Behavior Analysis* 26:37–52.

Neef, N. A., D. Shade, and M. S. Miller. 1994. "Assessing Influential Dimensions of Reinforcers on Choice in Students with Serious Emotional Disturbance." *Journal of Applied Behavior Analysis* 27:575–583.

Ormrod, J. E. 1999. *Human Learning.* 3rd ed. Columbus, Ohio: Merrill.

Osborne, J. G. 1969. "Free-Time As a Reinforcer in the Management of Classroom Behavior." *Journal of Applied Behavior Analysis* 2:113–118.

Palardy, M. J. 1987. "Mastery Learning: A Mixed View." *Education* 107 (4): 424–427.

Peha, J. M. 1995. "How K–12 Teachers Are Using Computer Networks." *Educational Leadership* 53 (2): 18–25.

Polloway, E. A., and J. R. Patton. 1993. *Strategies for Teaching Learners with Special Needs.* New York: Merrill.

Prawat, R. S. 1992. "From Individual Differences to Learning Communities— Our Changing Focus." *Educational Leadership* 49 (7): 9–13.

Rachlin, H. 1991. *Introduction to Modern Behaviorism.* 3rd ed. New York: Freeman.

Ryba, K., L. Shelby, and P. Nolan. 1995. "Computers Empower Students with Special Needs." *Educational Technology* 53:82.

Semb, G. B., J. A. Ellis, and J. Araujo. 1993. "Long-Term Memory for Knowledge Learned in School." *Journal of Educational Psychology* 55:305–316.

Skinner, B. F. 1954. "The Science of Learning and the Art of Teaching." *Harvard Educational Review* 24:86–97.

———. 1958. "Reinforcement Today." *American Psychologists* 13:94–99.

———. 1968. *The Technology of Teaching.* New York: Appleton-Century-Crofts.

———. 1973. "The Free and Happy Student." *Phi Delta Kappan* 55:13–16.

Skinner, B. F., and R. Epstein. 1982. *Skinner for the Classroom.* Champaign, Ill.: Research Press.

Slavin, R. E. 1987. "Ability Grouping and Student Achievement in Elementary Schools: A Best Evidence Synthesis." *Review of Educational Research* 57:243–386.

————. 1999. *Educational Psychology: Theory and Practice*. 6th ed. Boston: Allyn and Bacon.

Slavin, R. E. 2000. *Educational Psychology: Theory and Practice*. Boston: Allyn and Bacon.

Sussman, D. M. 1981. "PSI: Variations on a Theme." In *Behavior Modification: Contribution to Education*, ed. S. W. Bijou and R. Ruiz. Hillsdale, N.J.: Erlbaum.

Waal, F. B. 1999. "The End of the Nature versus Nature." *Scientific American* 6 (281): 94–99.

Walters, S. P. 1998. "Accessible Web Design." *Teaching Exceptional Children* 30 (6): 42–47.

Wasserman, E. A. 1993. "Comparative Cognition: Toward a General Understanding of Cognition in Behavior." *Psychology Science* 4:156–161.

Watson, J. B. 1925. *Behaviorism*. New York: Norton.

Wolfgang, C. H. 1995. *Solving Discipline Problems: Methods and Models for Today's Teachers*. Boston: Allyn and Bacon.

CHAPTER 3

Ivan P. Pavlov

Ivan P. Pavlov was born on September 14, 1849, in Russia. He was educated first at the church school in Ryazan and then at the theological seminary. He had planned on a career in theology, but was so influenced by Russian translations of Western scientific writings, and particularly with their Darwinian overtones, that he abandoned his religious training (Windholz, 1997). In 1870, he enrolled in physics and mathematics and took courses in natural science. Natural science caused him to become absorbed with physiology and medicine.

Five years later, in 1875, Pavlov completed the courses and was awarded the degree of candidate of Natural Sciences. He continued his education in physiology at the Academy of Medical Surgery and was awarded a gold medal four years later. In 1883, he developed the basic principles of the function of the heart and the nervous system. Pavlov's experiments showed that there was a basic pattern in the reflex regulation of the activity of the circulatory organs. His work earned him a Nobel Prize in 1904.

This research led the way for new advances in medicine. He clearly showed in one of his experiments that the nervous system plays a significant part in regulating the digestive process. His research into the digestive process led him to create a science of conditioned reflexes. From his research findings, Pavlov was able to study all psychic activity objectively (Pavlov, 1927).

Pavlov continued to conduct research with physiological topics for several years. It was not until he was at the age of fifty that he began to study classical conditioning, a study that lasted for over three decades. Pavlov considered himself a physiologist rather than a psychologist, even though his major contributions were directed at the development of theories of learning (Watson, 1971; Windholz, 1996a, 1996b).

CLASSICAL CONDITIONING

Pavlov's experiments with conditioning reflexes with his dog are well reported in the professional literature (Klein, 1996; Hergenhahn and Olson, 1997). He devised a series of experiments in classical conditioning, which is essentially sign language. In his experiments, he demonstrated the pairing of a neutral stimulus with an unconditioned stimulus until the former comes to substitute for the latter in eliciting a response. The first response to be conditioned by Pavlov was the salivary reflex.

According to Ormrod, Pavlov's experiment in conditioning his dog is reflected by a stimulus–response sequence (Ormrod, 1999). The sequence is a modified premise of her three-step method.

1. A neutral stimulus (NS) is a stimulus to which the organism does not respond. In the experiment, the bell was originally a neutral stimulus that did not elicit a salivation response.
2. The second stimulus is called an unconditioned stimulus (UCS) and the response is called an unconditioned response (UCR), because the organism responds to the stimulus unconditionally without having to learn to do so. In Pavlov's experiment, meat power was an UCS to which the dog responded with the UCR of salivation.
3. When steps 1 and 2 are paired, the NS now elicits a response. The NS has become a conditioned stimulus (CS) to which the dog has learned a conditioned response (CR). The UCS and UCR are an unlearned stimulus–response unit called a reflex.

The main features of Pavlov's classical conditioning procedure are discussed in this chapter. Before conditioning, the UCS naturally elicits the UCR. A NS (such as a tone) has no eliciting effect. During conditioning, the NS is paired with the UCS. Through its association with the UCS, the NS becomes a CS and elicits similar to the UCR. Classical conditioning is also referred to as learning through stimulus substitution, since the CS, after being paired with the UCS often enough, can then be substituted for it. The CS will evoke a similar, but weaker, response. It is also referred to as signal learning, because the CS serves as a signal for the occurrence of the UCS.

Most responses that can reliably be elicited by a stimulus can be classically conditioned. For example, the knee-jerk, eye-blink, and pupillary reflexes can all be conditioned to various stimuli (Lefrançois, 2000).

The more time between the signal and the subsequent event, the better the animal can prepare for the event, and this is of special importance when the event is noxious or potentially harmful. A longer preparation time requires a longer interval between the CS and the UCS, such as that which occurs in either delayed or trade conditioning, both of which require a nervous system that can maintain excitation after the stimulus has ceased to act. Such animals have more time to prepare for oncoming events, which means that they can employ strategy and tactics instead of only reflexes.

THE CLASSICAL CONDITIONING MODEL

Classical conditioning has been conducted on a number of organisms and humans (Lipsitt and Kaye, 1964; Reese and Lipsitt, 1970; Macfarlane, 1978; Thompson and McConnell, 1955). The classical conditioning model becomes active when two stimuli are presented to an organism at approximately the same time. When a stimulus elicits response, the stimulus brings about a response automatically within the organism; in essence, the organism has no control over the response (Hergenhahn and Olson, 1997; Hollis, 1997).

In classical conditioning, the CS precedes the UCS, and, as with most sequential events, the time relations between these two stimuli are crucial. Conditioning is faster when the CS is followed almost immediately by the UCS. The best interval in humans is about half a second, which is approximately the optimal interval between the warning stimulus and the signal to respond in a reaction time experiment. Half a second is also roughly the time estimated for the reticular formation to alert the cerebral cortex to its optimal level of arousal for acting on incoming stimuli. All these time relations suggest that the CS acts as a signal that prepares the organism for the oncoming UCS.

At intervals slower than half a second or greater than two seconds, conditioning is slower. In terms of the time interval between the CS and UCS, there are three possibilities: simultaneous, delayed, and trace conditioning (Klein, 1996).

Simultaneous Conditioning

The CS and UCS start and end at the same time, but very little conditioning results. An example according to Klein would be an individual walking into a fast food restaurant (Klein, 1996). The restaurant (CS) and food (UCS) would occur at the same time. This simultaneous conditioning in this case would lead to weak hunger conditioned to the restaurant.

Delayed Conditioning

The CS onset proceeds the UCS onset. When the CR first appears, it occurs immediately after the onset of the CS, but eventually it is delayed until just prior to the onset of the UCS. A dark sky that proceeds a severe storm is an example of delayed conditioning. A person having experienced this condition may become afraid when a dark sky appears.

Trace Conditioning

The CS starts and terminates before the onset of the UCS. Presumably, the response is conditioned to the neutral trace of the CS, hence, the name trace conditioning. With this conditioning, the CS is presented and terminated prior to the USC onset. A parent who calls a child to dinner is using trace conditioning (Klein, 1996).

Backward Conditioning

This time relation requires brief mention. In backward conditioning, the UCS precedes the CS. Tait and Saladin's explanation provides some clarity to backward conditioning (Tait and Saladin, 1986). They indicate that backward conditioning may not produce the intended CS but may result in the development of another type of CR. The backward conditioning paradigm is also a conditioned inhibition procedure where the CS is paired with the absence of the UCS. In some instances, a person would experience a conditioned inhibition rather than conditioned excitation when exposed to the CS.

EXTINCTION

So long as the CS and UCS are paired, the CR is likely to occur, but if the CS is presented repeatedly without the UCS, the CR gradually dissipates. This process is called extinction, and it continues until there is no longer any CR.

When the organism no longer responds to the CS, it might appear that the effects of the conditioning process are eliminated, but they are not. After a brief time, the CR reappears, though it is weaker. This phenomenon is called spontaneous recovery. It may require repeated extinctions to eliminate all the effects of the original conditioning.

HIGHER-ORDER CONDITIONING

A UCS is usually part of a stimulus response reflexive unit that is programmed in the nervous system. Pavlov's experiment with his dog provided an excellent example of higher-order conditioning. After the dog had been conditioned to salivate at the sound of a bell, the bell was later rang in conjunction with a NS such as a flash of light. This NS would also elicit a salivation response, even though it had never been directly associated with meat (Ormrod, 1999). The flash of light, through its association with the bell, would eventually elicit the conditioned reflection response, which is called higher-order conditioning. It consists of using a previous CS (the bell) as a UCS with which a new NS (the flash of light) can be paired to obtain another CS.

First-order conditioning is nothing more than the process of conditioning explained. Second-order conditioning consists of using the CS from first-order conditioning as the UCS in a subsequent conditioning procedure. Pavlov has demonstrated third-order conditioning, but it is extremely difficult to obtain.

Higher-order conditioning is difficult to accomplish because of the ever-present problem of extinction. When the CS is presented without the UCS, the CR is extinguished. Thus, when the light and the bell in my example are paired, the CR to the tone weakens because the original UCS (the electric shock) is absent. This tendency can be counteracted by interspersing trials of first-order conditioning (pairing of the bell with electric shock), thereby strengthening the original CR. These difficulties in obtaining higher-order conditioning underscore the limitations of classical conditioning: it cannot be separated very far from the unconditioned stimuli that comprise one-half of the innately programmed reflexive units.

DISCRIMINATION

Survival often involves a choice of alternative responses, and the ability to choose requires the ability to discriminate among objects and events in the environment. Such discrimination is easy to condition, even in so primitive an animal as the flatworm. Discrimination can be induced by two ways: prolonged training and differential reinforcement. First, if a CS is paired with a UCS many times, the tendency is to respond to stimuli related to the CS. But for those stimuli not identical to the CS, the response level decreases. The second way of bringing about discrimination is through differential reinforcement. This process involves presenting a high-frequency tone with a low-frequency tone that will occur during extinction. Only the high-frequency tone is followed by reinforcement after such training. When the animal is presented with tones other than high-frequency tones during extinction, it tends not to respond to them (Hergenhahn and Olson, 1997).

CLASSICAL CONDITIONING IN HUMAN LEARNING

The principles of classical conditioning have been successfully used to control or condition human behaviors in the areas of involuntary responses, fears, and phobias (Brunner, Goodnow, and Austin, 1956). Involuntary responses can be induced through hunger. When animals or people are exposed to food, they exhibit a set of UCRs that prepare them to digest, metabolize, and store ingested foods. These unconditioned feeding responses are involuntary and include the secretion of saliva, gastric juices, pancreatic enzymes, and insulin. Powley's research claims that these unconditioned feeding responses in humans can be controlled (Powley, 1977).

Miller's and Staats and Staats's research have reported the development of fear through classical conditioning in animals and humans (Miller, 1948; Staats and Staats, 1957). Their findings support the premise that fear is conditioning when a novel stimulus (CS) is associated with an aversive event. An example given by Klein provides some clarity to this premise (Klein, 1996). He states that an examination is an aversive event and explains that when an individual takes a test (UCS), the examination elicits an unconditioned pain reaction (UCR). The psychological distress experienced when an instructor hands you a test is one aspect of your pain reaction, and the increased physiological arousal is another part of your response to receiving an examination. Although the intensity of the aversive event may lesson while you are taking a test, you will not experience relief until you complete it.

More recently, Ormrod indicates that individuals who are unusually

afraid of failing may have previously associated failure with unpleasant ⟵
circumstances, such as associating failure with pain punishment (Ormrod,
1999). Educators should be careful to make certain that this type of association with failure does not become so strong a CS for children that they
resist engaging in new activities and attempting challenging problems.

SUMMARY

Pavlov's research in conditioning significantly impacted the development
of psychology in the world. His experiments with the salivation response
with his dog were instrumental in developing classical conditioning. The
impact of his work received world-wide recognition, and in 1904 he was
awarded a Nobel Prize in Medicine and Physiology for his work on diges-
tion (Smith, 1995).

Pavlov's experiments have provided a theoretical framework for the
continuation of scientific studies in contemporary psychology and related
medical research activities. Additionally, his research in classical conditioning has assisted us in understanding human fears and phobias, and
has provided a model for educators to employ in reducing, controlling, or
eliminating fears and phobias, as well as providing strategies for modifying and controlling deviant behaviors.

BIBLIOGRAPHY

Brunner, J. S., J. Goodnow, and G. Austin. 1956. *A Study of Thinking*. New York:
   Wiley.
Hergenhahn, B. R., and M. H. Olson. 1997. *An Introduction to Theories of Learn-
   ing*. Upper Saddle River, N.J.: Prentice Hall.
Hollis, K. L. 1997. "Contemporary Research on Pavlovian Conditioning: A
   'New' Functional Analysis." *American Psychologists* 52:956–965.
Klein, S. B. 1996. *Learning Principles and Applications*. 3rd ed. New York:
   McGraw-Hill.
Lefrançois, G. R. 2000. *Theories of Human Learning: What the Old Man Said*.
   4th ed. Pacific Grove, Calif.: Brooks/Cole.
Lipsitt, L. P., and H. Kaye. 1964. "Conditioning Sucking in the Human New-
   born." *Psychonomic Science* 1:29–30.
Macfarlane, A. 1978. "What a Baby Knows." *Human Nature* 1:74–81.
Miller, N. E. 1948. "Studies of Fear As an Acquirable Drive: Fear As Motivation

and Fear Reduction As Reinforcement in Learning of New Response." *Journal of Experimental Psychology* 38:89–101.

Ormrod, J. E. 1999. *Human Learning*. 3rd ed. Columbus, Ohio: Merrill.

Pavlov, I. P. 1927. *Conditioned Reflexes*. Trans. G. V. Anrep. London: Oxford University Press.

Powley, R. L. 1977. "The Ventro Media Hypothalamic Syndrome Satiety, and Acephalic Phase Hypothesis." *Psychological Review* 84:89–126.

Reese, H. W., and L. D. Lipsitt. 1970. *Experimental Child Psychology*. New York: Academic.

Smith, G. P. 1995. "Pavlov and Appetite." *Integrative Physiological and Behavioral Science* 30:169–174.

Staats, C. K., and A. W. Staats. 1957. "Meaning Established by Classical Conditioning." *Journal of Experimental Psychology* 54:74–82.

Tait, R. W., and M. E. Saladin. 1986. "Concurrent Development of Excitory and Inhibitory Associations during Back Conditioning." *Animal Learning and Behavior* 14:132–137.

Thompson, R., and J. McConnell. 1955. "Classical Conditioning in the Planarian, Dugesia Doroto Cephala." *Journal of Comparative and Physiological Psychology* 48:65–68.

Watson, R. I. 1971. *The Great Psychologists*. 3rd ed. Philadelphia, Penn.: Lippincott.

Windholz, G. 1996a. "Hypnosis and Inhibition As Viewed by Heidenhain and Pavlov." *Integrative Physiological and Behavioral Science* 31:155–162.

———. 1996b. "Pavlov's Conceptualization of Paranoia within the Theory of Higher Nervous Activity." *History of Psychiatry* 7:159–166.

———. 1997. "Ivan P. Pavlov: An Overview of His Life and Psychological Work." *American Psychologist* 52:941–946.

CHAPTER 4

Burrhus F. Skinner

Burrhus F. Skinner was an American psychologist who was one of the many giants of behavioral psychology in the twentieth century. He was born in Susquehanna, Pennsylvania, in 1904. Skinner, since his early days, was an avowed behaviorist who found psychology intriguing. In 1931, he received his Ph.D. in Psychology, and then spent several years conducting research projects. *The Behavior of Organisms* was his first major publication. It was published in 1938 and provided the framework for his principles of operant conditioning. He was famous for his popular book *Walden Two* (1948), which advanced scientific principles of human behavior. Through his writings and research, over a span of two decades, Skinner was recognized as the leader in the behaviorism movement. He held and promoted this leadership until his death (Skinner, 1954, 1958, 1971; Holland and Skinner, 1961).

RESPONDENTS AND OPERANT BEHAVIOR

In Lefrançois's view, responses elicited by a stimulus are called respondents (Lefrançois, 2000). Responses emitted by an organism are called operants. In respondent behavior, the organism acts on the environment. Other differences between the two behaviors may be seen in the following ways: respondent behaviors are shown by the organism's involuntary behaviors to a stimulus, whereas operant behaviors are more voluntary.

OPERANT CONDITIONING

Operant conditioning is a form of learning "in which the consequences of behavior lead to changes in the probability of its occurrence (Skinner,

1948)." Skinner prescribed to this theory and furthered it with his own work that evolved into what has been called the behavior analysis model, which is commonly referred to as behavior modification. This model is a systematic shaping process that uses positive and negative reinforcers to obtain desired behaviors or to extinguish inappropriate ones. This technique can be used in the context of child rearing or diminishing simple deviant social behaviors (e.g., getting towed if parked in a reserved parking space), but is most widely known for its use in the classroom. The technique has been well demonstrated by several authors (Ormrod, 1999; Hergenhahn and Olson, 1997). Its benefits are felt even more profoundly in the special education classroom, where behavior problems abound, as it is widely used to change inappropriate behaviors or teach appropriate ones. Skinner's entire theory is based on the use of reinforcers (Miller and Kelley, 1994; Hergenhahn and Olson, 1997; Klein, 1996; Covington, 1992).

Skinner experimented with the use of positive and negative reinforcers and the timing in which they were given in an effort to shape a desired behavior. He created a learning apparatus called the Skinnerean Box, which was designed for "teaching" rats to push a lever in order to get food pellets. Immediately after the rat made any movement toward the lever, it received a food pellet (positive reinforcer). With each successive move it made toward the lever, it was compensated with a food pellet and this reinforced the rat's movement toward the level (successive approximations). It was ultimately rewarded with food when it finally reached the lever and pushed down hard enough to receive the pellets from the dispenser (Iverson, 1992). This idea of shaping the rat's behavior was extended beyond the laboratory and used to shape human behavior as well (Delprato and Midley, 1992). Key components that are integral in achieving successful behavior modification are timing, consistency, and effectiveness of the reinforcers. Skinner discovered the importance of the timing of the reinforcer. If the food pellet was not given to the rat immediately after he moved toward the lever, the movement was not being reinforced. In order for behavior modification to be successful, the delay between the response and the reinforcer should be minimal. At the same time, Skinner concluded that consistency is equally important. Initially, the reinforcer must be given after every response; and then after some learning has taken place it is not always necessary, or in some cases desirable, to reinforce each response.

Lastly, Skinner discovered that the reinforcer being used must, in fact, be rewarding for the learner (Ormrod, 1999). If student's behavior is being reinforced with candy and the student hates candy, then little learning will occur. Therefore, it is often necessary to experiment with different options for different students. Another important factor is that not all reinforcers are contrived; natural consequences of one's actions can be an equally or more effective reinforcer. Skinner developed the concept of two kinds of reinforcers: primary and secondary. Primary reinforcers are innately reinforcing and have not been learned (i.e., food, warmth, and sexual gratification), while secondary reinforcers are learned through classical conditioning (Hergenhahn and Olson, 1997). When these two reinforcers are paired together, learning naturally occurs. For example, in teaching a dog to sit, a treat (primary reinforcer) is given each time the dog sits as the owner says "good dog" (secondary reinforcer). The dog eventually associates the treat with "good dog" and eventually is conditioned to accept "good dog" as the positive reinforcer in the absence of the treat. This pairing of reinforcers is done regularly without premeditation of child rearing, on the job, and in many other social situations.

REINFORCEMENT

Skinner considered that animal trainers, parents, and educators cannot realistically walk around with primary reinforcers in their pockets and devote all of their time to rewarding behaviors in a timely, consistent manner while keeping in mind all of the different reinforcers that are effective for each individual. With this in mind, Skinner developed six different schedules of reinforcement and tested each of their effects on behavior.

The first schedule is continuous reinforcement schedule, in which the investigator uses continuous reinforcement for every correct response made. The second schedule is fixed interval reinforcement schedule where the animal is reinforced for a response made only after a set interval of time. The third schedule is fixed ratio reinforcement schedule, which is employed whenever the response made by the animal is reinforced. The fourth schedule is variable interval reinforcement; with this schedule, the animal is reinforced for responses made at the end of time intervals of variable durations. The fifth schedule is variable ratio reinforcement where the reinforcer is received after a varying number of responses have occurred; this schedule produces the highest response rate.

The sixth schedule is concurrent schedules and matching law where reinforcement is delivered under different schedules.

POSITIVE AND NEGATIVE REINFORCEMENTS

According to Skinner, a positive reinforcer, either primary or secondary, is something that, when added to the situation by a certain response, increases the probability of that response's recurrence (Skinner, 1953). Skinner also utilized and experimented with negative reinforcers in an effort to shape behavior (Skinner, 1953). Negative reinforcers are often confused with punishment, when, in fact, they are quite the contrary. Negative reinforcers remove unpleasant situations and in doing so reinforce the behavior that aided the learner in escaping the unpleasant situation. Negative reinforcers support a behavior that stops a negative event from happening or prevents it from happening at all. Using another sidewalk on a rainy day rather than the usual one prevents you from getting splashed by the puddles as cars pass. The use of another sidewalk (target behavior) is reinforced by avoiding the wet splashes (negative reinforcer) punishment that otherwise would have occurred.

Punishment, unlike negative reinforcers, is a negative consequence that leads to the reduction in the frequency of the behavior that produced it. Punishment suppresses a response as long as it is applied; the habit is not weakened and will return. According to Skinner:

> punishment is designed to remove awkward, dangerous, or otherwise unwanted behavior from a repertoire on the assumption that a person who has been punished is less likely to behave in the same way again. Unfortunately, the matter is not that simple. Reward and punishment do not differ merely in the direction of the changes they induce. A child who has been severely punished for sex play is not necessarily less inclined to continue, and a man who has been imprisoned for violent assault is not necessarily less inclined toward violence. Punished behavior is likely to reappear after the punitive contingencies are withdrawn. (Skinner, 1971)

In summary, Skinner's major disagreement with punishment is that it is not effective in changing behavior in the long run.

According to Skinner, punishment is used so widely because it is reinforcing to the punisher (Skinner, 1953). He stated that we instinctively attack anyone whose behavior displeases us. The immediate effect of the practice is reinforcing enough to explain its currency.

Skinner has provided us with some alternatives to punishment.

1. Change the circumstance causing the undesirable behavior. For example, rearrange the seating of a child may reduce or eliminate the behavior.
2. The undesirable behavior can be satisfied by permitting the organism to perform the act until it is tired of it.
3. Some behaviors are considered normal for the development stage of the child; simply waiting for the child to outgrow the behavior is a recommended procedure.
4. Skinner recommended that letting time pass and ignoring the undesirable behavior may be an effective method for controlling the behavior.
5. Probably the most effective alternative process according to Skinner is extinction (Skinner, 1953). He stated further that behavior persists because it is being reinforced. To reduce or eliminate undesirable behavior, one needs to find the source of reinforcement and remove it.

EXTINCTION

Once the reinforcement has been withdrawn, the amount of time required before the organism stops responding deviates from organism to organism due to continuous and fixed schedules of reinforcement (Ormrod, 1999). When a response is not reinforced, it gradually returns to its baseline. During the initial stage of extinction, there may be a brief increase in the behavior being extinguished (Lerman and Iwata, 1995). Rachlin refers to this process as an extinction burst (Rachlin, 1991).

An excellent example according to Lefrançois is that a behavior that has been extinguished through withdrawal of reinforcement often reappears without any further conditioning when the animal is again placed under the same experimental conditions (Lefrançois, 2000). The extinction period following spontaneous recovery is almost invariably much shorter than the first. Assume that the pigeon that Skinner conditioned to peck at a disk is taken out of the cage and not allowed to return to it for a considerable period of time. If it does not peck at the disk when it is reintroduced into the cage, one can infer that forgetting has occurred. One of Skinner's experiments showed at least one pigeon that had still not forgotten the disk-pecking response after six years. He also reported one instance of a pigeon that emitted 10,000 pecks prior to extinction.

SHAPING

Slavin writes that shaping is employed in behavioral learning theories to refer to the teaching of new behaviors by reinforcing learners for approaching the desired final behavior (Slavin, 2000). Shaping is considered to be an important tool in classroom instruction. Teachers may model and teach skills to children step by step until the children are ready to perform certain tasks in the skills and finally to complete the total skill. Shaping is also employed in training animals to complete tasks or acts when they do not ordinarily perform. The environment must be controlled if shaping is to be effective. The Skinnerean Box is an excellent example of controlling the environment. The box included a metal bar that, when pushed down, caused a food tray to swing into reach long enough for the rat to grab a food pellet. By conducting the tasks, the rat was reinforced with food pellets.

CHAINING

"Chaining" may be defined as the linking of a sequence of responses. It is an important component used in operant conditioning. All training works backward from a primary reinforcer. The investigator reinforces one response, then two responses in a row, followed by reinforcing a sequence of three or more responses. Ormrod's example provides clarity to the process: "[S]tudents in a first-grade classroom might learn to put their work materials away, sit quietly at their desks, and then line up single file at the classroom door before going to lunch" (Ormrod, 1999). These behaviors or actions often require one step at a time, which is frequently identified as chaining.

PROGRAMMED LEARNING

Skinner's principles of learning have been applied to programmed learning. In Skinner's and Fletcher's views, programmed learning is most effective when the information to be learned is presented in small steps, when rapid feedback is given to the learners concerning the accuracy of their responses, and when the learners are permitted to learn at their own pace (Skinner, 1958; Fletcher, 1992). According to Skinner, a teaching machine meets the prerequisite for programmed learning. In an article written by Skinner in 1958, he outlined the values of teaching machines. Since his views on this matter have been succinctly reported elsewhere, I simply summarize them here. A teaching machine:

1. Simply brings the student into contact with the person who composed the materials it presents
2. Is a labor-saving device because it can bring one programmer into contact with many students
3. Provides constant interchange between program and student
4. Induces sustained activity
5. Insists that a given point be thoroughly understood, either frame by frame or set by set, before the student moves on
6. Presents just the material for which the student is ready
7. Assists the student in arriving at the correct answer
8. Reinforces the student for every correct response by using immediate feedback

Research findings involving the effectiveness of program learning are inconclusive. Research conducted by Schramm and Lumsdaine pinpointed the controversy in the field (Schramm, 1964; Lumsdaine, 1964). Approximately half of the studies summarized by Schramm found programmed learning to be effective when compared with traditional programs. Data from these studies tend to support the notion that additional research is needed to investigate the various components of programmed instruction that make it an effective teaching device.

The concepts of programmed learning have been infused into computer-assisted instruction. Computer software programs are used to instruct students in a variety of skills (Choate, 1977). Polloway and Patton allude to the value of computer-assisted instruction in teaching mathematics (Polloway and Patton, 1993). Bakken and Goldstein state that computers have the ability of presenting information in a multisensory mode, which makes them suitable for individuals with various types of disabilities (Bakken, 1998; Goldstein, 1998; Ryba, Shelby, and Nolan, 1995; Cornish, 1996).

These programmed devices have had minimum impact on educational practices today. However, I believe that the impact in the future will be significant on educational changes and reforms.

SUMMARY

Skinner's work in behaviorism makes him the indisputable spokesperson in the field (Skinner, 1953, 1954, 1958, 1966, 1971, 1989). He raised experimentation in animal behavior to a scientific level through the use of the Skinnerean Box. Other contributions include experimenting with the teaching machine and programmed learning. These experiments still have a significant impact on educational reforms today. It would be remiss if Skinner's contributions in operant conditioning were not summarized. His principles of operant conditioning were based on a system of controlling behavior through positive and negative reinforcement.

Few fields in American psychology have received more attention in the past decades than that of operant conditioning, and none has been attacked more vigorously by critics of all persuasions for its practices and theories, particularly in the area of educational and social control. Whatever the arguments for or against the methods or the theory of their operation, the fact remains that rigorous psychophysical methods have been successfully developed for animals with the aid of operant techniques.

Lefrançois sums up operant conditioning by stating that "it involves a change in the probability of a response as a function of events that immediately follow it. Events that increase the probability of a response are termed reinforcers. Aspects of the situation accompanying reinforcement become discriminative stimuli that serves as secondary reinforcers" (Lefrançois, 2000). These reinforcers may be positive or negative, primary or secondary, and a variety of reinforcement schedules may be applied to record and evaluate behaviors.

Skinner's experiments with humans and animals have been supported by a preponderance of research studies—many of which were conducted by him, as reflected throughout this chapter. Most of these studies support the premise of immediate consequences, which implies that behavioral changes are based on immediate reinforcement. In addition, pleasurable consequences increase the frequency of a behavior, whereas negative consequences reduce the frequency of behavior.

Skinner objected to speculation concerning unobserved behaviors. He believed that most theories of learning were wasteful and unproductive because they were not based on observable behaviors.

BIBLIOGRAPHY

Bakken, J. A. 1998. "Evaluating the World Wide Web." *Teaching Exceptional Children* 36 (6): 48–52.

Choate, J. S. 1977. *Successful Inclusion Teaching.* Boston: Allyn and Bacon.

Cornish, E. 1996. "The Cyberspace Out by 2025." *Education Digest* 46:4–9.

Covington, M. V. 1992. *Making the Grade: A Self-Worth Perspective on Motivation and School Reform.* Cambridge: Cambridge University Press.

Delprato, D. J., and B. D. Midley. 1992. "Some Fundamentals of B. F. Skinner's Behaviorism." *American Psychologist* 47:1507–1520.

Fletcher, J. D. 1992. "Individualized Systems of Instruction." In *Encyclopedia of Educational Research*, 6th ed., ed. M. C. Alkin. New York: Macmillan.

Goldstein, C. 1998. "Learning at Cyber Camp." *Teaching Exceptional Children* 30 (5): 16–26.

Hergenhahn, B. R., and M. H. Olson. 1997. *An Introduction to Theories of Learning.* Upper Saddle River, N.J.: Prentice Hall.

Holland, J. G., and B. A. Skinner. 1961. *The Analysis of Behavior: A Program for Self-Instruction.* New York: McGraw-Hill.

Iverson, I. H. 1992. "Skinner's Early Research: From Reflexology to Operant Conditioning." *America Psychologist* 47:1318–1328.

Klein, S. B. 1996. *Learning: Principles and Applications.* 3rd ed. New York: McGraw-Hill.

Lefrançois, G. R. 2000. *Theories of Human Learning: What the Old Man Said.* 4th ed. Pacific Grove, Calif.: Brooks/Cole.

Lerman, D. C., and B. A. Iwata. 1995. "Prevalence of the Extinction Burst and Its Attenuation during Treatment." *Journal of Applied Behavior Analysis* 28:93–94.

Lumsdaine, A. A. 1964. "Educational Technology, Programmed Learning, and Instructional Sciences." In *Theories of Learning and Instruction*, ed. E. R. Hilgard. Chicago: University of Chicago Press.

Miller, D. L., and M. L. Kelley. 1994. "The Use of Goal Setting and Contingency Contracting for Improving Children's Homework Performance." *Journal of Applied Behavior Analysis* 27:73–84.

Ormrod, J. 1999. *Human Learning.* 3rd ed. Columbus, Ohio: Merrill.

Polloway, E. A., and J. R. Patton. 1993. *Strategies for Teaching Learners with Special Needs.* New York: Merrill.

Rachlin, H. 1991. *Introduction to Modern Behaviorism.* 3rd ed. New York: Freeman.

Ryba, K., L. Shelby, and P. Nolan. 1995. "Computers Empower Students with Special Needs." *Educational Technology* 53:82.

Schramm, W. 1964. *The Research on Programmed Instruction: An Annotated Bibliography*. Washington, D.C.: U. S. Office of Education.

Skinner, B. F. 1938. *The Behavior of Organisms: An Experimental Analysis*. Englewood Cliffs, N.J.: Prentice Hall.

———. 1948. *Walden Two*. New York: Macmillan.

———. 1953. *Science and Human Behavior*. New York: Macmillan.

———. 1954. "The Science of Learning and the Art of Teaching." *Harvard Educational Review* 124:86–87.

———. 1958. "Teaching Machines." *Science* 128:969–977.

———. 1966. "What Is the Experimental Analysis of Behavior?" *Journal of Experimental Analysis of Behavior* 9:213–218.

———. 1971. *Beyond Freedom and Dignity*. New York: Knopf.

———. 1989. "The Origins of Cognitive Thought." *American Psychologist* 44:13–18.

Slavin, R. W. 2000. *Educational Psychology: Theory and practice*. 6th ed. Boston: Allyn and Bacon.

CHAPTER 5

Social Learning Theories

During the last two decades, we have witnessed the rediscovery, creation, or the validation of a great diversity of social learning theories. These theories have provided us with a common language concerning learning theories on academic performance of disabled and other individuals.

The study of social learning theories enables the school to better understand both how individuals think about school-related processes and how the children are likely to be feeling about themselves in relation to the process. The school's understanding of both the cognitive and the affective characteristics of individuals may be termed as "empathic." One way of showing empathy to children is through designing effective classroom environments that consider the cognitive and affect levels of the children (Butter, 1989; Hilliard, 1989).

The conceptual basis of this research is based on the social imitation theory of Bandura and Walters (Bandura and Walters, 1963). The common threads uniting these theories and concepts are imitation, modeling, and copying behavior intervention. Children imitate, model, and copy behavioral techniques from their environments. These models and techniques are frequently inappropriate for the school environment and create conflict and tension between children and the school. Learning, culture, and behavioral styles of these children should be incorporated and integrated into a total learning packet. Social learning theories also provide a concrete framework for the schools to begin to implement additional social skills strategies into the curriculum.

Throughout the latter half of the twentieth century social learning theory emerged as an integral part of behaviorism. As researchers defined learning paradigms, while the opponents of classical and operant conditioning offered a lawful relationship of behavior and the environment, social learning theory postulated that an individual could acquire responses by observing and subsequently imitating the behavior of others in the environment (Rotter, 1966; Bandura, 1965; Coleman, 1986).

"Social learning theory" is defined as a psychological theory that emphasizes the learning of socially expected, appropriate, and desirable behavior (Kahn and Cangemi, 1979; Rotter, 1966). Social learning theorists view behavior as an interaction between an individual and the environment. From its inception, social learning theory was an attempt to integrate the stimulus–response and the cognitive theories. Advocates of this school of thought felt that theorists must include both behavioral and internal constructs in any theory of human behavior and learning (Rotter, 1966; Bandura, 1963).

LEV VYGOTSKY'S THEORY

Lev Vygotsky's theory, according to Moll, lends support to the concept that natural properties as well as social relations and constraints make possible the social construction of a child's higher psychological processes (Moll, 1991). The three major components of Vygotsky's theory are: (1) the internalization of culture means; (2) the interpersonal or social process of mediation; and (3) a child's knowledge is formed within the zone of proximal developmental cognitive space defined by social relational boundaries.

One of the major postulates of Vygotsky's theory, according to Moll, is that there is a functional relationship between the effects of the culture on cognitive development and biological growth (Moll, 1991). The physical, biological, and neurological determinants are more readily understood and generally agreed on. However, the impact of the cultural determinants are not as easily understood. The cultural determinants include social processes that transform naturally through the mastery and use of cultural signs. In essence, on the one hand the natural development of children's behavior form the biological conditions necessary to develop higher psychological processes; on the other hand culture provides the conditions by which the higher psychological processes may be realized.

COMMONALITY AMONG THEORIES

The common threads uniting these theories and concepts are imitation, modeling, and copying behavior (Bandura and Walters, 1963). Individuals imitate, model, and copy behaviors directly from their environments. These models and techniques are, however, considered inappropriate and create conflict and tension between children, society, and the school. Learning, culture, and behavioral styles of individuals should be, as much as possible, incorporated and integrated into a total learning packet. Social learning theories provide a concrete framework for society and the school to begin to implement additional social skills strategies into the curriculum.

"Social skills" is a phrase used to describe a wide range of behaviors varying in complexity and is thought to be necessary for effective social function and academic success. Behaviors that constitute social skills development may vary depending on the situation, role, sex, age, and disabling conditions of individuals.

SOCIAL COGNITIVE THEORY

By 1986, Bandura defined his position by using new terminology. "Social learning theory" was replaced by the term "social cognitive theory" (Bandura, 1989; Rosenstock, Strecher, and Becker, 1988; Corcoran, 1991).

Social cognitive theory is an attempt to explain human behavior from a natural science perspective by integrating what is known about both the effects of the environment and the role of cognition. It suggests that people are not merely products of their environment nor are they driven to behave as they do by internal forces. Social cognitive theory presents a cognitive interactional model of human functioning that describes behavior results from reciprocal influences among the social, physical, personal, thinking, feeling, and perception environments and the individual's behavior itself (Kauffman, 1993). In summation, social cognitive theory reconceptualizes that thought and other personal factors, behavior, and the environment all operate as interacting determinants. Because of the reciprocal causation, therapeutic efforts can be directed at all three determinants. Psychosocial functioning is improved by altering faculty thought patterns, by increasing behavioral competencies and skills in dealing with situational demands, and by altering adverse social conditions (Bandura, 1986). Bandura used the term "triadic reciprocality" to describe the social cognitive model. Because we have systems with which to code, retain, and process information, several human attributes are incorporated into social cognitive theory.

Social learning theory is concerned with acquisition of new behaviors that occur as unlearned or previously learned responses that are modified or combined into more complete behaviors. This process, according to social learning theory, is sped up by direct reinforcement or expected reinforcement through imitation (Miller and Dollard, 1941).

NEAL E. MILLER AND JOHN DOLLARD

Neal E. Miller and John Dollard were influenced by the earlier work of Hull (Miller and Dollard, 1941). Theories developed by Miller and Dollard investigated the circumstances under which a response and a cue stimulus become connected. Accordingly, both a cue and a response must be present in order for social learning to exist. Four factors of psychological principles are outlined by Miller and Dollard: drive, cure, response, and reward.

Drive

"Drive" is defined as the first factor in learning that impels action or response. It is the motivating factor that allows the individual to view a situation and react toward a stimulus. Individuals have primary or innate drives and secondary or acquired drives. The behavior that the drive leads to will be learned if it results in a reduction of drive (Miller and Dollard, 1941). Reinforcement always results from reduction of drive (Kahn and Cangemi, 1979).

Cues

Cues determine when the individual will respond, where, and which response he/she will make. In social learning, the individual waits for cues from society and then responds to those cues. Society can control the individual by sending out various cues and rewarding the response, either positively or negatively. The presence or absence of cues, number of cues, and/or types of cues can determine the resulting amount and type of learning that occurs.

Response

The response is the most integral part of assessing whether or not the individual has learned, and to what degree learning exists. It is the result of the individual's reaction elicited by cues.

Reward

Reward determines if the response will be repeated. If a response is not rewarded, the tendency to repeat that response is weakened. Similarly, responses that are rewarded are likely to be repeated. Moreover, a connection can be made between the stimulus and the reward, thereby strengthening the response. Rewards may be positive or negative and can themselves become a motivating factor or drive.

Miller and Dollard outlined the following phrases to describe imitation (Miller and Dollard, 1941).

Same Behavior

Same behavior is created by two people who perform the same act in response to independent stimulation by the same cue. Each has learned independently to make the response. The behavior may be learned with or without independent aides.

Matched-Dependent Behavior

Matched-dependent behavior primarily consists of leadership by which followers are not presently aware of the consequences of their action, but rely totally on the leadership of others and follow without question. The individual is controlled by the cues that the leader exhibits and the response from the individual becomes a predictable source for the leader to maintain. Most behavior is demonstrated in this matched-dependent mode. No immediate reward criteria need be present at this time. The actions of the individual can become motivating within themselves. The participation and interaction the individual is allowed to take part in becomes the rewarding factor.

Copying Behavior

Copying behavior is demonstrated when an individual duplicates his/ her attitudes and responses so that they match that which has been deemed socially acceptable by the peer group of the individual. The individual is rewarded for modeling after a select group of peers and the acceptance of their norms. Miller and Dollard have suggested that the child's tendency to copy is an acquired secondary drive that can account for the psychoanalytic concept of identification (Miller and Dollard, 1941).

JULIAN B. ROTTER

Julian B. Rotter combined a social learning framework and behavioral approaches with applications for clinical, personality, and social psychology (Rotter, 1954, 1966, 1990). While Rotter was inspired through his work with his former teacher Kurt Lewin, he rejected Lewin's and Hull's position because he felt that they did not conceptualize past experiences. Thus, they did not explain and predict all behavior. According to Rotter: "Cognitive approaches were of little value in predicting the behavior of rats; and approaches that did not take into account the fact that human beings think, generalize along semantic lines, and are motivated by social goals and reinforced by social reinforcements, were extremely limited in their explanations or predictions" (Rotter, 1966). Rotter turned into the learning theorist, wherein his thinking was strongly influenced by Alfred Adler. Beginning in 1946, immediately following World War II, Rotter culminated work from his master's thesis and his doctoral dissertation and published it as *Social Learning and Clinical Psychology* (1954).

From a constructs point of view, Rotter outlined seven principles of social learning theory:

1. The unit of investigation for the study of personality is the interaction of the individual and his/her meaningful environment. This principle describes the social learning position of an interactionist approach.
2. Personality constructs are not dependent for explanation on constructs in any other field. Rotter contended with this principle that scientific constructs should be consistent across all fields of science.
3. Behavior as described by personality constructs takes place in space and time. According to Rotter, any constructs that describe events themselves are rejected because constructs must describe physical as well as psychological variables.
4. Not all behavior of an organism may be usefully described with per-

sonality constructs. Behavior that may be usefully described by personality constructs appears in organisms at a particular level or stage of complexity and development. This postulate recognizes that events are amenable to specific terms. Likewise, they are not amenable to others.

5. Personality has unity. In this context, Rotter defines "unity" in terms of relative stability and interdependence. The presence or relative stability does not, however, exclude specificity of response and change.

6. Behavior as described by personality constructs has a directionality aspect. Behavior is said to be goal directed. This principle is the motivational focus of social learning theory. Social learning theorists identify specific events that have a known effect either for groups or for individuals as reinforcers. Environmental conditions that determine the direction of behavior also refer to goals or reinforcement. When reference is made to the individual determining the direction, Rotter calls these needs. Both goals and needs are inferred from referents to the interaction of the person with his/her meaningful environment. Learned behavior is goal-oriented and new goals derive their importance for the individual from their associations with earlier goals.

7. The occurrence of a behavior of a person is determined not only by the nature or importance of goals and reinforcements, but also by the person's anticipation or expectancy that these goals will occur. This principle is an attempt to determine how an individual in a given situation behaves in terms of potential reinforcers (Rotter, 1966).

Rotter's expectancy–reinforcement theory stresses that the major basic modes of behavior are learned in social situations and are intricately fused with needs required for their satisfaction (Kahn and Cangemi, 1979).

Internal versus external control, that is, control of reinforcement often referred to as locus of control, is firmly embedded in Rotter's social learning theory (Rotter, 1954, 1966, 1990; Strickland, 1989). Internal versus external control refers to the degree to which persons expect that a reinforcement or an outcome of their behavior is contingent on their behavior or personal characteristic versus the degree to which persons expect that the reinforcement or outcome is a function of chance, luck, or fate or is under the powerful influence of others.

Basic to Rotter's position is the fact that reinforcement acts to strengthen an expectancy that a particular behavior will be followed by that reinforcement in the future. Once an expectancy for a reinforcement sequence is built, the failure of the reinforcement to occur will reduce or extinguish the expectancy. As an infant grows and has more experiences, he/she differentiates casual events from the events that are reinforcing. Expectancies also generalize along a gradient from a specific situation to a series of situations that are perceived as related or similar (Rotter, 1966).

ALBERT BANDURA

Albert Bandura is considered the forerunner of social learning theory and is most often associated with empirical research in the area (Bandura, 1965, 1989; Coleman, 1986; Evans, 1989; Tudge and Winterhoff, 1991; Bandura and Walters, 1963; Weignan, Kuttschreuter, and Baarda, 1992).

Because concerns with subjective measurement create skepticism among scientists regarding social learning theory, Bandura insisted on experimental controls. Thus, he was able to transcend from empirical observations to experimental validity (Rotter, 1966; Bandura and Walters, 1963; Tudge and Winterhoff, 1991). Bandura wanted a broader meaning of behaviorism that would include learning from the behavior of others. He, too, was dissatisfied with the stimulus–response theorists who contended that people acquire competencies and new patterns of behavior through response consequences (Bandura, 1986). He could not imagine how a culture could transmit its language and mores through trial and error (Evans, 1989).

Bandura's major concern was in the social transmission of behavior. Two prevailing principles support the theory. The first is the element of observational learning and the second is the inclusion of a model or an individual who might serve as an example for another (Kahn and Cangemi, 1979; Bandura, 1966). Learning through imitation is called observational learning (Bandura and Walters, 1963). Modeling is a process of teaching through example that produces learning through imitation. The basic assumptions underlying Bandura's position is that behavior is learned and organized through central integrative mechanisms prior to motor execution (Bandura, 1971).

Observational Learning

Individuals acquire cognitive representations of behavior by observing models as previously indicated. These cognitive representations are in the form of memory codes stored in long-term memory. They may be either visual imagery codes or verbal propositional codes. Bandura used the terms "observational learning" and "modeling" interchangeably to refer to learning that takes place in a social context. He preferred the term "modeling" (or "observational learning") over the term "imitation" because he believed that imitation is only one way in which we learn from models (Mussen, 1983).

Many behaviors are learned without the benefit of reinforcement. Individuals learn many things by observing others (Best, 1993). That is, other people serve as behavioral models. This is the main principle of social learning theory proposed by Bandura and his colleagues (Bandura and Walters, 1963). What is the difference between observational learning and imitation? Take the following episode as an example. Suppose you watch someone at a party eat a mint from a tray of candies. The person turns blue, falls to the floor, and thrashes about while moaning loudly. You then eat a mint from the same tray. Even though you imitated the model's behavior, you can conclude that you learned very little from observing the model. McCormick conducted a similar study having a skilled gymnast watching another gymnast's routine (McCormick and Pressley, 1997). The skilled gymnast had no trouble performing the acts, whereas a less skilled gymnast would.

In observational learning, people learn through vicarious experiences. That is, when they see others experience reinforcements and punishments, they form expectations about the reinforcements or punishments that they might receive for their own behaviors. In an experiment, Bandura had young children view a film in which a child exhibited some very novel physical and verbal aggressive behaviors to a set of toys (Bandura, 1965). At the completion of the film, the child model was either punished for the aggression (spanked and verbally rebuked), reinforced for it (given soft drinks, candy, and praise), or provided no consequences. After watching the film, the children were left alone in the room where the film was made with an opportunity to play with the toys seen in the film. Children who watched the film in which the child model was spanked for aggression were much more likely to exhibit the aggressive behaviors when interacting with the toys than if they had watched the film depicting reward or no consequences for the aggression. Then, all children in the experiment were offered stickers and fruit juice if they would show the experimenter the aggressive behaviors that the film model exhibited. The children had little difficulty reproducing the behavior.

McCormick and Pressley view this as a situation where the children had clearly learned the aggressive behaviors in question because they could reproduce those behaviors when given an incentive to do so (McCormick and Pressley, 1997). However, they were less likely to perform the aggressive behaviors when given an incentive to do so. They were even less likely to perform the aggressive behaviors after viewing the film in which the child model had been punished because they had learned to expect punishment for aggressive behavior from the film. Performance of a behavior depends on knowing a response as well as the expectation of reinforcements. Data from Bandura's study suggested the fun of playing with the toys aggressively was not worth the risk of getting spanked or verbally rebuked if no reward was given. Social learning theory stresses not only principles of behavioral learning theory, but also many aspects of cognitive theory as well.

Modeling and Imitation

Bandura believed that the basic way that children learn is through imitation of models in their social environment and the primary mechanism driving development is observation (Bandura, 1965). Imitation is to copy, to follow a model, or to repeat, rehearse, or reproduce (Bandura and Walters, 1963).

Bandura identified two kinds of processes by which children acquire attitudes, values, and patterns of social behavior. Direct imitation is described as explicit directives about what adults, most often parents and teachers, want the child to learn; they attempt to shape the child's behavior through rewards and punishments and/or through direct instruction. Active imitation, through which personality patterns are primarily acquired, consists of parental attitudes and behaviors, most of which the parents have not attempted to teach (Bandura, 1967; Kahn and Cangemi, 1979).

Bandura pointed out that human subjects in social settings can acquire new behaviors simply by seeing them presented by a model. He maintains that even if the observer does not make the response him/herself and even if at the time neither he/she nor the model is reinforced for the behavior, the observer may learn the response so that he/she can perform it later. The observer acquires internal representational responses that mediate subsequent behavioral reproduction or performance (Bandura, 1989).

A second subprocess is retention of the observed behavior. Bandura contended that observational learning can be retained over long periods of time without overt response. Retention depends in part on sufficient coding or mediating the event and on covert rehearsals.

A third subprocess is motoric reproduction. The observer may be able to imagine and to code behaviors of which he/she is motorically incapable. Motor responses are most readily acquired when the observer already possesses the competent skills and needs only to synthesize them into new patterns.

Several constructs have been applied to the modeling process. The first construct, imitation, is the process wherein the person copies exactly what he/she sees the model doing. The model's example is repeated, rehearsed, or reproduced. The observer's next step is identification, that is, the process that requires incorporation of personality patterns. The observer has to determine how and/or if the behavior response pattern embodies his/her personality. In most cases, the observer performs the learned behavior embellished with his/her idiosyncrasies rather than imitating the model's actions precisely. Bandura felt that imitation was too narrow, and identification, too diffuse. The third construct is social facilitation. In this process, new competencies are not acquired and inhibitions serve as social guides (Bandura and Walters, 1963).

Actual performance depends on incentive or motivation. The absence of positive incentives or negative sanctions may inhibit the response or the individual may have a reason to make the response. For example, parental prohibitions against foul language by their child and/or the child that is not given an opportunity to talk, dress, or feed him/herself may have acquired the necessary responses through observations, but this child will not deem it necessary to actually perform the response. Bandura acknowledged the important influences of personal factors, endowed potentialities, and acquired competencies, and stressed reciprocity between internal mechanism and the social environment (Moore, 1987).

According to Bandura, there are three effects of modeling influences (Bandura, 1977). First, modeling can facilitate the acquisition of new behaviors that did not exist in the observer's repertoire. Second, previously acquired responses can strengthen or weaken inhibitory responses in the observer (disinhibitory effect). Finally, observation can serve to elicit a response that has been previously exhibited by the model. This response facilitation effect was demonstrated in studies conducted by Bandura in which children observed aggressive behaviors by models who were rewarded or punished for their aggressive acts (Bandura, 1965,

1977). Voluminous amounts of literature support the use of modeling as an effective teaching strategy (Bandura, Ross, and Ross, 1963; Tudge and Winterhoff, 1991, 1993; Bandura, 1986, 1989; Bandura, Gusec, and Mendlove, 1967).

During the 1960s, Bandura and Walters conducted a now-classic series of experiments on imitation (Bandura and Walters, 1963). By introducing actions of the model as the independent variable, Bandura and Walters were able to observe the effects on the behavior of children who had observed the model. Furthermore, by systematically varying the behavioral characteristics of the models (e.g., from nuturant to powerful, to cold, to neutral) they were able to assert the kinds of persons who were the most effective models (Damon, 1977). They noted specifically that other adults, peers, and symbolic models are significant in the learning process of children. When exposed to conflicting role standards as represented by adults, peers, and other observed models, children will adopt different standards than if adults alone provided the model. Peer modeling, however, is no more effective than child–adult interaction. The attitude of the child toward the model, whether or not the model is rewarded for his/her behavior, and the personal characteristics of the model are more important to Bandura (Bandura, 1986, 1989).

Vicarious learning as it relates to television viewing has been investigated extensively (Bandura and Walters, 1963; Bandura, Gusec, and Mendlove, 1966; Bandura, Ross, and Ross, 1961, 1963). Bandura's work in the 1960s and 1970s demonstrated the powerful effects of both live and filmed models on young children's behavior. Viewing of television violence was found to correlate significantly with children's aggressive behavior (Eron, 1987).

Self-Efficacy

Bandura's most recent emphasis has been on individual factors in social-interactive contexts. Introduced in 1977, Bandura continued several decades of research regarding the basic source of motivation (Bandura, 1976, 1977). He outlined a theoretical framework in which the concept of self-efficacy received a central role for analyzing the changes achieved in clinical treatment of fearful and avoidant behavior. Because the results of his research showed good maintenance and transfer, the concept of self-efficacy was expanded by adding a program of self-directed mastery (Carroll, 1993). Bandura agreed that if individuals are allowed to succeed on their own, they will not attribute their success to the use of mastery aides or to the therapist. This clinical tool restored an individual's coping capabilities. He felt that the treatments that were most effective were built on an "empowerment model." Continued research suggested to the investigators that they could predict with considerable accuracy the speed of therapeutic change and the degree of generality from the extent to which the individuals' perceived efficacy was enhanced. Bandura felt strongly that if you really wanted to help people you must provide them with competencies, build a strong belief, and create opportunities for them to develop the competencies (Evans, 1989; Bandura, 1995).

Self-efficacy theory addresses the origins of beliefs of personal efficacy, their structure and function, the processes through which they operate, and their diverse effects (Bandura, 1995). Four main sources of self-efficacy are cited (Bandura, 1977). The most effective way of creating a strong sense of self-efficacy is through mastery experiences. As individuals master skills, they tend to raise their expectations about their capabilities. Vicarious experiences provided by social models is the second method of creating efficacy beliefs. Seeing people who are similar succeed raises the observer's level of aspiration. Bandura noted, however, that this influence is most effective when the observer perceives him/herself to be similar to the model (Bandura, 1977). Social persuasion or verbally encouraging persons that they have what it takes to succeed is regarded by Bandura as a weaker influence. Finally, emotional arousal is the source that serves as an indicator to an individual that he/she is not coping well with a situation, the self-regulating capacity.

As Bandura examined psychological principles as a means of creating and strengthening expectations of personal efficacy, he made a distinction between efficacy expectations and response outcome expectancies (Bandura, 1977). "Outcome expectancy" is defined as the individual's estimate that a given behavior will lead to specific outcomes. An efficacy expectation is the conviction that one can successfully execute the behavior that is necessary to produce the outcomes.

Perceived self-efficacy is referred to as an individual's act of raising or lowering his/her self-efficacy beliefs. A major goal of self-efficacy research is an investigation of the conditions under which self-efficacy beliefs alter the resulting changes. The effects of self-efficacy in regulating human functioning are evident in human cognitive motivational effect and selectional process (Bandura, 1989, 1995). There are three levels of self-efficacy theory that are applied to cognition of interest to educators.

The first application is concerned with how children perceived self-efficacy affects their rate of learning. This level of self-efficacy concerns the students' belief in their capacities to master academic affairs. In 1991, Moulton, Brown, and Lent conducted a meta-analysis to determine the relations of self-efficacy beliefs to academic outcomes. Results revealed positive and significant relationships between self-efficacy beliefs, academic performance, and persistence outcomes across a wide variety of subjects, experimental designs, and assessment methods. Moulton, Brown, and Lent supported an earlier study by Schunk (Schunk, 1987). A second level of application examines how teachers' perceptions of their instructional efficacy affects children academically. The classroom atmosphere is partially determined by the teachers' belief in their own instructional efficacy and how it affects children academically. The recommendation for teachers is to teach children the cognitive tools with which to achieve and enhance their skills of efficacy so that they can use the skills effectively. Bandura felt that skills are a general rather than a fixed trait (Bandura, 1989). In addition, people with the same skills can perform poorly, adequately, or extraordinarily depending on how well they use the subskills that they have developed. The third level of application is concerned with the perceived efficacy of the school. Collective efficacy of the school as a whole fosters academic achievement of the children in the school and creates an environment conducive to learning (Evans, 1989; Ashton and Webb, 1986).

Self-efficacy has been employed to enhance the academic skills of children who are learning disabled (Schunk, 1987); to generate health-related action (Bandura, 1995; Rosenstock, Strecher, and Becker, 1988); to train self-management (Frayne and Lantham, 1987) in achievement predictions in marketing (Kalechstein and Norwicki, 1993); to train self-confidence in sports (George, 1994), career choice, and development and addictive behavior (Bandura, 1995); and in many other applications that are too numerous to mention here.

SUMMARY

As with information processing theory, social learning theory is a framework or general theoretical approach that encompasses the work of many theorists. The approach originated in the 1930s and 1940s by Miller, Dollard, and their associates, who proposed that imitation is the primary learning mechanism for most social behaviors. Subsequently, the social learning theory was spearheaded by Bandura and his colleagues (Bandura and Walters, 1963), who initially attempted to explain the acquisition of aggression and other social behaviors through the mechanisms of observation and vicarious reinforcement.

Bandura laid out the conceptual framework of his approach in his book *Social Learning Theory* (1977). His theory is based on a model of reciprocal determinism. This means that Bandura rejected both the humanist/existentialist position viewing people as free agents and the behaviorist position viewing behavior as controlled by the environment. Rather, external determinants behavior (such as rewards and punishments) and internal determinants (such as thoughts, expectations, and beliefs) are considered part of a system of interlocking determinants that influence not only behavior, but also the various parts of the system. Each part of the system, behavior, cognition, and environmental influences affects each of the other parts. People are neither free agents nor passive reactors to external pressures. Instead, through self-regulatory processes, they have the ability to exercise some measure of control over their own actions. As self-regulation results from symbolic processing of information, Bandura in his theorizing assigned an increasingly prominent role to cognition. In 1986, he started calling his approach social cognitive theory, rather than social learning theory.

Bandura's theory is similar to behavioral learning theory in that it is primarily concerned with behavioral change. The question lies in the definition of learning. Does behavior learning produce a relatively permanent change in behavior? A major difference between them lies in their concepts of how people acquire complex, new behaviors. Bandura found it hard to believe that learning a relatively permanent change in behavior is acquired through reinforcements as Burrhus F. Skinner claims. Reinforcement is the concept behaviorists use to describe the acquisition of complex behaviors. It is a process in which the organism is initially reinforced for responses that faintly resemble some target behavior. Then, over time, reinforcement is gradually reserved for behaviors that become increasingly similar to the target behavior until, at last, the target behavior is achieved. Bandura offered the example of language where the child masters thousands of words and complex syntax and grammar by the time he/she enters school (Bandura, 1986). The rapidly and seeming ease with which children acquire language does not fit well with the tedious process of reinforcing. Bandura pointed out that cognitive and social development would be greatly retarded if we learned only through the effects of our own actions. Fortunately, most human behavior is learned by observing the behavior of others.

Many of the differences between Bandura's and other theoretical approaches to human learning are made apparent by contrasting their views of where the causes of human behavior are located. Personal determinism theorists claim that behavior is a function of instincts, traits, drives, beliefs, or motivational forces within the individual. Most cognitive theorists take the interactional view that behavior is determined by the interaction of internal forces and environmental influences. That is, they believe that people's thoughts and beliefs interact with information from the environment to produce behavior. However, this model does not take into account how a person's behavior may lead to environmental changes that, in turn, may influence how he/she thinks about a situation.

Bandura viewed the relationship of behavior, person, and environment as a three-way reciprocal process called triadic reciprocality. Bandura suggested that the person, the environment, and the person's behavior itself all interact to produce the person's subsequent behavior. In other words, none of the three components can be understood in isolation of the others as a determiner of human behavior. Bandura further stated that behavior can also create environments: "We are all acquainted with problem-prone individuals who, through their obnoxious conduct, predictably breed negative social climates wherever they go. Others are equally skilled at bringing out the best in those with whom they interact" (Bandura, 1977). Bandura pointed out that the relative influence exerted by personal, behavioral, and environmental factors will vary across individuals and circumstances (Bandura, 1986). In some cases, environmental conditions are all-powerful. For example, if people are dropped into deep water, they will engage in swimming behavior regardless of any of the differences in their cognitive processes and behavior repertories.

The application of Bandura's social learning principles to social situations have wide implementations for the school and other social agencies charged with instructing disabled individuals. The principles outlined in this chapter have been successfully demonstrated with many groups, including disabled individuals. Applications of these principles do not require extensive training or preparation.

According to Bandura, most human behavior can be self-regulated by individuals if they are given practical models to imitate (Bandura, 1977). He further articulated that an individual's moral behavior has to be internalized for immoral behaviors to be changed. In essence, individuals must observe and be given practical models to observe, which will aid them in internalizing their behaviors.

BIBLIOGRAPHY

Ashton, P. T., and R. B. Webb. 1986. *Making a Difference: Teacher's Sense of Efficacy and Student Achievement*. White Plains, N.Y.: Longman.

Bandura, A. 1965. *Social Learning and Personality*. New York: Holt, Rinehart, and Winston.

———. 1971. "Psychotherapy Based upon Modeling Principles." In *Handbook of Psychotherapy and Behavior Change*, ed. A. E. Bergin and S. L. Garfield. Englewood Cliffs, N.J.: Prentice Hall.

———. 1976. "Social Learning Analysis of Aggression." In *Analysis of Delinquency and Aggression*, ed. E. Ribes-Inesta and A. Bandura. Hillsdale, N.J.: Halsted.

———. 1977. "Self-Efficacy toward a Unifying Theory of Behavior Change." *Psychological Review* 84:191–215.

———. 1977. *Social Learning Theory*. Englewood Cliffs, N.J.: Prentice Hall.

———. 1986. *Social Foundations of Thought and Action: A Social Cognitive Theory*. Englewood Cliffs, N.J.: Prentice Hall.

———. 1989. "Human Agency in Social Cognitive Theory." *American Psychologist* 44:1175–1184.

———. 1995. *Self-Efficacy in Changing Societies*. Cambridge, Mass.: Harvard University Press.

Bandura, A., and R. H. Walters. 1963. *Social Learning and Personality Development*. New York: Holt, Rinehart, and Winston.

Bandura, A., J. E. Gusec, and F. L. Menlove. 1966. "Observational Learning As a Function of Symbolization and Incentive Set." *Child Development* 37:499–506.

———. 1967. "Vicarious Extinction of Avoidance Behavior." *Journal of Personality and Social Behavior* 5:16–23.

Bandura, A., D. Ross, and S. A. Ross. 1961. "Transmission of Aggression through Imitation of Aggressive Models." *Journal of Abnormal and Social Psychology* 63:575–582.

Best, D. L. 1993. "Inducing Children to Generate Mnemonic Organization Strategies: An Examination of Long-Term Retention and Materials." *Developmental Psychology* 29:325.

Butter, O. B. 1989. "Early Help for Kids at Risk: Our Nations Best Investment." *NEA Today* 7:51–53.

Carroll, J. 1993. "Self-Efficacy Related to Transfer of Learning and Theory-Based Instructional Design." *Journal of Adult Education* 22:37–43.

Coleman, M. 1986. *Behavior Disorders: Theory and Practice*. Englewood Cliffs, N.J.: Prentice Hall.

Corcoran, K. J. 1991. "Efficacy, Skills, Reinforcement, and Choice Behavior." *American Psychology* (February) 46:155–157.

Damon, W. 1977. *The Social World of the Child*. San Francisco, Calif.: Jossey-Bass.

Eron, L. 1987. "The Development of Aggressive Behavior from the Perspective of a Developing Behaviorism." *American Psychologist* 42:435–442.

Evans, R. 1989. *Albert Bandura: The Man and His Ideas—A Dialogue*. New York: Praeger.

Frayne, C., and F. Lantham. 1987. "Application of Social Learning Theory to Employee Self-Management of Attendance." *Journal of Applied Psychology* 72:383–392.

George, T. 1994. "Self-Confidence and Baseball Performance: A Causal Examination of Self-Efficacy Theory." *Journal of Sport and Exercise Psychology* 16:381–389.

Hilliard, A. G. 1989. "Teachers and Cultural Styles in a Pluralistic Society." *NEA Today* 7:65–69.

Kahn, K., and J. Cangemi. 1979. "Social Learning Theory: The Role of Imitation and Modeling in Learning Socially Desirable Behavior." *Education* 100:41–46.

Kalechstein, A., and S. Norwicki. 1993. "Social Learning Theory and Prediction of Achievement in Telemarketers." *Journal of Social Psychology* 134:547–548.

Kauffman, J. 1993. *Characteristics of Emotional and Behavioral Disorders of Children and Youth*. New York: Merrill.

McCormick, C. B., and M. Pressley. 1997. *Educational Psychology: Learning, Instructions, and Assessments*. New York: Longman.

Miller, N. E., and J. Dollard. 1941. *Social Learning and Imitation*. New Haven, Conn.: Yale University Press.

Moll, I. 1991. "The Material and the Social in Vgotsky's Theory of Cognitive Development." Cleaning House on Teacher Education, ED352186.

Moore, S. 1987. "Piaget and Bandura: The Need for a Unified Theory of Learning." Paper presented at the biennial meeting of the Society for Research in Child Development, Baltimore, Md., April 23–26, 1987.

Moulton, A. K., S. Brown, and R. Lent. 1991. "Relation of Self-Efficacy Beliefs in Academic Outcomes: A Meta-Analytic Investigation." *Journal of Counseling Psychology* 38:30–38.

Mussen, P. H. 1983. *Handbook on Child Psychology*. 4th ed. New York: Wiley.

Rosenstock, I., V. Strecher, and M. Becker. 1988. "Contribution of HBM to Self-Efficacy Theory." *Health Education Quarterly* 15:175–183.

Rotter, J. 1954. *Social Learning and Clinical Psychology*. New York: Prentice Hall.

———. 1966. "Generalized Expectancies for Internal versus External Control of Reinforcement." *Psychological Monographs: General and Applied* 80:80.

———. 1990. "Internal versus External Control of Reinforcement: A Case History Variable." *American Psychologist* 45:489–493.

Schunk, D. 1987. "Peer Models and Children's Behavior Change." *Review of Educational Research* 57:149–174.

Strickland, F. 1989. "Internal–External Control Expectancies from Contingency to Creativity." *American Psychologist* 44:1–12.

Tudge, R., and P. Winterhoff. 1991. "Vzgotsky, Piaget, and Bandura: Perspectives on the Relations between the Social World and Cognitive Development." *Human Development* 36:61–81.

Weignan, O., O. Kuttschreuter, and B. Baarda. 1992. "A Longitudinal Study of the Effects of Television Viewing on Aggressive and Prosocial Behaviors." *British Journal of Social Psychology* 31:147–164.

CHAPTER 6

Application of Social Learning Theories

The major emphasis of social learning theories is primarily on environmental learner interaction. The learning of behaviors that are socially accepted, as well as learning ones that are not, is called social learning. This view is supported by Stuart (Stuart, 1989). He maintains that social learning theories attempt to describe the process by which we come to know what behaviors should or should not be projected when we are in different types of social situations. The theories themselves are learning theories that have been applied to social situations. These theories have been generally behavioristic rather than cognitive (Bandura, 1970), and they do not separate the parts from the whole; instead, they have as a major underlying concept the holistic and interactive nature of development. Various areas of development of the self do not exist separately from one another, and movement toward maturity in one area can affect movement and learning in another area. Social learning theories also address individual differences and how such factors as personality temperament and sociological influences may interact with the developmental process (Moll, 1991).

They assist us in identifying how different individuals may manage, delay, progress through, or retreat from developmental tasks. These theories also suggest that there are persistent individual differences such as cognitive style, temperament, or ethnic background that interact with development. Additionally, these theories are a source of knowledge about individual types and styles that may be critical to our understanding of differing sources or reward and punishment for students.

Research is congruent in the fact that observational learning offers an important vehicle in teaching youth and adults (Kazdin, 1980). According to Charles, special education was the first segment of public education to recognize the power of Bandura's work (Charles, 1985). Modeling, when used in conjunction with behavior modification, produced results that surpassed those of any previous technique. The early evidence summarized by Bandura and Walters indicated that all children with a history of failure, and institutionalized children more specifically, are more prone than other children to social influence (Bandura and Walters, 1963). Thus, special educators have applied modeling procedures to teach new behaviors, to increase behaviors, and to reduce or eliminate undesirable behaviors. Zaragoza, Vaughn, and McIntosh review twenty-seven studies that examined social skills intervention for children with behavioral problems (Zaragoza, Vaughn, and McIntosh, 1991). The most frequently used interventions were coaching, modeling, rehearsing, giving feedback, or providing reinforcement. Twenty-six of the twenty-seven studies reported some type of improvement in the social behaviors. The results of this research yielded positive changes in the self, teacher, and parental perceptions.

APPLICATION OF MODELING TECHNIQUES

Charles believes that the powers of modeling are even more notable in the regular classroom (Charles, 1985). Modeling, he contends, is their most effective method of teaching many of the objectives in the three domains of learning: psychomotor, cognitive, and affective. Bandura expanded the concept of modeling to include symbolic modeling (Bandura, 1971). Bandura concluded that images of reality are shaped by what we see and hear rather than by our own direct experiences. We have images of reality that we have never experienced personally. A theory of psychology should, thus, be in step with social reality.

During the years that followed, Bandura identified internal processes that underlie modeling (Bandura, 1989). These processes are referred to as self-efficacy (self-efficacy is discussed later in this chapter). Bandura identified information abilities as mediating links between stimulus and response (Bandura, 1995). Observers function as active agents who transform, classify, and organize meaningful stimuli.

AGGRESSION

"Aggression" is defined as behavior that results in personal injury and in destruction of property (Bandura, 1976). In reference to the theories of aggression, Bandura's first position, the one in which he remained, was that the instinct theories did not explain how children from high-risk environments develop prosocial styles. Conversely, they did not explain how children from advantaged backgrounds and disabled individuals develop serious antisocial patterns of behavior. The drive-reduction theorists' view was that aggression had cathartic effects. Conditions that were likely to be frustrating to the child heightened the drive level, thereby leading to aggression. Once the aggressive drive was reduced, the belief was that the likelihood of participation in aggressive behavior was abated (Eron, 1987; Evans, 1989; Bandura, 1971). According to Bandura, a complete theory of aggression must explain how aggression develops, what provokes aggression, and what maintains aggressive acts. He points out that individuals can acquire aggressive styles of conduct either by observing aggressive models or through direct combat experience—individuals are not born with repertories of aggressive behavior. Contrary to existing theories, Bandura's research showed that frustration could produce any variety of reactions and one does not need frustration to become aggressive. Moreover, he demonstrated that exposure to aggressive models tended to increase aggression (Evans, 1989). These findings have significant implication for reducing aggressive behaviors in individuals. Social forces determine the form that aggression takes, where and when it will be expressed, and who are selected as targets (Bandura, 1976).

The different forms of aggressive elicitors are delineated to include modeling influences, aversive treatment, anticipated positive consequences, instructional control, and delusional control (Bandura, 1976). In search of a common element among the stressors within the environment that elicits aggression, he concluded that there is one common trait: they all produce a negative effect.

The third major feature concerns the conditions that sustain aggressive behavior. Bandura proposed that behavior is controlled by its consequences (Bandura, 1973). Therefore, aggression can be induced. However, social learning theory distinguishes the three forms of reinforcement that must be considered. These include direct internal reinforcement, vicarious or observed reinforcement, and self-reinforcement.

ANGER AND HOSTILITY

The aforementioned studies have consistently shown that negative behaviors such as anger and hostility are learned behaviors that children imitate from their environments. These behaviors manifest themselves in hostile and destructive patterns of behavior, which frequently cannot be controlled by the schools, thus, creating conflict and tension between children, parents, and the schools (Matsueda and Heimer, 1987).

Expressing anger and hostility constructively requires a great deal of inner control. Internal awareness of anger must first be recognized. If one is not aware of his/her anger, it cannot be controlled. When anger is repressed or ignored, it will surface later and add to one's frustration. Usually by this time, anger will be expressed in aggressive behaviors such as attempts to harm someone, destroy something, insults, and hostile statements and actions. Aggressive behaviors manifest themselves in ways that infringe on the rights of others.

Controlling anger and managing feelings are essential in developing appropriate interpersonal skills. Individuals should be taught how to control anger through application of the following:

1. Recognizing and describing anger
2. Finding appropriate ways of expressing anger
3. Analyzing and understanding factors responsible for anger
4. Managing anger by looking at events differently or talking oneself out of anger
5. Learning how to repress feelings
6. Expressing anger constructively
7. Experimenting with various and alternative ways of expressing anger

Teachers may employ a variety of strategies to assist students in controlling or reducing anger. Role-playing, creative dramatics, physical activities, time out, relaxation therapy, writing and talking out feelings, assertive behavioral techniques, managing provocations, and resolving interpersonal conflicts through cooperative approaches are, to name a few, strategies and techniques that teachers may employ.

SOCIAL SKILLS/TEACHING STRATEGIES

Teaching Apology Strategies

Apologies can restore relationships, heal humiliations, and generate forgiveness if taught appropriately. They are a powerful social skill that

generally is not considered to be important by the school. It may be concluded that the school considers this skill to be a function of the home. As
reflected throughout this book, the school must assume the leadership in
teaching all social skills. This approach is especially true for a significant
number of individuals with disabilities.

Like all social skills, appropriate ways to apologize must be taught, otherwise, they can strain relationships, create grudges, and instill bitter ven-
geances. Apologies are a show of strength because not only do they
restore the self-concepts of those offended, but they also make us more
sensitive to the feelings and needs of others. Specific strategies have been
outlined and developed to assist educators in teaching appropriate ways
that individuals with disabilities can apologize without diminishing their
"egos."

The examples of anger and hostility and the teaching of apologizing
and other social skills strategies have been observed and associated with
many of the poor social skills shown by many individuals. These skills
appear to interface and interact, and are associated with many other poor
social skills.

Teaching Self-Regulation Skills

Instructional programs must be developed and designed to enable individuals to gain knowledge about appropriate interpersonal skills and to
employ this newly acquired knowledge in solving their social problems.
In order for this goal to be accomplished, they must be taught effective
ways of internalizing their behaviors and assessing how their behaviors
affect others. Helping individuals develop self-regulation skills appears to
be an excellent technique for bringing behaviors to the conscious level
where they can be controlled. Some of the more commonly used self-
regulation skills are summarized.

Be Aware of One's Thinking Patterns

Provide "think-aloud" activities and model behaviors to reflect solving
problems by working through tasks and asking questions such as: (1)
What is needed to solve the problem? (2) Things are not working out,
should I try another way? (3) What assistance do I need to solve the problem? As the teacher performs these think-aloud activities, he/she may ask
for input from the students' viewpoint that is relevant to the type of self-

regulation skills being demonstrated. Those skills may have to be modeled and demonstrated several times. Provide opportunities for individuals with disabilities to demonstrate them individually and in cooperative groups, as well as evaluate the effectiveness of their actions.

Making a Plan

Have individuals identify specific examples where self-regulation is useful. Motivation may come from a story, file, tape, or creative dramatic activities. Instruct them to develop a plan to reduce, correct, or eliminate the undesired behaviors. As they demonstrate the behaviors, the teacher should reinforce and praise them.

Develop and Evaluate Long-Term Goals

Employ self-regulation strategies to assist individuals with disabilities in accomplishing long-term goals. Have them to identify social and behavioral goals. Record the goals and assist them in making a plan as outlined previously. Provide a scheduled time to meet with them to determine how well the goals are being achieved. In some instances, the goals will need to be modified or adapted in order to focus on specific behaviors. Self-regulation strategies make actions more controllable by making one aware of his/her own behavior. Once awareness is achieved, the plan outlined earlier may be taught to bring behaviors under control. These strategies frequently will need to be adapted and modified to meet the uniqueness of the class. A variety of techniques and strategies may be used to aid the teacher in developing the skills of self-regulation:

1. Role-playing activities
2. Classifying behaviors and identifying types of self-regulation strategies to employ
3. Working in cooperative groups
4. Positively reinforce the mental habits
5. Reading and developing stories
6. Being sensitive to feedback and criticism
7. Teaching self-monitoring skills
8. Seeking outside advice when needed
9. Evaluating progress made

Self-regulation strategies are one of several strategies, which may be used to teach appropriate social skills to individuals. Appropriate social skills are essential for developing personal relationships and accepting the roles of authority figures. Social behaviors are learned, therefore, they can be changed and modified with appropriate intervention. They require that an individual evaluate the situation, choose the appropriate social skills, and perform the social tasks appropriately (Katz, 1991). Unfortunately, many individuals have not been exposed to appropriate social models or do not possess enough prerequisite skills, such as maturity and self-control, to successfully perform the social skills. Development of social skills requires that individuals have appropriate models to copy and imitate, to recognize nonverbal clues, and to adjust their behaviors accordingly.

Matsueda's research (Matsueda and Heimer, 1987) supports the findings of Katz (Katz, 1991); it indicates that negative behaviors are learned behaviors, which children imitate from their environments. The schools view these behaviors as hostile and destructive and respond to children in a negative fashion, thus, creating conflict and tension between schools and children.

Several researchers have directly or indirectly implied that social skills must be taught and integrated into the curriculum and assume a position of primacy along with the basic three Rs (reading, writing, and arithmetic) (Hilliard, 1989; Bilken, 1989; Taylor, 1992; Hatch and Johnson, 1990; Forest, 1990; Collins and Hatch, 1992; Kagan, 1989; Johnson and Johnson, 1990).

Findings from other studies support the aforementioned research by concluding that many individuals with disabilities may have developed or adapted alternative ways and styles of coping with problems within their communities. These behavioral styles are frequently in conflict with the school and society in general and may be viewed as negative or destructive. Behavioral styles and models copied and imitated by many individuals may serve them well in their environments but are frequently viewed as dysfunctional by the school (Taylor, 1992, 1998).

INTEGRATIVE ASPECTS OF SOCIAL SKILLS DEVELOPMENT

As indicated throughout this text, one of the major reasons that individuals' behaviors are frequently rejected by the school and social institutions may be attributed to the failure of them to display appropriate social skills needed for different social interactions. The types of role modes to which they have been exposed to do not frequently provide them with the appropriate behaviors to copy or transfer to other social functions in our society.

Various types of social skills instruction must be developed and systematically taught to individuals. The earlier the intervention, the sooner negative behaviors can be addressed, eradicated, or reduced. Both the home and the school should play dominant roles in developing prosocial skills for individuals (Oswald and Sinah-Nirbay, 1992; Walker et al., 1992).

The school may be the most appropriate agency along with parental input to conduct the social skills training or intervention. Teaching students prosocial skills necessary to cope with the social demands of society creates a climate in which positive relationships can exist and empower students to direct their own successes. A safe, supportive environment tends to facilitate learning. Prosocial skills taught and practiced daily in a nurturing environment assist in reducing negative behavior and in promoting positive ones.

Social skills of individuals are developed through interactions with family, school, and community. Social skills are shaped by reinforcement received as a result of interaction with the environment. Often, children do not learn effectively from past experiences. Frequently, thcy are enabled to transfer one social reaction to another socially acceptable situation; thus, their behaviors are frequently interpreted as immature, inept, or intrusive. This negative feedback prohibits future social interactions. This is especially true for individuals with disabilities.

Research findings suggest that a significant relationship exists between social skills intervention and academic achievement. Many social skills procedures, such as attending and positive interaction techniques, have been shown to increase academic performance. Oswald and Sinah-Nirbay write that social skills interventions appear to work in naturalistic environment (Oswald and Sinah-Nirbay, 1992). Similar findings by Walker et al. indicate that the probability of individuals failing and not adjusting to school and peer acceptance are significant (Walker et al., 1992). They further articulate that some individuals do not have sufficient social skills to be successful in school. Finally, they voice that there is an urgent need for social skills training that should be integrated into the curriculum.

Individuals are faced with double challenges; lack of appropriate social training may not permit many of them to engage productively in many social events. Special techniques and interventions related to remediating poor or inappropriate skills must be addressed early in their school experiences in order to bring social skills up to accepted school standards. According to Taylor, early intervention is needed to expose individuals with disabilities to appropriate social models (Taylor, 1992).

Many individual cultural experiences have not provided them with appropriate social skills to be successful in the larger community or to cope with appropriate social behavior. Changing inappropriate social behavior involves infusing principles of social learning theories, such as modeling, imitation, and behavioral techniques, with social skills instruction. Once social skills deficits have been identified, the aforementioned social learning principles may be used to reinforce or reward appropriate social behavior (Taylor, 1998).

Research findings have clearly demonstrated that diverse groups of children are at risk for developing appropriate interpersonal skills (Achenbach and Zigler, 1968; Coleman, 1986; Cummings and Rodda, 1989; Kauffman, 1993). Social skills deficiencies are commonly observed in this population. Several factors may attribute to these deficiencies such as child-rearing practices, deprived cultural environments, and lack of understanding the social expectations or rules. These deficiencies may lead to demonstrations of inappropriate or inadequate social behaviors.

Social skills are learned throughout a lifetime from imitating or modeling both negative and positive behaviors. Consequently, many individuals lack basic interpersonal skills. These individuals are frequently at a disadvantaged in society. Some individuals tend to feel in adequate and use unproductive, inadequate, and socially unacceptable ways of relating and communicating with others.

Many individuals may have developed or adapted alternative ways and styles of coping with problems. These behavioral styles are frequently in conflict with the school and society in general and may be viewed as negative or destructive. Behavioral styles and models copied and imitated by individuals may serve them well in their environments, but are frequently viewed as dysfunctional by the school and society (Carroll, 1993; Damon, 1997).

The ability of many individuals to function satisfactorily in social groups and to maintain dispositions, habits, and attitudes customarily associated with character and personality is usually below expected levels set by the school. They are more likely than other children to be rejected by their peers; have fewer, less rigid controls over their impulses; have learned hostile and destructive patterns of behavior; and often seem unable to respond to traditional classroom instruction. Individuals imitate behavior techniques from their environments (Taylor, 1992; Ashton and Webb, 1986).

The importance and values of interpersonal skills instruction has been minimized in the schools. Mastering of these skills requires training and practice in order for children to interact appropriately with others. Interpersonal skills allow children to take appropriate social behaviors, understand individuals' responses to the behaviors, and respond appropriately to them. Lack of this development may lead to feelings of rejection and isolation in a classroom setting. There is also ample evidence to suggest that children's social difficulties may emanate from vastly different deficit areas. These deficit areas must be identified and remediated during the early years. Schools must design direct and immediate intervention programs that will permit individuals to experience success (Brody and Stoneman, 1977; Oswald and Sinah-Nirbay, 1992; Ayers, 1989).

COGNITIVE BEHAVIOR MODIFICATION

Social learning theory has also influenced cognitive behavior modification (Bandura, 1977). A major assumption of social learning theory is the notion that affective, cognitive, and behavior variables interact in the learning process. For example, the extent to which a child understands the cognitive concepts of place value will affect how well he/she performs the behavior of computing three-digit subtraction problems with regrouping (refer to chapter 11 for concept learning strategies). Motivation and other affective variables also interact. In cognitive behavior modification, modeling is used as a primary means of instruction.

Research in social learning theory as well as in cognitive behavior modification supports the notion that modeling is very effective when used to teach children with disabilities. With cognitive behavior modification, students are asked not only to watch observable behaviors as the instructor performs the task, but also to listen to the instructor's self-talk. In this way, the instructor is modeling both observable behaviors and the unobservable thinking processes associated with those behaviors. Being able to model the unobservable thinking processes is an important component for teaching such cognitive skills as verbal math problem solving, finding the main idea in a paragraph, editing written work, and solving social problems. In most instances, the person modeling is the teacher or a peer, but video puppets have also been used. Vaughn, Ridley, and Bullock used puppets as models for teaching interpersonal skills to young, aggressive children (Vaughn, Ridley, and Bullock, 1984). The puppets were used to demonstrate appropriate social behaviors and strategies for solving inter-personal problems. Another effective cognitive behavior modification concept is self-verbalization, which is often used when teaching children with behavior problems. Strategies include teacher modeling, guided practice, and the gradual fading of teacher cueing. First, the teacher describes and models self-verbalization. Then, the teacher provides exter-nal support and guidance as students attempt to apply the approach to problems.

Cognitive behavior modification is designed to actively involve stu-dents in learning. Meichenbaum characterized the student as a collabora-tor in learning. General guidelines to consider when using this type of modification include:

1. Analyze the target behavior carefully
2. Determine if and what strategies the student is already using
3. Select strategy steps that are as similar as possible to the strategy steps used by problem solvers
4. Work with the student in developing the strategy steps
5. Teach the prerequisite skills
6. Teach the strategy steps using modeling, self-instruction, and self-regulation
7. Give explicit feedback
8. Teach strategy generalization
9. Help the students maintain the strategy (Meichenbaum, 1983)

From its inception, social learning theory has served as a useful frame-work for the understanding of both normal and abnormal human behavior. A major contribution that has important implications for the modification of human behavior is the theory's distinction between learning and per-formance. In a now-classic series of experiments, Bandura and his associ-ates teased apart the roles of observation and reinforcement in learning and were able to demonstrate that people learn through mere observation.

In a study of aggression, an adult model hit and kicked a life-size inflated clown doll, with children watching the attack in person or on a television screen. Other children watched the model perform some innoc-uous behavior. Later, the children were allowed to play in the room with the doll. All children who had witnessed the aggression, either in person or on television, viciously attacked the doll, while those who had observed the model's innocuous behavior did not display aggression towards the doll. Moreover, it was clearly shown that the children modeled their aggressive behaviors after the adult. This study accomplished its purpose by demonstrating that observational learning occurs in the absence of direct reinforcement (Bandura, Ross, and Ross, 1961).

SELF-REGULATION OF BEHAVIOR

According to Bandura, "If actions were determined solely by external rewards and punishments, people would behave like weathervanes, constantly shifting in different directions to conform to the momentary influences impinging upon them. Self-regulation refers to the learner monitoring his or her thinking and actions through language mediation"(Bandura, 1986). When Meichenbaum developed his cognitive behavior modification training for the self-control of hyperactive children, he used Lev Vygotsky's notions about how language affects socialization and the learning process (Meichenbaum, 1977). Vygotsky suggested that children become socialized when using verbal self-regulation (Vygotsky, 1978). Children first use language to mediate their actions by overtly engaging in self-instruction and self-monitoring. Later, this language mediation becomes covert.

SELF-OBSERVATION

Studies demonstrate that learning is enhanced when individuals have knowledge of and apply appropriate monitoring or executive strategies during the learning process. In order to influence their own actions, people need to monitor relevant aspects of their behaviors. Naturally, the behaviors that are monitored must be appropriate to the situation. Several factors influence whether self-observation will produce effective goals or standard setting and self-evaluation that will, in turn, lead to changes in behavior (Meichenbaum, 1977; Schunk, 1991; Yell, 1993).

Focusing on immediate behavior is more effective than monitoring the future effects of behavior. Another factor is whether an individual focuses on his/her successes or failures. Self-monitoring one's successes increase desired behavior, whereas observing one's failures causes little change or lowers performance. Helping students to pay more attention to their successes will increase their self-efficacy (Hamilton and Ghatala, 1994).

SELF-EFFICACY

According to Bandura, another factor that influences people's motivation to perform modeled activities is their perceived efficacy (Bandura, 1995). "Self-efficacy" is an academic term that refers to how capable someone judges him/herself to be in a given situation. It is a person's sense of "I can do it" or "I cannot do it." In addition to its informative and motivational role, reinforcement, by both direct and vicarious experience, influences performance by its effects on self-efficacy. That is, seeing other people succeed or fail (or succeeding or failing oneself) affects a person's judgment of his/her own capabilities.

Perceptions of self-efficacy can have diverse effects on behavior, thought patterns, and emotional reactions. One's choice of activities and environments is influenced by one's perceived efficacy. Individuals tend to avoid tasks and situations that they believe exceed their capabilities, but they undertake tasks they feel capable of handling (Bandura, 1977). For example, students who do not view themselves as capable in math might attempt to avoid taking math classes. However, students with high self-efficacy for math will choose more math electives. Perceived efficacy influences the amount of effort people will expend and how long they will persist at a task in the face of difficulty.

One's perceived self-efficacy may or may not correspond to one's real self-efficacy. People may believe their self-efficacy is low when in reality it is high, and vice versa. The situation is best when one's aspirations are in line with one's capabilities. On the one hand, people who continually attempt to do things beyond their capabilities experience frustration and despair and may eventually give up on almost anything. On the other hand, if people with high self-efficacy do not adequately challenge themselves their personal growth may be inhibited. The development of perceived self-efficacy and its impact on self-regulated behavior are topics about which Bandura has written extensively (Bandura, 1986).

Students with or without learning disabilities who believe they are capable of reaching a desired goal or of attaining a certain level of performance have a high level of perceived self-efficacy (Schunk, 1991).

High self-efficacy in any given domain is important because it motivates future attempts at tasks in the same domain. For example, one motivation for a child with cerebral palsy to attempt tracing the letters of the alphabet is previous success in developing a functional pencil grip and successfully tracing horizontal and vertical lines. If the child's tracing letters improves, then self-efficacy in handwriting increases even more, which in turn, motivates future attempts to write. What if the tracing of letters goes badly? Self-efficacy in handwriting is likely to decline. Self-efficacy is determined in part by present attempts at learning and performance; it then affects future attempts at learning and performance.

Teachers can help students with learning and behavior problems identify and use appropriate internal evaluative standards by teaching them to set goals that are specific, proximal, and challenging. Specific goals clearly designate the type and amount of effort needed and provide unambiguous standards for judging performance. Specific goals are much more effective in directing behavior than global or generals goals (Schunk, 1991). Proximal goals refer to immediate performance on tasks rather than to some distant future goal. Finally, goals that are effective in directing behavior are challenging rather than too easy or too difficult.

Teachers can model goal setting. In doing so, a teacher can point out how he/she selects attainable yet challenging goals, describing how goals that are too easy and those that are unattainable can be impractical and frustrating. He/she can emphasize knowledge when setting goals and focus on setting self-improvement goals. Again, teachers must remember that only tasks that are challenging for the learner, but not so difficult that progress is impossible, are capable of providing information to students that increases self-efficacy.

SUMMARY

Social learning theory was born into a climate in which two competing and diametrically opposed schools of thought dominated psychology. On the one hand, psychologists who advocated psychodynamic theories postulated that human behavior is governed by motivational forces operating in the form of largely unconscious needs, drives, and impulses. These impulse theories tended to give circular explanations, attributing behavior to inner causes that were inferred from the very behavior they were supposed to cause. They also tended to provide explanations after the fact, rather than predicting events, and had very limited empirical support.

On the other hand, there were various types of behavior theory that shifted the focus of the causal analysis from hypothetical internal determinants of behavior to external publicly observable causes. Behaviorists were able to show that actions commonly attributed to inner causes could be produced, eliminated, and reinstated in the person's external environment. This led to the proposition that people's behavior is caused by factors residing in the environment.

Social learning theory presents a theory of human behavior that to some extent incorporates both viewpoints. According to Bandura, people are neither driven by inner force nor buffeted by environmental stimuli; instead, psychological functioning is best explained in terms of continuous reciprocal interaction and external causes. This assumption, termed "reciprocal determinism," became one of the dominant viewpoints in psychology.

An initial exposition of social learning theory was presented in Bandura and Walters's text *Social Learning and Personality Development* (1963). This formulation drew heavily on the procedures and principles of operant and classical conditioning. In his book *Principles of Behavior Modification* (1969), Bandura placed much greater emphasis on symbolic events and self-regulatory processes. He argued that complex human behavior could not be satisfactorily explained by the narrow set of learning principles behaviorists had derived from animal studies. He incorporated principles derived from developmental, social, and cognitive psychology into social learning theory.

During the 1970s, psychology had grown increasingly cognitive. This development was reflected in Bandura's 1977 book *Social Learning Theory*, which presented self-efficacy theory as the central mechanism through which people control their own behavior. Over the following decade, the influence of cognitive psychology on Bandura's work grew stronger. In his book *Social Foundation of Thought and Action: A Social Cognitive Theory* (1986), he finally disavowed his roots in learning theory and renamed his approach social cognitive theory. This theory accorded central roles to cognitive, vicarious, self-reflective, and self-regulatory processes. Social learning/social cognitive theory became the dominant conceptual approach within the field of behavior therapy. It has provided the conceptual framework for numerous interventions for a wide variety of psychological disorders and probably will remain popular for a long time. In 1981, Bandura was honored with the Award for Distinguished Scientific Contribution to Psychology from the American Psychological Foundation in recognition for his work.

Social learning theories offer the school a common context through which environment, developmental sequence, and early experiences of individuals' development can be understood and researched. These theories enable educators to better understand how individuals think, how they feel about themselves, and how to become aware of factors in the environment precipitating cognitive and affective problems that may have some bearing on academic performance. The relationship between social learning theories and the academic performance of individuals is not well established. Most research reported today simply indicates that there is a causal relationship. There is a dire need to conduct empirical studies to determine to what degree social learning theories impact the academic performance of these individuals.

Social learning theories appear to be an appropriate approach for integration skills for individuals. These theories provide teachers with a common language by which they can communicate about the effects of social learning theories on academic performance.

The study of social learning theories enables the school to better understand how individuals think about school-related processes and how they are likely to be feeling about themselves in relation to these processes. The school's understanding of both the cognitive and the affective characteristics of individuals with disabilities may be termed as "empathic." One way of showing empathy to children is through designing effective classroom environments that consider the cognitive and affective levels of the children.

Social development is a major area in which many individuals need assistance. They frequently have developed inappropriate interpersonal skills that are not accepted by the school. Inability to conform to expected social standards may result in unacceptable social skills that are essential for developing personal relationships and accepting the role of authority figures (Taylor, 1992). Research findings by Hilliard and Johnson and Johnson support the notion that the culture plays a dominant role in shaping behavior (Hilliard, 1989; Johnson and Johnson, 1990). Children model and imitate behaviors from their environments. Innovative ways must be found by the schools to provide appropriate role models for individuals to imitate and copy.

BIBLIOGRAPHY

Achenback, T., and E. Zigler. 1968. "Cue-Learning and Problem Learning Strategies in Normal and Retarded Children." *Child Development* 39:837–848.

Ashton, P. T., and R. B. Webb. 1986. *Making a Difference: Teacher's Sense of Efficacy and Student Achievement.* White Plains, N.Y.: Longman.

Ayers, W. 1989. "Childhood at Risk." *Educational Leadership* 46:70–72.

Bandura, A. 1969. *Principles of Behavior Modification.* New York: Rinehart & Wilson.

———. 1970. *A Social Learning Theory.* Englewood Cliffs, N.J.: Prentice Hall.

———. 1971. "Psychotherapy Based upon Modeling Principles." In *Handbook of Psychotherapy and Behavior Change,* ed. A. E. Bergin and S. L. Garfield. Englewood Cliffs, N.J.: Prentice Hall.

———.1973. *Aggression: A Social Learning Analysis.* Englewood Cliffs, N.J.: Prentice Hall.

———. 1976. "Social Learning Analysis of Aggression." In *Analysis of Delinquency and Aggression,* ed. E. Ribes-Inesta and A. Bandura. Englewood Cliffs, N.J.: Prentice Hall.

———. 1977. *Social Learning Theory.* Englewood Cliffs, N.J.: Prentice Hall.

———. 1986. *Social Foundation of Thought and Action: A Social Cognitive Theory.* Englewood Cliffs, N.J.: Prentice Hall.

———. 1989. "Human Agency in Social Cognitive Theory." *American Psychologist* 44:1175–1184.

———. 1995. *Self-Efficacy in Changing Societies.* Cambridge: Cambridge University Press.

Bandura, A., D. Ross, and S. A. Ross. 1961. "Transmission of Aggression through Imitation of Aggressive Models." *Journal of Abnormal and Social Psychology* 63:575–582.

Bandura, A., and R. H. Walters. 1963. *Social Learning and Personality Development.* New York: Holt, Rinehart, and Winston.

Bilken, D. 1989. "Making Differences Ordinary." In *Educating All Children in the Mainstream of Regular Education,* ed. W. Stainback and M. Forest. Baltimore, Md.: Paul H. Brookes.

Brody, G., and Z. Stoneman. 1977. "Social Competencies in the Developmental Disabled: Some Suggestions for Research and Training." *Mental Retardation* 15:41–43.

Carroll, J. 1993. "Self-Efficacy Related to Transfer of Learning and Theory-Based Instructional Design." *Journal of Adult Education* 22:37–43.

Charles, C. M. 1985. *Building Classroom Discipline.* White Plains, N.Y.: Longman.

Coleman, M. 1986. *Behavior Disorders: Theory and Practice.* Englewood Cliffs, N.J.: Prentice Hall.

Collins, T. W., and J. A. Hatch. 1992. "Supporting the Social–Emotional Growth of Young Children." *Dimensions of Early Childhood* 27:17–21.

Cummings, C., and A. Rodda. 1989. "Advocacy, Prejudice, and Role Modeling in the Deaf Community." *Journal of Social Psychology* 129:5–12.

Damon, W. 1997. *The Social World of the Child.* San Francisco, Calif.: Jossey-Bass.

Eron, L. 1987. "The Development of Aggressive Behavior from the Perspective of a Developing Behaviorism." *American Psychologist* 42:435–442.

Evans, R. 1989. *Albert Bandura: The Man and His Ideas—A Dialogue.* New York: Praeger.

Forest, M. 1990. "Maps and Cities." Presentation at Peak Parent Center Workshop, Colorado Springs, Colo.

Hamilton, R., and E. Ghatala. 1994. *Learning and Instruction.* Houston, Tex.: McGraw-Hill.

Hatch, T., and R. Johnson. 1990. "Social Skills for Successful Group Work." *Educational Leadership* 47:29–33.

Hilliard, A. G. 1989. "Teachers and Cultural Styles in a Pluralistic Society." *NEA Today* 7:65–69.

Johnson, W., and R. Johnson. 1990. "Social Skills for Successful Group Work." *Educational Leadership* 47:29–33.

Kagan, S. L. 1989. "Early Care and Education: Beyond the School House Doors." *Phi Delta Kappan* 71:107–112.

Katz, L. G. 1991. "The Teacher's Role in Social Development of Young Children." Clearinghouse on Elementary and Early Childhood Education. ERIC. ED 331642.

Kauffman, J. 1993. *Characteristics of Emotional and Behavioral Disorders of Children and Youth.* New York: Merrill.

Kazdin, A. 1980. *Behavior Modification in Applied Settings.* Homewood, Ill.: Dorsey.

Matsueda, R. L., and K. Heimer. 1987. "Race, Family Structure, and Delinquency: A Test Differential Association and Social Control Theories." *American Sociological Review* 52 (December): 826–840.

Meichenbaum, D. 1977. *Cognitive Behavior Modification: An Integrated Approach.* New York: Plenum.

———. 1983. "Teaching Thinking: A Cognitive Behavior Approach." In *Interdisciplinary Voices in Learning Disabilities and Remedial Education.* Austin, Tex.: Pro-Ed.

Moll, I. 1991. "The Material and the Social in Vygotsky's Theory of Cognitive Development." Clearinghouse on Teacher Education. ERIC. ED 352186.

Oswald, D. P., and N. Sinah-Nirbay. 1992. "Behavior Modification." in *Current Research on Social Behavior.* 16:443–447.

Schunk, D. H. 1991. "Self-Efficacy and Academic Motivation." *Educational Psychologist* 26 (2): 206–232.

Stuart, R. B. 1989. "Social Learning Theory: A Vanishing or Expanding Presence?" *Psychology: A Journal of Human Behavior* 26:35–50.

Taylor, G. 1992. "Impact of Social Learning Theory on Educating Deprived Minority Children." Clearinghouse on Teacher Education. ERIC. ED 349260.

———. 1998. *Curriculum Strategies for Teaching Social Skills to the Disabled.* Springfield, Ill.: Thomas.

Vaughn, S. R., C. A. Ridley, and D. D. Bullock. 1984. "Interpersonal Problem Solving Skills Training with Aggressive Young Children." *Journal of Applied Developmental Psychology* 5:213–223.

Vygotsky, L. S. 1978. *Mind in Society: The Development of Higher Psychological Processes.* Cambridge, Mass.: Harvard University Press.

Walker, H., M. Irvin, K. Larry, J. Noell, and H. S. George. 1992. "A Construct Score Approach to the Assessment of Social Competence." *Behavior Modification* 16:449–452.

Yell, M. L. 1993. "Cognitive Behavior Therapy." In *Behavior Management Application for Teachers and Parents*, ed. T. J. Zirpoli and K. J. Melloy. Columbus, Ohio: Macmillan.

Zaragoza, N., S. Vaughn, and R. McIntosh. 1991. "Social Skill Intervention and Children with Behavior Problems: A Review." *Behavioral Disorders* 16:260–275.

CHAPTER 7

Direct Intervention Techniques
for Teaching Social Skills

Intervention should reflect the assessed needs of individuals. Teacher-made checklists that outline social skills development may be used. There are several approaches that may be used to promote skills of individuals through a model called direct instruction. The model was designed by Carnine (Carnine, 1991). Carnine, Granzin, and Becker's direct instruction is based on a set of general principles about effective instruction (Carnine, Granzin, and Becker, 1988). Using this approach, students are expected to draw their own conclusions relevant to the problem.

Goldstein and McGinnis support the concept of direct instruction (Goldstein and McGinnis, 1984). They indicate that modeling, role-playing, practicing, and giving feedback are principal procedures and techniques used to teach social skills. Additional instruction using the techniques addressed in this chapter can facilitate the teaching of social skills through direct instruction.

Direct instruction implies that the teacher is directly intervening to bring about a desired change by providing basic information for children to master the task, which is a prerequisite. Direct instruction may be used with any subject area to assist children in learning basic skills, as well as employing the concept of task analysis (step-by-step sequence of learning a task). I have decided to accent social skills because I believe that they are prerequisites to academic and physical skills.

Bandura provided us with the conceptual framework for using direct instruction (Bandura, 1970). He advanced the concept of social learning theory and behavioral modeling (refer to chapter 5 for additional details). He advocated that much of what the student learns is through modeling from observing others. Carefully and systematically conducted information gained through modeling may be transferred to other academic, social, and nonacademic functions. Specific techniques for using effective modeling strategies are delineated later in this chapter.

SKILLSTREAMING

Skillstreaming is a comprehensive social skills program developed by Goldstein and McGinnis (Goldstein and McGinnis, 1984). In this program, social skills are clustered in several categories with specific skills to be demonstrated. Clear directions are provided for forming the skill-streaming groups, group meetings, and rules. Activities include meeting, role-playing, giving feedback, and the transfer of training. The program is designed to foster human interaction skills needed to perform appropriate social acts. Feedback is received in the form of praise, encouragement, and constructive criticism, and is designed to reinforce correct performance of the skills.

COGNITIVE BEHAVIOR MODIFICATION

These techniques focus on having individuals to think and internalize their feelings and behaviors before reacting. The process involves them learning responses from the environment by listening, observing, and imitating others in their environments. Both cognition and language processes are mediated in solving problems and developing patterns (Gresham, 1985).

Cognitive behavioral strategies are designed to increase self-control of behavior through self-monitoring, self-evaluation, and self-reinforcement. These strategies are designed to assist children in internalizing their behaviors, to compare their behaviors against predetermined standards, and for children to provide positive and negative feedback to themselves. Research findings indicate that there is a positive relationship between what individuals think about themselves and the types of behaviors they display (Rizzo and Zabel, 1988). Matching the cognitive and affective processes in designing learning experiences for individuals appears to be realistic and achievable within the school.

BEHAVIORAL MODIFICATION TECHNIQUES

Behavioral modification techniques may provide the teacher with strategies for assisting individuals in performing desirable and appropriate behaviors, as well as promoting socially acceptable behaviors. These techniques are designed to provide teachers, educators, and parents with a method to modify individuals' behaviors to the extent that when they are emitted in a variety of situations, they are consistently more appropriate than inappropriate (Aksamit, 1990; Shores, Gunter, and Jack, 1993).

There are some cautions for using behavioral strategies in the classroom. The chief purpose of the teacher's using these techniques is to change or modify behaviors. The teacher is not generally concerned with the cause of the behaviors, but rather with observing and recording overt behaviors. These behavioral responses may be measured and quantified in any attempt to explain behaviors. Motivation and the dynamic causes of the behaviors are primary concerns for the teacher.

In spite of the cautions involving behavioral modification techniques, most of the research supports their use (Salend and Whittaker, 1992; Lane and McWhirter, 1992; Rizzo and Zabel, 1988; Katz, 1991; Taylor, 1992). The major concerns voiced are that the techniques must be systematically employed, that the environmental constraints must be considered, and that the teachers, educators, and parents must be well versed in using the techniques.

There are many effective ways in which behavior can be modified. Contingency contracting, the task-centered approach, peer mediation, and proximity control are four of the most promising techniques to employ.

Contingency Contracting

This technique involves pupils in planning and executing contracts. Gradually, pupils take over record keeping, analyze their own behavior, and even suggest the timing for cessation of contracts. Microcontracts are made with the pupil in which he/she agrees to execute some amount of low-probability behavior after which he/she may engage immediately in some high-probability behavior (Premack Principle) for a specified time.

Task-Centered Approach

The task-centered approach to learning is another approach for modifying behaviors of individuals. This system provides individuals a highly structured learning environment. Individuals may be experiencing difficulty because they cannot grasp certain social skill concepts. Behavioral problems may stem from the frustration of repeated failure, such as poor attention or the inability to work independently or in groups. Elements in the task-centered approach may include activities to promote:

1. Attention-level tasks designed to gain and hold the individual's attention
2. Development of visual and auditory discrimination activities as needed
3. Interpretation and reaction to social level tasks emphasizing skills related to social interaction
4. Limitation of social exchanges, the development of verbal and social courtesies, and group participation activities

Peer Mediation Strategies

Peer mediation strategies have been successfully employed to manage behavior. The model is student-driven and enables students to make decisions about issues and conflicts that impact their lives. The model requires that students exercise self-regulation strategies, which involve generating socially appropriate behavior in the absence of external control imposed by teachers or other authorities. To be effective, the concept must be practiced by individuals and frequently reinforced by the teachers through role models and demonstrations of prosocial skills.

Several investigations have shown that negative behaviors and discipline problems decrease when using this strategy. There is an increase in cooperative relationships and academic development. Findings also show an increase in task behaviors (Salend and Whittaker, 1992; Lane and McWhirter, 1992). Implications for using this strategy with individuals may assist them in internalizing appropriate behaviors and significantly influence developing appropriate social skills (Storey, 1992; Odom and Strain, 1984).

Several studies have investigated the importance of using microcomputers to improve interpersonal skills of individuals. Students tended to make less error in subject areas when they worked in groups. Individuals' behaviors also improved. They tended to imitate the behaviors of their nondisabled peers by increasing their personal and social awareness skills and competencies. Nondisabled peers tended to accept disabled individuals more readily with the use of computers (Hines, 1990; Cosden, 1985; Hedley, 1987; Thorkildsen, 1985).

Proximity Control

Studies show that teacher movement in the class may provide effective control of student behaviors by bringing the teacher and student into closer proximity. It is believed that this close proximity will improve interaction between student and teacher (Shores, Gunter, and Jack, 1993; Aksamit, 1990; Banbury and Herbert, 1992; Denny, Epstein, and Rose, 1992).

The technique is easily implemented. The teacher stands close to pupils or arranges his/her desk to be closer to their desks. It is believed that this close proximity provides an external type of control for pupils. Denny, Epstein, and Rose find that teachers generally are not taking advantage of this technique (Denny, Epstein, and Rose, 1992). They recommended that teachers move freely throughout the room and monitor activities.

COACHING

Appropriate coaching techniques may be employed by teachers to develop social skills for individuals. Some of the more commonly known techniques include:

1. Participation
2. Paying attention
3. Cooperation
4. Taking turns
5. Sharing
6. Communication
7. Offering assistance and encouragement

These techniques are designed to make individuals cognizant of using alternative methods to solving problems; anticipating the consequences of their behaviors; and developing plans for successfully coping with problems.

CUING

Cuing is a technique employed to remind students to act appropriately just before the correct action is expected rather than after it is performed incorrectly. This technique is an excellent way of reminding students about prior standards and instruction. A major advantage of this technique is that it can be employed anywhere using a variety of techniques such as glances, hand signals, painting, nodding or shaking the head, and holding up the hand.

Cuing can be utilized without interrupting the instructional program or planned activities for disabled individuals. The technique assists in reducing negative practices and prevents students from performing inappropriate behaviors.

Successful implementation of this technique requires the students to thoroughly understand the requirement, as well as recognizing the specific cue. Failure to get the students to understand may result in confusing the students, especially when they are held accountable for not responding appropriately to the intended cue.

MODELING

Modeling assumes that an individual will imitate the behaviors displayed by others. The process is considered important because disabled, as well as all individuals, acquire social skills through replicating behaviors demonstrated by others. Educators and adults may employ modeling techniques to change and influence behaviors of children by demonstrating appropriate skills to model. The impact and importance of this valuable technique is frequently overlooked by teachers. Teachers frequently do not assess the impact of their behaviors on children.

Modeling, if used appropriately, may influence or change behaviors more effectively than positive behavior. This is premised on the fact that once a behavior pattern is learned through imitation, it is maintained without employing positive reinforcement techniques. Teachers should be apprised and cognizant of the importance of modeling and promoting appropriate social skills of individuals. Additionally, they should be trained and exposed to various techniques to facilitate the process. Children do not automatically imitate models they see. Several factors are involved: (1) establishing rapport between teachers and children; (2) reinforcing consequences for demonstrating or not demonstrating the modeled behavior; and (3) determining the appropriate setting for modeling certain behaviors.

Individuals should be taught how to show or demonstrate positive behaviors in structured situations. The technique provides for the structured learning of appropriate behaviors through examples and demonstration by others. Internal or incidental modeling may occur at any time; however, a regular structured time or period of the day is recommended in order to develop structure in a variety of social conditions. Teaching behavioral skills through modeling is best accomplished by beginning with impersonal situations that most students encounter, such as the correct way to show respect to others. As individuals master the modeling process, additional behavioral problems may be emphasized.

Modeling activities may be infused throughout the curriculum at random, however, a specific time is recommended for modeling instruction. Activities should be planned based on the assessed needs of the class and be flexible enough to allow for changes when situations dictate.

ROLE-PLAYING

Role-playing is an excellent technique for allowing individuals to act out both appropriate and inappropriate behaviors without embarrassment or experiencing the consequences of their actions. It permits individuals to experience hypothetical conditions that may cause some anxiety or emotional responses in ways that may enable them to better understand themselves. Once entrenched, these activities may be transferred to real-life experiences. Role-playing may assist individuals in learning appropriate social skills through developing appropriate models by observing and discussing alternative behavioral approaches. It may be conducted in any type of classroom structure, level, or group size, and it may be individually or grouped induced. Through appropriate observations and assessment procedures, areas of intervention may be identified for role-playing activities.

Role-playing assists individuals in identifying and solving problems within a group context. It is also beneficial to shy students by encouraging their interactions with classmates without aversive consequences. As with most group activities, role-playing must be structured by the teacher. Activities should be designed to reduce, minimize, correct, or eliminate identified areas of deficits through the assessment process. Gills lists the following advantages of role-playing:

1. Allows the student to express hidden feelings
2. Is student-centered and addresses itself to the needs and concerns of the student
3. Permits the group to control the content and pace
4. Enables the student to empathize with others and to understand their problems
5. Portrays generalized social problems and dynamics of group interaction, both formal and informal
6. Gives more reality and immediacy to academic descriptive material (e.g., history, geography, social skills, and English)
7. Enables the student to discuss private issues and problems
8. Provides an opportunity for nonarticulate students and emphasizes the importance of nonverbal and emotional responses
9. Gives practice in various types of behavior (Gills, 1991)

Disadvantages include:

1. The teacher can lose control over what is learned and the order in which it is learned
2. Simplifications can mislead
3. It may dominate the learning experiences to the exclusion of solid theory and facts
4. It is dependent on the personality, quality, and mix of the teacher and students
5. It may be seen as too entertaining and frivolous

Gills investigated the effects of role-playing, modeling, and videotape playback on the self-concept of elementary school children (Gills, 1991). The Piers-Harris children's self-concept scale was employed on a pre- and posttest basis. Intervention was for a six-month period. Data showed that the combination of role-playing, modeling, and videotape playback had some effect on various dimensions of self-concept.

VIDEOTAPE MODELING

Videotape modeling is an effective measure to improve self-concept of individuals. They may be encouraged to analyze classroom behavior and patterns of interaction through reviewing videotapes. This technique can show individuals the behaviors expected before they are exposed to them in various settings. Videotape modeling affords the teachers the opportunity to reproduce the natural conditions of any behavior in the classroom setting. It may also provide realistic training that can be transferred to real experiences inside and outside of the classroom (Banbury and Herbert, 1992; Shores, Gunter, and Jack, 1993).

For learners, educators may employ this technique to bridge the gap between transferring modeling skills to real-life situations. It has proved to be an effective tool to teach prosocial skills to this group.

COOPERATIVE LEARNING

A basic definition of "cooperative learning" is a method of learning through the use of groups. Five basic elements of cooperative learning are:

1. Positive interdependence
2. Individual accountability
3. Group processing
4. Small group/social skills
5. Face-to-face primitive interaction

A cooperative learning group is one in which two or more students are working together toward a common goal in which every member of the group is included. Cooperative learning seems ideal for mainstreaming. Learning together in small groups provides a sense of responsibility and an understanding of the importance of cooperation among youngsters. Also, individuals have the opportunity to socialize and interact with each other (Adams, 1990; Slavin, 1984; Johnson and Johnson, 1983; Gemma, 1989; Slavin and Oickle, 1981).

Cooperative learning strategies have the power to transform classrooms by encouraging communities of caring, supportive students whose achievements improve and whose social skills grow. Harnessing and directing the power of cooperative learning strategies present a challenge to the classroom teacher. Decisions about the content appropriateness of the structures, the necessary management routines, and the current social skills development of individuals call for special teacher preparation (Johnson and Johnson, 1988). For successful outcomes with students, teachers also need to follow-up and have the cooperation of peer coaches, administrative support, parent understanding, and time to adapt to the strategies (Slavin, 1991).

While cooperative models replace individual seat work, they continue to require individual accountability. Teachers who use cooperative structures recognize that it is important for students to both cooperate and compete.

Cooperative learning organizes students to work together in structured groups toward a common goal. Among the best known cooperative structures are Jigsaw, Student Teams Achievement Divisions, Think-Pair-Share, Group Investigation, Circle of Learning, and Simple Structures. To use a cooperative structure effectively, teachers need to make some preliminary decisions. According to Kagan, the following questions should be asked:

1. What kind of cognitive and academic development does it foster?
2. What kind of social development does it foster?
3. Where in the lesson plan (content) does it best fit? (Kagan, 1990)

Teachers also need to examine what conditions increase the effect of cooperative strategies. Positive interdependence, face-to-face (primitive) interaction, individual accountability, and group processing affect cooperative learning outcomes.

The benefits of cooperative learning appear to be reflected in the following:

1. Academic gains, especially among disabled and low-achieving students
2. Improved race relations among students in integrated classrooms
3. Improved social and affective development among all students (Kagan, 1990; Johnson and Johnson, 1983; Slavin, 1991)

Cooperative learning practices vary tremendously. The models can be complex or simple. Whatever their design, cooperative strategies include:

1. A common goal
2. A structured task
3. A structured team
4. Clear roles
5. Designated time frame

6. Individual accountability
7. A structured process

We need cooperative learning structures in our classroom because many traditional socialization practices are absent. Not all students come to school with a social orientation, and students appear to master content more efficiently with these structures (Kagan, 1990; Cosden, 1985). The preponderance of research indicates that cooperative learning strategies motivate students to care about each other and to share responsibility in completing tasks.

COOPERATIVE LEARNING VERSUS PEER TUTORING

It is frequently assumed by some parents that cooperative learning is another concept of peer tutoring, but there are many significant differences between cooperative learning and peer tutoring. In cooperative learning, everyone is responsible for learning and nobody is acting as a teacher or as a tutor. However, in peer tutoring one child has the role of teacher and another as student or teacher. The tutor already knows that subject and material and teaches it to a peer who needs individualized remedial help to master a specific skill. In cooperative learning, the initial teaching comes not from a student but from the teacher, because some students grasp concepts quickly and some slowly. These students reinforce what they have just learned by explaining concepts and skills to teammates who need help (Slavin, 1991). Cooperative work puts a heterogeneous group of students together to share ideas and knowledge.

SPECIAL GROUP ACTIVITIES

In a paper presented at the annual meeting of the American Education Research Association, Dorr-Bremme advanced some unique techniques for improving social identity in kindergarten and first grade (Dorr-Bremme, 1992). Students sat in groups and planned daily activities, which were videotaped. Analysis of the videotapes revealed several dimensions of social identity to be important, such as academic capability, maturity, talkativeness, independence, aggressiveness, ability to follow through, and leadership ability. The teacher responded to students individually and as circle participants, depending on how the behavior was viewed. Findings indicated that social identity was the combined responsibility of everyone in the classroom interacting to bring about the most positive social behavior. Interactions between individual students and the teacher were minimized.

GROUP-PLAY ACTIVITIES

The values and benefits of group-play therapy cannot be overemphasized when employed with many individuals. These activities may assist individuals in developing appropriate interpersonal skills and relationships. Many individuals tend to settle differences with peers by physical means. This trend may be attributed to poor impulse control, poor modeling and imitation strategies, and an inability to internalize their behaviors (Coker and Thyer, 1990; Istre, 1993; Goldstein and Goldstein, 1990).

In order for individuals to internalize their behaviors, activities must be designed to bring behaviors to the conscience level. Individuals frequently have problems in self-control that may be designed to enable individuals to cope with problems that may cause loss of control. Properly employed, these activities will assist individuals in understanding the consequences of their behaviors. Once individuals understand the consequences of their behaviors, they are moving toward self-management.

SOCIAL-COGNITIVE APPROACHES

These techniques are designed to instruct individuals to deal more effectively with social matters through self-correction and problem solving. Self-monitoring or instruction involves verbal prompting by the student concerning his/her social behavior. Verbal prompting may be overt or covert. The approach is designed to help students maintain better control over their behaviors.

MAKING BETTER CHOICES

This social-cognitive approach is designed to assist individuals in making better choices. Group lessons are developed around improving social skills. Lessons are designed to promote forethought before engaging in a behavior and to examine the consequences of the behavior. The major components of this program include the following cognitive sequence:

1. Stop (inhibit response)
2. Plan (behaviors leading to positive behaviors)
3. Do (follow plan and monitor behavior)
4. Check (evaluate the success of the plan)

These steps should be practiced by individuals and reinforced by the teacher. Various social skills are identified by the teacher for the students to practice. Progress reports should be kept and assessed periodically by both the teacher and students.

ROLE OF THE SCHOOL IN A BEHAVIORAL SETTING

A meaningful course of action for dealing with negative behavior would be to isolate the behavior and then to quantify, record, and observe the number of acts involved. When this determination has been made, the teacher is equipped to undertake a course of action to change the negative behaviors. Social skills training is the technique advocate. Analysis of the behavior may lead the teacher to pursue a course of action.

Individuals enter school with a wide range of learning abilities, interests, motivations, personalities, attitudes, cultural orientations, and socioeconomic statuses. These traits and abilities must be recognized and incorporated into the instructional program. Promoting positive behavior may take several forms such as using praise frequently, eye contact, special signals, and having individual conferences with pupils.

Individuals enter school with set behavioral styles. Frequently, these styles are inappropriate for the school. Several techniques are recommended to change inappropriate behaviors in the classroom:

1. Have teachers raise their tolerance levels. Teachers generally expect individuals to perform up to acceptable standards. Additionally, it is assumed that students have been taught appropriate social skills at home. Whereas this assumption may be true for most pupils, frequently, it is not true for pupils with disabilities. By the teacher's

recognizing causal factors, such as environment, culture, and value, tolerance levels may be raised.

2. Change teacher expectations for pupils. Pupils generally live up to expectations of teachers. Teachers should expect positive behaviors from children. To accomplish this goal, behaviors will sometimes have to be modeled. It is also recommended that individual time be allowed for certain pupils, through interviews and individual conferences where the teacher honestly relates how the child's behavior is objectionable.

3. A teacher's behavior toward a pupil. A pupil uses the teacher's overt behavior as a mirror for a picture of his/her strength in the classroom. When a positive reflection is projected, this increases the achievement level. When the message is overtly or covertly negative, the pupil has nothing to support his/her efforts. If there is little positive interaction between the pupil and teacher, the pupil may conclude that his/her behavior is not approved by the teacher. Because the pupil depends so heavily on the teacher's behavior for clues, it is crucial that the teacher objectively analyze his/her interaction with individuals.

SUMMARY

Most learning is social and is mediated by other people. Consequently, pupils profit when working in groups. Individual and group activities have proven to be successful in teaching appropriate social skills. Behavioral intervention techniques have proven to be equally successful. There are many individual and group experiences designed to promote social growth among and between children. One of the most promising techniques is cooperative learning, because it appears to help improve social skills of individuals. As the term implies, students work together in groups to help each other attain the behavioral objective when engaged in cooperative learning. Students benefit both socially and academically when participating in group activities. Therefore, the individual's social skills are being dually challenged and developed.

Although cooperative models call for group activities, they require individual accountability. And teachers who use such structures of cooperative learning recognize the need of reaching every student to cooperate and compete while working toward the group goal. The most widely used cooperatively learning programs are Jigsaw, Student Teams Achievement Divisions, Think-Pair-Share, Group Investigation, and Circle of Learning.

With the movements of mainstreaming and inclusion, more and more individuals with disabilities will be interacting with their peers. Some of them may engage in offensive behaviors because of their inability to interact positively. Others have difficulties in communication, which may also result in integration failure (Kaplan, 1996). Teachers must recognize the importance and need for improved interpersonal relationships or increased interaction among all students.

Most individuals with disabilities do not meet academic success due partly to their inability to implement the above social skills or techniques. These techniques are designed to reduce students' isolation and increase students' abilities to react and work with other students toward the solution of common problems. Teachers should experiment with various forms of individual, group, and behavioral intervention strategies to improve social skills of individuals (Taylor, 1992). Since most behaviors are learned, they can be changed through behavioral intervention strategies; once social skills are learned through the application of these techniques, they become automatic.

Lutfiyya's approach outlines three strategies needed for successful group facilitation: facilitation, interpretation, and accommodation (Lutfiyya, 1991). He concludes that all three approaches depend on cooperation within the group. Roles are shared by all involved. Although this approach is primarily used to diagnose and evaluate individuals with disabilities, implications for group planning are clear.

Social skills interventions are needed if individuals are to be successfully integrated into the mainstream. Activities such as greeting, sharing, cooperation, assisting, complementing, and inviting should be developed and modeled. Social skills development assists individuals in several ways:

1. Social competence helps compensate for academic deficits
2. Social skills are needed for success in the mainstream and in employment
3. Social skills training helps derive maximum benefit from academic and/or vocational instruction
4. Social competence is fundamental to good interpersonal relationships and fosters improved leisure and recreational activities

With these in mind, it is incumbent upon our educational systems to focus on designing social skills curricular for all students.

The teaching of social skills for students can be as subtle as the teacher incidentally modeling the correct social behavior in a classroom situation to overt direct instruction in the form of approaches or techniques such as skillstreaming, coaching cooperative learning, structured modeling, role-playing, or creative dramatics. The manner in which social skills are taught and the specific teacher characteristics that are used can determine the quality of the entire educational experience for the student.

Positive behavior is a prerequisite for attaining the other skills necessary for school success. For whatever reason, social skills are a major deficit area for some students. Social skills include the ability to follow instruction, accept criticism, disagree appropriately, greet someone, make a request, and reinforce and compliment others, as well as acceptable ways of getting attention. Thus, activities should be infused throughout the curriculum (Anita and Kreimeyer, 1992).

BIBLIOGRAPHY

Adams, D. N. 1990. "Involving Students in Cooperative Learning." *Teaching Pre-k* 8:51–52.

Aksamit, D. L. 1990. "Practicing Teachers' Perceptions of Their Pre-service Preparation for Mainstreaming." *Teacher Education and Special Education* 13:21–29.

Anita, S. D., and K. Kreimeyer. 1992. "Project Interact: Intervention for Social Integration of Young Hearing-Impaired Children." Office of Special Education and Rehabilitative Services.

Banbury, M. M., and C. R. Herbert. 1992. "Do You See What I Mean?" *Teaching Exceptional Children* 24:34–48.

Bandura, A. 1970. *A Social Learning Theory.* Englewood Cliffs, N.J.: Prentice Hall.

Carnine, D. 1991. "Curricular Interventions for Teaching Higher Order-Thinking for All Students: Introduction to the Special Series." *Journal of Learning Disabilities* 24 (5): 261–269.

Carnine, D., A. Granzin, and W. Becker. 1988. "Direct Instruction." In *Alternative Education Delivery Systems: Enhancing Instructional Options for All Students*, ed. J. Braden, J. Zims, and M. Curtis. Washington, D.C.: National Association for School Psychologists.

Coker, K. H., and B. A. Thyer. 1990. "School and Family-Based Treatment of

Children with Attention-Deficit Hyperactivity Disorder: Families in Society." *Journal of Contemporary Human Services*: 276–281.

Cosden, M. 1985. "The Effects of Cooperative and Individual Goal Structure on Learning Disabled and Nondisabled Students." *Teaching Exceptional Children* 52:103–114.

Denny, R. K., M. N. Epstein, and E. Rose. 1992. "Direct Observation of Adolescent with Behavioral Disorders and Their Nonhandicapped Peers in Mainstream." *Vocational Education Classrooms, Behavioral Disorders* 18:333–341.

Dorr-Bremme, D. W. 1992. "Discourse and Society Identify in Kindergarten–First Grade Classroom." Clearinghouse for Teacher Education. ERIC. ED 3542111.

Gemma, A. 1989. "Social Skills Instruction in Mainstreamed Preschool Classroom." Clearinghouse for Teacher Education. ERIC. ED 326033.

Gills, W. 1991. "Jewish Day Schools and African-American Youth." *Journal of Negro Education* 60:566–580.

Goldstein, A., and E. McGinnis. 1984. *Skillstreaming Elementary Children*. Chicago: Research Press.

Goldstein, S., and M. Goldstein. 1990. *Managing Attention Disorders in Children: A Guide for Practitioners*. New York: Wiley.

Gresham, F. M. 1985. "Utility of Cognitive-Behavioral Procedures for Social Skills Training with Children: Critical Review." *Journal of Abnormal Child Psychology* 13:491.

Hedley, C. N. 1987. "What's New in Software? Computer Programs for Social Skills." *Journal of Reading, Writing, and Learning Disabilities International* 3:187–191.

Hines, M. S. 1990. "Error Monitoring by Learning Handicapped Students Engaged in Collaborative Microcomputer-Based Writing." *Journal of Special Education* 23:407–422.

Istre, S. M. 1993. "Social Skills of Preadolescent Boys with Attention Deficit Hyperactivity Disorder." Ph.D. diss., Oklahoma State University. Abstract in *Dissertation Abstracts International* 53:4064.

Johnson, D. W., R. Johnson, and E. Holubec. 1988. *Cooperation in the Classroom*. Edina, Minn.: International.

Johnson, R. T., and D. W. Johnson. 1983. "Effects on Cooperative, Competitive, and Individualistic Learning Experiences on Social Development." *Exceptional Children* 49:323–329.

Kagan, S. 1990. "The Structural Approach to Cooperative Learning." *Educational Leadership* 47:12–15.

Kaplan, P. 1996. *Pathways for Exceptional Children*. Minneapolis, Minn.: West Publishing Company.

Katz, L. G. 1991. "The Teacher's Role in Social Development of Young Children." Clearinghouse on Elementary and Early Childhood Education. ERIC. ED 331642

Lane, P. S., and McWhirter. 1992. "A Peer Mediation Model: Conflict Resolution for Elementary and Middle School." *Elementary School Guidance and Counseling* 27:15–21.

Lutfiyya, Z. 1991. *Tony Sati and Bakery—The Roles of Facilitation, Accommodation, and Interpretation.* Syracuse, N.Y.: Center on Human Policy, Syracuse University.

Odom, S. L., and P. S. Strain. 1984. "Classroom-Based Social Skills Instruction for Severely Handicapped Preschool Children." *Topics in Early Childhood Special Education* 4:97–116.

Rizzo, J. V., and R. H. Zabel. 1988. *Educating Children and Adolescents with Behavioral Disorders: An Integrative Approach.* Boston: Allyn and Bacon.

Salend, S. J., and C. R. Whittaker. 1992. "Group Evaluation: A Collaborative, Peer-Mediated Behavior Management System." *Exceptional Children* 59:203–209.

Shores, R. E., P. L. Gunter, and S. L. Jack. 1993. "Classroom Management Strategies: Are They Settling for Coercion?" *Behavior Disorders* 18:92–102.

Slavin, R. E. 1984. "Effects on Team Assisted Individualization on the Mathematics Achievements of Academically Handicapped and Nonhandicapped Students." *Journal of Educational Psychology* 76:813–819.

———. 1991. *Using Student Team Learning.* Baltimore, Md.: Center for Social Organization of Schools, Johns Hopkins University.

Slavin, R. E., and E. Oickle. 1981. "Effects of Cooperative Learning Teams on Student Achievement and Race Relations: Treatment by Race Interactions." *Sociology of Education* 54:174–180.

Storey, K. 1992. "A Follow-up of Social Skills Instruction for Preschoolers with Developmental Delays." *Education and Treatment of Children* 15:125–139.

Taylor, G. 1992. "Impact of Social Learning Theory on Educating Deprived/Minority Children." *Clearinghouse for Teacher Education* ERIC. 349260.

Thorkildsen, R. 1985. "Using an Interactive Videodisc Program to Teach Social Skills to Handicapped Children." *American Annals of the Deaf* 130:383–385.

CHAPTER 8

Cognitive Psychology

The study of cognition in psychology during the last four decades is more intense now than at any previous time. With the recognition that complex internal processing is involved in most learning and perception, and with a continual widening of the definition of cognition in this chapter, a number of examples are given, and from these examples it will be clear how broad the current conception really is. Currently, not only are all the major academic skills, ranging from reading to mathematics and science, included under cognition, but also much that is classically considered as part of perception. In fact, it has become increasingly difficult to draw any sharp line between cognition and perception (Ormrod, 1999).

From a theoretical standpoint, there are many different approaches to cognition, but it is fair to say that none of them currently dominate the scene. As in the case of an exact definition of cognition, it is also not possible to give a precise definition or to delineate sharply the key theoretical concepts in the various approaches to cognitive theory. Without too much injustice, however, the current theories can be grouped into four classes, and the four main sections of this chapter are organized to represent each of the four main theoretical approaches.

In brief terms, the four approaches are behavioral, developmental, information processing, and linguistic in orientation. The behavioral approach to cognition is typically represented by stimulus–response theorists like Estes, the developmental approach by Jean Piaget, and the information-processing approach by Newell and Simon (Newell and Simon, 1972), as well as current work in artificial intelligence. The linguistic approach has been most stimulated by Chomsky (Chomsky, 1957), but the large amount of literature on semantics derives not from the linguistic tradition of Chomsky and his colleagues, but rather from that of logicians and philosophers. Some attention will be given to both of these linguistic approaches.

Without attempting anything like an adequate or complete survey, I also indicate for these approaches some of the relevant studies directly concerned with the cognitive capacities of children with disabilities.

As I turn to these four theoretical approaches to cognition, it is important to emphasize that each is incomplete and unsatisfactory in several ways. There are some reasons of a real synthesis of theoretical ideas that have been emerging in psychology from a number of different viewpoints, but it is premature to indicate the lines of this synthesis. It is clear, however, that what once appeared as sharp conceptual differences between behavioral approaches on the one hand, and information-processing approaches on the other, has with time increasingly become less clear and less distinct. More is said about such a synthesis in the final section.

BEHAVIORAL APPROACH

The behavioral approach to cognition in the form of concept formation may be illustrated by the application of the simple all-or-none conditioning model. Bower and Estes showed that a simple conditioning model could give an excellent account of paired-associate learning (Bower, 1961; Estes, 1961). In paired-associate experiments, the learner is shown, for example, a nonsense syllable and is asked to learn to associate with it the response of pressing a left or right key. Given a list of, say, twenty nonsense syllables, with half of them randomly assigned to the left key and half of them to the right key, the scientific problem is to give an exact account of the course of learning. The naive idea most of us have is that on each trial, with exposure to the stimulus and an indication of what is the correct response, learning will gradually occur. One traditional way of expressing this is that the connection or response strength will gradually build up from trial to trial.

The experiments reported by Bower and Estes showed that in simple paired-associate learning the situation is somewhat different. The evidence is fairly clear that in the kind of paired-associate experiment just described the learner does not improve incrementally, but rather learns the association between a stimulus and responds on an all-or-none basis. There is no improvement in the probability of his/her making a correct response until he/she fully learns the association. The theory of such experiments can be stated rather explicitly within a classical stimulus–response framework. The only important concepts are those of conditioning a response to a stimulus and sampling the stimuli on a given trial, together with the reinforcement that serves as a correction procedure when incorrect responses are made or that informs the learner that a correct response has been made (Ormrod, 1999).

In the Bower and Estes models, there are two essential assumptions. First, until the single stimulus element is conditioned there is a constant guessing probability (p) that the learner responds correctly (c) and that the single stimulus element will be conditioned to the correct response. The only change in this model in order to apply it to concept learning is that the concept rather than the single stimulus element is now that to which the correct response is conditioned.

In essence, according to Slavin in paired-associate learning the student must associate response with each stimulus (Slavin, 2000). Techniques to improve students' responses include imagery, the keyword method, serial and free-recall learning, loci method, peg word method, and initial-letter strategies. For specific examples concerning the use of these paired-associate learning techniques, refer to Slavin (Slavin, 2000). Paired-associate learning involves learning a sequence of information in the correct order. The aforementioned strategies will aid students in associating with stimuli.

DEVELOPMENTAL APPROACH

A major approach to cognition has been to describe in explicit terms the sequence of concept development in children from birth to adolescence (Piaget, 1952). Without question, the outstanding effort has been that of Piaget and his collaborators. The studies have ranged over most of the topics one would like to see included in a broad theory of cognition and have covered more conceptual ground than the behavioral approach just discussed.

The Piagetian developmental approach studies the four following concepts: the child's understanding of spatial concepts, including both two- and three-dimensional concepts; the development of geometrical concepts; the development of concept of distance conservation; and the spatial coordinate system. Extensive and controversial studies on the concepts of conservation of mass, weight, and volume were also conducted.

Additional studies were concerned with the development of number concepts and set concepts closely related to those of number concepts; for example, the notion of two sets being equivalent, that is, having the same cardinality. Still other studies have been devoted to the development of the concepts of causality and also of morality in children.

Those who want to get a deeper feeling for the Piagetian approach to cognition can look at either some of the many books of Piaget that have been translated into English or at some of the excellent readers composed of shorter articles that have appeared in recent years.

The enormous body of research studies generated by Piaget and his collaborators has given us an overview of the cognitive development of the child unequaled by any of the other approaches to cognition. The attempt has been to map out in broad terms the cognitive development along every major dimension of intellectual or perceptual skill. To a lesser extent than one might expect, this conceptual apparatus and approach to cognition has not been extensively applied to children with disabilities.

Granted that the developmental approach of Piaget has given by far the most extensive analysis of the whole range of cognitive concepts, it is natural to ask why this approach has not been uniformly adopted by most investigators and conceded to be the soundest approach to cognition. There are, I think, three reasons for reservations about the Piagetian approach to cognition. These reasons can be given and seriously held to without at the same time denigrating the great value of work that Piaget and his collaborators have done.

One objection to the developmental Piagetian approach to cognition is the lack of emphasis and attention given to language development. The linguistic approach that is discussed in the next section emphasizes the overwhelming importance of language development for the cognitive development of a child and its advocates find far too little attention paid to the problems of language development in the Piagetian viewpoint.

The second objection has been a methodological one by many experimental psychologists to the quality of the experimental data reported by Piaget and his collaborators. The standard objection has been not that well-designed experiments have been used as a basis for the conclusions drawn, but rather that empirical methods have been based too much on anecdotal methods, or at the least, open-ended interviews in which children are verbally interrogated about their understanding of concepts and relevant cognitive tasks. This criticism is less valid than it was a decade ago, because much of the emphasis, especially on the part of American investigators following the Piaget line of development, has been on the careful design of experiments to test Piagetian concepts. There now exists a rather substantial literature of an experimentally sound character in the Piagetian tradition, and the reader will find current issues of journals like *Developmental Psychology* and the *Journal of Experimental Child Psychology* full of carefully designed experiments that clearly grow out of this tradition.

The third line of criticism of the Piagetian approach is the lack of clarity in the development of key concepts and the absence of sharply defined experimental tests of the key concepts. To illustrate the problem and to provide a comparison with the earlier discussion of all-or-none conditioning as a behavioral approach, I paraphrase and present briefly an analysis I have given elsewhere of Piaget's concept of stages.

I use Piaget's concept of stages because it is central to much of his work in development and because it has become increasingly important in developmental psycholinguistics. I hasten to add, however, that a similar analysis could be given of other key concepts. An instance of how Piaget uses the concept of stages can be gained from the following quotation, in which the analysis of three stages of multiple seriation is discussed by Piaget.

> We shall distinguish three stages, corresponding to the usual three levels. During stage I, there are no seriations in the strict sense. The child's constructions are intermediate between classification and seriation. During stage II, there is seriation, but only according to one of the criteria, or else the child switches from one criterion to the other. . . . Finally, during stage III (starting at 7–8 years), the child reaches a muliplicative arrangement based on the twofold seriation of the set of elements. (Piaget, 1960)

There is in this passage, as elsewhere in the writings of Piaget, little indication that matters could be otherwise—that development could be incremental and continuous and that stages may be an artificial device with no real scientific content. No one denies that children develop in some sequential fashion as they acquire new capacities and skills. The problem is in determining whether they proceed in stages or continuously. We could of course artificially and conventionally divide any period of incremental development and label it as a particular "stage." In principle, the issue about stages versus incremental acquisition of concepts is exactly the issue faced by the behavioral approach in comparing the all-or-none conditioning model with the ordinary incremental model.

In other places, Piaget does comment on the question of the actual existence of stages, but he does not address the matter in ways that seem scientifically sound. Piaget writes as follows:

> I now come to the big problem: the problem of the very existence of stages; do there exist steps in development or is complete continuity observed? . . . [W]hen we are faced macroscopically with a certain discontinuity we never know whether there do not exist small transformations which we do not manage to measure on our scale of approximation. In other words, continuity would depend fundamentally on a question of scale; for a certain scale of measurement we obtain discontinuity. Of course this argument is quite valid, because the very manner of defining continuity and discontinuity implies that these ideas remain fundamentally relative to the scale of measurement or observation. This, then, is the alternative which confronts us: either a basic continuity or else development by steps, which would allow us to speak of stages at least to our scale of approximation. (Piaget, 1960)

The confusion in this passage is in the introduction of the spurious issue of the scale of measurement. Obviously, this is an issue to be discussed in a refined analysis but, as the literature on all-or-none conditioning model versus incremental models shows, a perfectly good and sound prior investigation exists at a given level of measurement, namely, the level of standard experimental studies. What Piaget does not seem to recognize is the existence of a clear alternative and the necessity of testing for the presence or absence of this alternative in providing a more correct account of the sequential development that occurs in a child.

This discussion of stages is meant to indicate the tension that exists in any fair evaluation of the work of Piaget and his collaborators. Regardless, they have without doubt contributed enormously to the current intense interest in cognition, especially in the cognitive development of children. Piaget and his collaborators have put the problem in a proper perspective by insisting on investigating not just a few skills and concepts, but the entire range that we intuitively expect and believe are part of the child's developing competence. Meanwhile, both the theory and experimentation have often been loose and more suggestive than definitive. Methodological and theoretical criticisms are easy to formulate. Certainly, deeper clarification of both the experimental methodology and the theory is required before widespread applications to the critical problems of development in children with disabilities are extensively pursued.

INFORMATION-PROCESSING APPROACH

The information-processing approach to cognition has been deeply influenced by related developments in computer science and the widespread impact of computers themselves since the early 1950s. A good example of any early influential article in this approach to cognition is Newell, Shaw, and Simon (Newell, Shaw, and Simon, 1958). An influential book of the early 1960s was that edited by Feigenbaum and Feldman (Feigenbaum and Feldman, 1963).

In broad terms, the difference between the information-processing approach and the developmental approach of Piaget is that Piaget was primarily concerned with the characterization of tasks and the sequence in which the child learned to solve these tasks; in contrast, the information-processing approach is concerned with the processing apparatus necessary to handle even the most elementary forms of cognition.

As the name suggests, the information-processing approach has been influenced by the organization of information processing in computers. There is concern that the major aspects of information processing that have been the focus of computer organization should also be given attention in any conception of human processing. It is important not to be misunderstood on this point. Investigators like Mayer and Wittrock and Reisberg are far too sophisticated to think that the present stage of computer development provides anything like an adequate model of human processing (Mayer, 1996; Reisberg, 1977). Although they do not put it in so many words, it is probably fair to say that they would regard the problems of computer organization as indicating some of the necessary but not sufficient conditions for information processing in humans.

The major feature of the information-processing approach that differs from either the behavioral or developmental approach is the emphasis on the detailed steps a person or child takes in solving a concept, and the detailed analysis of the verbal protocol that can be obtained from him/her in the process of mastering a problem. The information-processing approach is like the developmental approach and at the same time it mirrors the behavioral approach in its emphasis on a highly detailed analysis of the structure and content of the protocol.

As is characteristic of other areas of psychology, the different approaches also tend to develop different types of tasks considered typical of cognition. The information-processing approach, especially in the work of Newell and Simon, is concerned with cryptarithmetic, simple logical inference, and the kind of problem solving that goes into complex games like chess (Newell and Simon, 1972).

The most characteristic and important feature of the information-processing approach is the attempt to simulate by a computer program the detailed processing in which a human subject engages in problem solving. This has proven to be both a strength and weakness of this approach to cognition. It is a strength because of the effort to capture as much as possible the explicit details of the human subject's thought processes in mastering a cognitive problem; in this ambition, it goes far beyond anything that has yet been attempted in the behavioral approach. The weakness of the approach is methodological. It centers around the difficulty of evaluating whether or not the simulation, even at the level of individual subjects, provides a good match to the actual ongoing processing in the human subject. The very complexity of the simulation raises new methodological problems that do not arise in the same form in either the behavioral or developmental approaches to cognition.

Recently, the broad spectrum of problems attacked under the heading of artificial intelligence by computer scientists has also provided a broader-based approach to cognition than the particular approach of Newell and Simon (Newell and Simon, 1972). It is not that the approach via artificial intelligence is in contradiction with that of Newell and Simon; rather, it is that new components with a different emphasis have been added. The work of Minsky and Papert has been especially influential in this development (Minsky and Papert, 1969). They have taken this approach at a mathematical level in their book *Perceptrons* (1969), and still more explicitly in their recent analysis of the close relation between artificial intelligence and the development of a child's intelligence. Perhaps the most characteristic feature of their recent work is the emphasis on a procedure or program on the one hand, and the process of debugging the procedure or the program on the other. The idea that learning a cognitive skill is primarily a matter of learning a procedure that itself might be broken into separate procedures, and that each of these separate procedures must go through a process of debugging similar to debugging a computer program is an important insight not previously exploited in any detail. There is now a widespread belief that we must be able to conceptualize the internal programs that an organism uses in solving a conceptual or perceptual problem.

Today, researchers and psychologists have discovered that individuals do not just absorb information at face value, rather they do a great deal with the information they acquire and actively try to organize and make sense of it (Ormrod, 1999). It is commonly agreed by most cognitive theorists that learning is a process of constructing knowledge from information an individual receives rather than directly receiving information through the five senses (Leinhardt, 1994; Collins and Green, 1992; Driver, 1995; Marshall, 1992; Mayer, 1996; Spivey, 1997). Most of the theorists refer to constructing knowledge from information received as constructivism rather than information-processing theory (Holloway, 1999; Brooks and Brooks, 1999). Individuals receive and react to information through individual and social constructivism. An example of individual constructivism may be found in Piaget's theory of cognitive structure, where a child constructs knowledge for his/herself rather than absorbing it exactly as perceived. Social constructivism theories imply how individuals work as a team to make sense of their surroundings.

LINGUISTIC APPROACH

An excellent expression of the linguistic approach to cognition is found in Chomsky (Chomsky, 1972). At the outset, an important difference to be noted about the linguistic approach in contrast to the three other approaches discussed already is that the linguistic approach does not in principle propose to be a general theory of cognition, but rather it concentrates on that significant part of cognition that is language dependent or consists of language skills themselves. Linguistics like Chomsky consider the phenomenon of cognitive psychology and, consequently, believe that a large place should be occupied by the linguistic approach to cognition, even if it is not meant to encompass all cognitive phenomena.

Linguists and psycholinguists with a strong linguistic orientation have been insistent that none of the other approaches to cognition provide anything like an adequate detailed theory of language performance in either children or adults. Indeed, it is customary for linguists like Chomsky to insist that even their own theories offer only the barest beginning of an adequate approach to the analysis of language. Long ago, Aristotle defined man as a rational animal, but much is to be said for the viewpoint that man should rather be defined as a talking animal. The linguistic approach to cognition insists on the central place of language in the cognitive behavior of man and rightly denies the adequacy of any theory of cognition that cannot account for major aspects of language behavior.

The linguistic viewpoint has emphasized understanding the complex and sometimes bewildering grammar of spoken language. There is, however, another aspect of language with a long tradition of analysis that is equally important from a cognitive standpoint. I have in mind the theory of meaning and reference, or what is usually termed the semantics of a language. This semantics tradition derives more from philosophy and logic than from linguistic. In support of this view, Houston states that because different sentences may have the same meaning, this indicates the philosophical and logical view rather than the linguistic approach (Houston, 1986). Psycholinguists have recommended a procedure for finding out the semantic or the meaning of a sentence. Forster and Wanner and Maratsas recommend that the sentence be divided into clauses (Forster, 1979; Wanner and Maratsas, 1978). This view is supported by Foder, Bever, and Garrett (Foder, Bever, and Garrett, 1974). They articulate that once a sentence has been divided into clauses, its meaning can be determined.

Methods that provide detailed descriptions of the grammatical and semantic structure of an individual's speech will continue to be developed. As this development continues, we will have a deeper understanding of cognition in the development of procedural grammars and semantics that yields not only a proper analysis of the structure of an individual's speech, but also provides the necessary mechanisms for generating the speech, both in its grammatical and semantical feature.

Klein states that language serves three important functions (Klein, 1996). It allows us to communicate with each other, it facilitates our thinking processes, and it enables us to recall information beyond the limits of our memory stores. The study of the meaning of language, called semantics, has shown that the same sentence can have different meanings and different sentences can have the same meaning.

A COMPARISON BETWEEN COGNITIVE AND BEHAVIORAL PSYCHOLOGY

Most cognitive research has dealt with higher mental process with humans, whereas behavioral research has centered its efforts on animal research. Standards for conducting studies with humans and animals differ significantly. Topics relevant to comprehension, understanding, memory, concept formation, and other high mental processes cannot be successfully conducted using animals.

Another major difference between the two paradigms may be in the major goals of the two approaches. Behaviorists attempt to establish relationships that exist between behavior and its antecedents as well as its consequences, where as cognitive theorists attempt to make plausible and useful information about the processes that intervene between input and output. Additionally, Lefrançois reflects that cognitive theories tend to be less ambitious in scope than behavior theories (Lefrançois, 2000). He furthered voices that there have been few attempts to build systematic inclusive cognitive theories that can explain all human learning and behavior. Emphasis in the last several decades has been on intensive research in specific areas, rather than on the construction of general systems.

SUMMARY

In the behavioral approach, learning theory is applied to mental development, for example, by Estes (Estes, 1961). Suppes shows how the simple all-or-none conditioning model applies to concept formation in children (Suppes, 1969) and reviews Zeaman and House's application of an extension of this model to children with disabilities. Relative to disabilities, he recommends a procedure not followed in practice to date, namely, an estimation of parameters of the learning models for individual subjects or for groups of subjects stratified according to mental age.

The developmental approach, dominated by Piaget, has made very considerable progress in describing the sequence of concept development in children, but has not been applied extensively to children with disabilities. Suppes advances three reasons for holding reservations about the viewpoint associated with Piaget, but none of the drawbacks are intrinsic to the approach. With work over time, it could prove highly fruitful in understanding the problems of development in children with disabilities.

The essence of the information-processing approach to cognition is a concern with the processing apparatus that appears to be necessary and with a detailed analysis of the steps a child takes in attaining a concept. Newell and Simon attempted to stimulate human information processing in a computer program (Newell and Simon, 1972), and Suppes touched on the strengths and weaknesses of this stratagem (Suppes, 1969). Minsky and Papert suggested that formulating and debugging the separate procedures (subroutines) of a larger procedure (program) is the process people follow in solving a conceptual problem (Minsky and Papert, 1969), and Suppes illustrated with some of his own work how an analysis along these lines might go (Suppes, 1969). If through research in the years ahead such analyses are made of the tasks and processes children with disabilities should master and follow, they also could contribute substantially to solving practical problems of instruction.

The linguistic approach focuses on what many consider to be the most important part of cognition, the part that is language dependent. The linguist's work on syntax is best represented by Chomsky, while the contribution of philosophers and logicians to semantics was mainly by Tarski (Chomsky, 1957). As Suppes pointed out, we should like a detailed account of both the grammar and meaning of speech of young children. He included in his article a review of some studies of retarded and deaf children. He also picked up again the matter of sensory substitution (Suppes, 1969).

The major thrust of cognitive psychology is to research and place emphasis on perceptual and cognitive processes where as behavioral psychology attempts to establish relationships that exist between behavior and its antecedents as well as its consequences. Individuals are prompted to use higher thinking processes to perceive, arrive at understanding, process information, and solve problems. Both cognitive and behavioral theorists support the idea that learning should be studied objectively. Refer to chapter 2 for additional major contributions made to learning theory by cognitive psychologists.

BIBLIOGRAPHY

Bower, G. H. 1961. "Application of a Model to Paired-Associate Learning." *Psychometrika* 26:255–280.

Brooks, J. G., and M. G. Brooks. 1999. "The Courage to Be Constructivist." *Educational Leadership* 57:18–24.

Chomsky, N. 1957. *Syntactic Structures*. The Hague: Mouton.

———. 1972. *Language and Mind*. New York: Harcourt Brace.

Collins, E., and J. Green. 1992. "Learning Classroom Settings: Making or Breaking a Culture." In *Redefining Student Learning: Roots of Educational Change*, ed. H. H. Marshall. Norwood, N.J.: Ablex.

Driver, R. 1995. "Constructivist Approaches Science Teaching." In *Constructivism in Education*, ed. L. P. Steffe and J. Gale. Hillsdale, N.J.: Erlbaum.

Estes, W. K. 1961. "New Developments in Statistical Behavior Theory: Differential Tests of Axioms for Associative Learning." *Psychometrika* 26:73–84

Feigenbaum, E. A., and J. Feldman. 1963. *Computers and Thought*. New York: McGraw-Hill.

Foder, J. A., T. G. Bever, and M. F. Garrett. 1974. *The Psychology of Language: An Introduction to Psycholinguistics and Generative Grammar*. New York: McGraw-Hill.

Forster, K. 1979. "Levels of Processing and the Structure of the Language Processor." In *Sentence Processing*, ed. W. E. Cooper and T. Walker. Hillsdale, N.J.: Erlbaum.

Holloway, J. H. 1999. Caution: "Constructivism Ahead." *Educational Leadership*, 57:85–86.

Houston, J. P. 1986. *Fundamentals of Learning and Memory*. 3rd ed. Orlando, Fla.: Harcourt Brace Jovanovich.

Klein, S. B. 1996. *Learning: Principles and Application*. 3rd ed. New York: McGraw-Hill.

Lefrançois, G. R. 2000. *Theories of Human Learning: What the Old Man Said*. Belmont, Calif.: Wadsworth.

Leinhardt, G. 1994. "History: A Time to Be Mindful." In *Teaching and Learning in History*, ed. G. Leinhardt, I. L. Beck, and C. Stainton. Hillsdale, N.J.: Erlbaum.

Marshall, H. H. 1992. *Redefining Student Learning: Roots of Educational Change*. Norwood, N.J.: Ablex.

Mayer, R. 1996. "Learners As Information Processors: Legacies and Limitations of Educational Psychology's Second Metaphor." *Educational Psychology* 31:151–161.

Minsky, M., and S. Papert. 1969. *Perceptrons*. Cambridge: MIT Press.

Newell, A., and H. A. Simon. 1972. *Human Problem Solving*. Englewood Cliffs, N.J.: Prentice Hall.

Newell, A., J. C. Shaw, and H. A. Simon. 1958. "Elements of a Theory of Human Problem Solving." *Psychological Review* 65:155–166.

Ormrod, J. E. 1999. *Human Learning*. 3rd ed. Columbus, Ohio: Merrill.

Piaget, J. 1952. *The Origins of Intelligence in Children*. New York: Basic.

———. 1960. Discussion in *Discussions on Child Development*, ed. J. M. Tanner and B. Inhelder. New York: International Universities Press.

Reisberg, D. 1977. *Cognition: Exploring the Science of the Mind*. New York: Norton.

Slavin, R. E. 2000. *Educational Psychology: Theory and Practice*. Boston: Allyn and Bacon.

Spivey, N. N. 1997. *The Constructivist Metaphor: Reading, Writing, and the Making of Meaning*. San Diego, Calif.: Academic.

Suppes, P. 1969. "Stimulus: Response Theory of Finite Automata." *Journal of Mathematical Psychology* 6:327–355.

Wanner, E., and M. Maratsas. 1978. "An ATN Approach to Comprehension." In *Linguistic Theory and Psychological Reality*, ed. M. Halle, J. Bresnan, and G. A. Miller. Cambridge: MIT Press.

CHAPTER 9

Cognitive Theories of Learning

In the preceding chapter, I established the relationship between cognitive psychology and cognitive theories of learning. In essence, cognitive psychology provided the framework for our present assumptions underlining cognitive learning theories. I alluded to the important work of Chomsky in formulating our present understanding of cognitive theory (Chomsky, 1957). Works by Brunner as well as countless others were instrumental in developing cognitive theory as a science (Brunner, 1961a, 1961b).

By the early 1900s, cognitive psychology was denouncing the stimulus–response (S–R) theory of learning and was formulating its own theory based on cognitive psychology. The movement was led by Edward C. Tolman, Jean Piaget, Lev Vygotsky, and several Gestalt psychologists. The impact and influence of their works today is shaping education reforms in educational practices.

EDWARD C. TOLMAN

Edward C. Tolman is considered to be a behaviorist, but his theory was basically cognitive. He believed that learning was internal and included a holistic view of learning. This concept was in contrast to the one advocated by behaviorists. Tolman's theory was based on a mechanistic view of learning. His theory attempted to emphasize and tried to understand the predictable nature of human behavior. Tolman adapted several ideas from behaviorists and according to Ormrod postulated the following principles in his purposive behaviorism (Ormrod, 1999).

   1. Behavior should be studied at a molar level. This view was in contrast to early behaviorist beliefs. They attempted to reduce behavior

to simple S–R responses. Refer to chapters 2 and 4 for additional behaviorist views on learning. Tolman opposed this S–R view; he related that behaviors are too complex to be regulated to simple S–R reflexes and that a total approach must be used when analyzing behavior.

2. Learning can occur without reinforcement. Tolman and Hovzik opposed this view. Their blocked-path study supported his theory that learning can occur without reinforcement (Tolman and Hovzik, 1930). This classical study involved three groups of rats who ran a different maze under different reinforcement conditions. Rats in group 1 were reinforced with food each time they successfully ran the maze. Group 2 rats received no reinforcement for successfully completing the maze. Group 3 rats were not reinforced during the first ten days, but were reinforced on the eleventh day. Findings showed that the performance rats in groups 2 and 3 improved even though they did not receive reinforcement. Once the rats in group 3 began receiving reinforcements, their performance in the maze equaled and in most cases surpassed group 1's performance. Results suggest that reinforcement is not as important to learning as advocated by behaviorists and that organisms develop cognitive maps of their environments. A cognitive map may be defined as an internal organization of relationships between goals and behaviors.

3. Learning can occur without a change in behavior. Most behaviorists will adamantly denounce this statement. Tolman stated that learning can occur without a change in behavior. He defined this type of learning as latent learning. The Tolman and Hovzik study reported earlier provides us with an example of latent learning. Rats in groups 1 and 3 must have equally learned the same amount during the first ten days, even though their behaviors did not reflect such learning. In essence, the amounts of learning were not observed. Tolman proclaimed that reinforcement influences performance rather than learning, in that it increases the likelihood that learned behavior will be displayed.

4. Intervening variables must be considered. Variables such as drive, habit, strength, and incentive play critical roles in learning. All behavior has a purpose and all actions are directed toward the accomplishment of some goal. The intervening variable listed earlier contributed significantly to promoting or impeding learning (Tolman, Ritchie, and Kalish, 1946).

5. Behavior is purposive. Tolman supported the formulation of S–R connections provided that they are part of a process that produces a certain goal. He proposed that individuals arrive and activities are directed at achieving the goal. The behavior has a purpose, which is the achievement of the goal. According to Tolman, there are certain events in the environment that convey information relevant to achieving one's goals. Goals can be successfully met only after one has mastered the events leading to the rewards or punishment in one's environment. The anticipation of future rewards stimulates activities to guide our behavior toward achieving the goal. The role of punishment indicates negative activities that impede the achievement of goals. Tolman's theory implies that behavior has a purpose that is goal directed. Consequently, this theory of learning is frequently referred to as "purposive behaviorism."

6. Expectations affect behavior. When an organism learns that certain behaviors produce certain results, expectations are formed concerning the behaviors. The organism expects a particular action to lead to a designated goal. Individuals also expect specific outcomes to produce certain results. If goals are not achieved, individuals continue to search for the reward that will satisfy the goal. Tolman indicated the importance of knowledge gained through experience.

7. Learning results in an organized body of information. Information is organized through what Tolman referred to as "cognitive maps." He proposed that organisms develop cognitive maps of their environments by organizing information and knowing the location of them. Tolman, Ritchie, and Kalish's experiment with rats gave some clarity to the term (Tolman, Ritchie, and Kalish, 1946). Rats ran several times through a series of mazes. Data suggested that the rats learned how the mazes were arranged. Some of the entrances leading to some of the alleys leading to food were blocked, so the rats had to choose other alleys to arrive at the food. The rats were able to locate the alley that was not blocked and provided a shortcut to the food. According to Tolman, rats integrated their experiences into a body of information (cognitive maps) from which they figured out the shortest route to the food.

Tolman's principal contribution to the development of psychological theory lies not so much in advances in knowledge and prediction made possible by his work as in the fact that it represents a transition from behavioristic to more cognitive interpretations. It departs from behavioristic theories such as those of Burrhus F. Skinner, John B. Watson, and Edwin R. Guthrie, which rejected speculation about events that might intervene between stimuli and responses by emphasizing the importance of cognitive variables such as expectancies (Lefrançois, 2000).

Classroom Application

Tolman suggested that our behavior is goal-oriented. We are motivated to reach specific goals and continue to drive until we obtain them. It is incumbent upon teachers to construct learning activities that will motivate the achievement of positive goals for children.

JEAN PIAGET

Jean Piaget's theory is basically cognitive and developmental. Much of it was based on the study of his own children. The method that he developed for studying his children was called the clinical method. He interviewed children and used their questions for follow-up questions. Initially, the method did not receive much support because it was considered too subjective by theorists. However, today the theory has stood the test of time and is considered a scientific approach for studying children. Piaget's work is considered the most comprehensive theory on intellectual development, as it incorporates a variety of topics involving cognitive development. Papert writes that Piaget found the secrets of human learning and knowledge hidden behind the cute and seemingly illogical notions of children (Papert, 1999).

Overview of Piaget's Contributions

According to Papert, Piaget grew up near Lake of Neuchâtel in a quiet region of Switzerland known for its wines and watchmaking (Papert, 1999). His father was a professor of medieval studies and his mother a strict Calvinist. He was a child prodigy who soon became interested in the scientific study of nature. At the age of ten, his observations led to questions that could be answered only by access to the university library. Piaget wrote and published a short note on the sighting of an albino sparrow in the hope that this would influence the librarian to stop treating him like a child. It worked. Piaget was launched on a path that would lead to his doctorate in zoology and a lifelong conviction that the way to understand anything is to understand how it evolves. Piaget published nearly sixty scholarly books, and in 1924 was appointed director of the International Bureau of Education. In 1955, he established the Center for Genetic Epistemology. In 1980, he died in Geneva.

Piaget articulated that it is not until the growing child reaches the two operational stages that he/she begins to acquire the concepts of conservation. He interpreted the concepts of conservation to the idea that the mass of an objective remains constant no matter how much the form changes. He demonstrated this concept with the following example. A five-year-old is given two tumblers, each half-full of water. When asked, the child will agree that there is the same amount of water in each tumbler. However, if the water is poured from one glass into a tall narrow container, the child will reply that there is more water in the tall glass. The child, according to Piaget, has no concept of the conservation of matters. Most children develop this concept by the time they reach their eighth birthday. This illustration demonstrates that knowledge can be described in terms of structures that change with development. Piaget advanced the concept of scheme. He defined "scheme" as the basic structure through which an individual's knowledge is mentally represented. As children develop mentally, physically, and socially, new schemes develop and old schemes are either integrated or modified into cognitive structures (Ormrod, 1999).

As children develop, their movements become more complex and coordinated as they react with their environments. This process according to Piaget is called adaptation (Piaget, 1959). Both assimilation and accommodation involve modifying one's perception of the environment to fit a scheme. An individual must have an advanced knowledge of the condition to effectively use assimilation. According to Piaget, the sucking scheme permits infants to assimilate a nipple to the behavior of sucking. Accommodation involves modifying a scheme to fit the environment, in essence, accommodation requires a change in understanding. The integration of the two leads to adaptation. The balance between assimilation and accommodation, according to Piaget, is an equilibrium, in which individuals can explain new events in terms of their existing schemes. When events cannot be explained in relationship to existing schemes, such events may create disequilibrium. Individuals must integrate their schemes in order to understand and explain conditions that create disequilibrium. This process from equilibrium to disequilibrium and back to equilibrium is referred to as equilibration, a process that leads to a balance between assimilation and accommodation.

Piaget is credited with upsetting the world of developmental psychology, and has done more than any other theorist to challenge psychologists' belief in the S–R theory concerning child psychology then all the humanistic psychologists combined. He believed that reflexes and other automatic patterns of behavior had a minor role in the development of human intelligence. He postulated that only in the first few days of the infant's life that his/her behavior depends on automatic behavioral reaction. Initially, this view of infancy was radically opposed to current theoretical beliefs. His views sharply opposed the traditional behaviorist theory, which maintained that humans seek to escape from stimulation and excitation, while his view maintained that the infant frequently actively seeks stimulation. Today, Piaget's theory relevant to the aforementioned topic has stood the test of time. His child development theory has been scientifically validated.

According to Piaget's view of intelligence, the child passes through four major stages: sensorimotor, preoperational, concrete operational, and formal operational. This theory maintains that all children go through these stages in an orderly sequence, however, some children can pass through the stages at different rates. Research findings by De Ribaupierre and Rieben support the earlier premise (De Ribaupierre and Rieben, 1995). Conclusions drawn by Crain indicate that individuals may perform tasks with different stages at the same time, especially when they have mastered tasks in the formal stage (Crain, 1985).

Sensorimotor Stage (Birth to Age Two)

During this stage, infants are exploring their world through the use of their senses and motor skills. Through interaction with the environment, infants achieve a major intellectual breakthrough. Children no longer believe that objects do not exist when they are out of sight. All infants have innate behavior called reflexes, such as sucking and grasping objects. From these basic reflexes, more complex behaviors develop to form advanced schemes. Much of the learning during this stage is by trial and error. According to Piaget, by the end of the sensorimotor stage, children have progressed from trial-and-error stages to a more planned approach to problem solving.

Preoperational Stage (Ages Two to Seven)

Piaget further proclaimed that infants do not possess schemes that enable them to think about objects other than those directly in front of them. Children at this stage of development are unable to think critically because they lack the cognitive structures necessary for critical thinking. They are limited because they are learning by doing, which is known as the preoperational stage.

Language develops at a rapid rate during this stage. Children learn to use their cognitive abilities to form new mental schemes. This stage is characterized by thinking that is often illogical, such as children's reaction to the conservation of liquid problem. Children were given glasses of several different sizes with the same amount of water. Most children picked the taller glass as having the most water.

According to Piaget, the children's thinking depends more on perception than logic during this stage. Also, children develop cognitive structures that allow them to represent objects or events via symbols such as language, mental images, and gestures. Despite the accomplishments of this stage, Piaget emphasized that children in this stage of development are unable to solve many problems that are critical to logical reasoning. The thinking of children in this stage is rigid, inflexible, and strongly influenced by the effects of momentary experience (Berk, 1991). A major limitation in children in the preoperational stage is that of egocentrism. Preoperational children are unaware of points of view other than their own, and they think everyone experiences the world in the same way as they do. Piaget suggested that egocentrism is largely responsible for the rigidity and illogical nature of young children's thinking. Egocentric thinking is not reflective thought, which critically examines, rethinks, and restructures an aspect of the environment.

Another limitation of preoperational thinking is the problem of conservation, that is, the idea that certain physical attributes of an object remain the same even though its external appearance changes. Preoperational children are easily distracted by the concrete, perceptual appearance of objects, and often focus their attention on one detail of a situation to the neglect of other important features (Berk, 1991).

The most important limitation of preoperational thought is its irreversibility. Reversibility, the main characteristic of logical operation, refers to the ability to mentally go through a series of reasonings or transformations in a problem and then reverse direction and return to the starting point (Berk, 1991). Because children in this stage are incapable of reversible thinking, their reasoning about events often consists of collections of logically disconnected facts and contradictions. Children in this stage tend to provide explanations by linking together two events that occurred close in time and space, as if one caused the other. Children in this stage are less likely to use inductive or deductive reasoning.

Concrete Operational Stage (Ages Seven to Eleven)

According to Piaget, this stage is a major turning point in cognitive development because children's thinking parallels adults. During this stage, children begin to think logically about the conservation problem presented in the preoperational stage. Children can only apply their logical operations to concrete and observable objects and events. During this stage, children have problems dealing with abstract information. They cannot successfully distinguish between logic and reality. Seriation is an important task that children learn during this stage. The task involves arranging things in a logical order. To accomplish this task, children must be able to order and classify objects by some standard or criterion. During this stage, children can perform relatively well on a variety of problems that involve operational thinking like conservation, transitivity, and hierarchical classification as well as problems that require them to reason about spatial relationships. The accomplishment of this feat enables children to become more critical thinkers.

Although thinking is much more adultlike than it was earlier, the stage of concrete operations suffers from one important limitation. Children in this stage can only think in an organized, logical fashion when dealing with concrete, tangible information they can directly perceive. Their mental operations do not work when applied to information that is abstract and hypothetical. Thoughts about abstract concepts such as force, acceleration, and inertia are beyond children in this stage. The concrete operational approach does not address potential relationships that are not easily detected in the real work or that might not exist at all (Berk, 1991).

Formal Operational Stage (Ages Eleven to Adulthood)

During this stage, children develop the ability to reason with abstract and hypothetical information. Proportional thinking also develops, which is essential to understanding scientific and mathematical reason, through which they begin to understand the concept of proportion. Children have also developed the skills to test hypotheses by holding selected variables constant. They are able to evaluate the logic and quality of their thought processes and to make necessary corrections. In formal operations, children apply their logic directly to real objects. The abilities that make up formal operational thought, thinking abstractly, testing hypotheses, and forming concepts are critical to the learning of higher-order skills (Brunner, 1961). According to Piaget, the formal operational stage brings cognitive development to a close (Berk, 1991).

Piaget is considered to be the giant in developmental psychology. His research refutes the behaviorist view of learning. He believed that stimulus responses and other automatic patterns advocated by behaviorists have a minor role in the development of human intelligence. According to Piaget, the stages of intellectual development are limited by maturation. Certain physiological changes must be evident for children to complete tasks in certain stages.

Piaget's theory of cognitive development is very much related to critical thinking skills. He suggested that the acquisition of knowledge is the result of interaction between the learner and the environment. Learning is, thus, facilitated by the child's acquisition of new skills and experiences (Berk, 1991). It is these new skills and experiences, according to Piaget, that allow children to become progressively more capable of critical thinking. The Piagetian perspective would suggest that teaching critical thinking skills to very young children is not helpful because of their undeveloped cognitive structures.

Classroom Application

The impact of Piaget's theories of learning and education is successfully summarized by Berk:

1. A focus on the process of children's thinking, not just its products. Educators must understand the processes employed by children to arrive at their answers and to provide appropriate strategies based on their cognitive functioning.
2. Recognition of the importance of children's self-initiated involvement in the learning process. Teachers should employ the discovery method in their classrooms.
3. A deep emphasis on practices geared toward making children think

like adults. Piagetian-based education denounces this type of education, which according to Piaget's theory may be worse than no teaching at all.

4. Acceptance of individual differences in development progression. Teachers must recognize that, according to Piaget, all children go through the same developmental sequence, but they do so at different rates. Consequently, instructional strategies should be geared toward reaching the individual needs of children through individual and small-group activities (Berk, 1991).

LEV VYGOTSKY

Lev Vygotsky's theory according to Ormrod and Moll lends support to the concept that natural properties as well as social relationships and constraints make possible the social construction of a child's higher psychological processes (Ormrod, 1999; Moll, 1991). The three major components of Vygotskian theory are: (1) the internalization of auxiliary culture means; (2) the interpersonal or social process of mediation; and (3) a child's knowledge is formed with the zone of proximal development, a cognitive space that is defined by social relational boundaries.

Vygotsky supported the view that many learning and thinking processes have their beginnings in social interactions with others. According to Vygotsky, the process through social activities that evolve into internal mental activities is called "internalization." Internalizing one's behavior can change one's view toward a situation, it provides for an individual to look at a situation from different angles on his/her own, as well as improving one's interpersonal communication skills.

There are many tasks in which children can perform with the assistance of others, rather than on their own. This process is known as the zone of proximal development. Vygotsky indicated that children learn very little from performing tasks in which they can complete independently. Instead, they develop primarily by attempting tasks in collaboration with others.

One of the major tenets of Vygotsky's theory is that there is a functional relationship between the effects of the culture on cognitive development and biological growth, whereas the physical, biological, and neurological determinants are more readily understood and agreed on, the impact of the culture determinants is not as easily understood. Cultural determinants include social processes that transform naturally through the mastery and use of culture signs. In essence, the natural development of children's behavior forms the biological conditions necessary to develop higher psychological processes. Culture, in turn, provides the conditions by which the higher psychological processes may be realized.

Classroom Application

Vygotskian theory has several applications for classroom use. One is the framework for setting up cooperative learning arrangements in the classroom. Another application is giving students more responsibility for their own learning by actively involving them in the learning process as resources and group leaders. The curriculum should be developmentally appropriate and include independent activities as well as performing activities with the assistance of others.

GESTALT PSYCHOLOGY

Gestalt psychologists supported the importance of organizational processes in perception, learning, and problem solving. They also believed that individual's were predisposed to organize information in particular ways (Ormrod, 1999). Max Wertheimer, Wolfgang Köhler, and Kurt Koffka were German psychologists who developed and field tested the theory. The results of their experimentations assisted in advancing some basic concepts of the theory.

Wertheimer is usually credited with starting the movement (Wertheimer, 1912). His experiment involved a description and analysis of an optical illusion known as the Phi Phenomenon. While riding a train, Wertheimer observed that when two lights blink on and off in a sequential manner and rate, they often appeared to be one light moving back and forth. Based on this observation, Wertheimer concluded that perception of an experience is sometimes different from the experience itself. Wertheimer's experiment was instrumental in formulating one of the basic ideas and principles of Gestalt psychology: perception is often different from reality. Gestalt psychologists supported the principle that human experience cannot be studied successfully in isolation. They advanced the concept that "the whole is more than the sum of its parts. Consequently, a combination of elements must be evident to show a whole pattern" (Wertheimer, 1912). Murray provides additional information concerning the whole concept (Murray, 1995). He states that the whole is different from the parts and uses music to clarify this concept. He relates that when listening to music, the overall perception is not of isolated notes but rather of bars or passages. He further articulates that physical objects derive their identity not only from the parts that compose them, but also from the manner in which these parts are combined.

Köhler's research with chickens demonstrated the importance of the interrelationships among elements. This transposition experiment was conducted with hens using the following experimental procedures:

1. Hens were shown two sheets of gray paper, a light and a dark shade
2. Grain was placed on both sheets, but the hens were only permitted to fed from the dark gray sheet
3. Then the hens were shown a sheet of paper the same shade in which they had previously fed from, along with a sheet of an even darker shade (Köhler, 1929)

The hens tended to go to the darker of the two sheets. Results tend to support that the hens had been conditioned to go to the dark shade because initially they were fed from the darker sheet.

Advocates of this theory believe that the organism structures and organizes experiences by forming and imposing structure and organization on situations or conditions. Individuals tend to organize experiences in particular, similar, and predictable ways. Gestaltists advanced several laws to explain how individuals organize their experiences.

The first is the Law of Proximity. This law implies that individuals tend to perceive as a unit those things that are close together in space. The second is the Law of Similarity. It states that individuals tend to perceive as a unit things that are similar to one another. The third is the Law of Closure. It implies that individuals tend to fill in missing pieces to form a complete picture. The fourth is the Law of Pragnanz. This law proposes that individuals always organize their experiences as simply, concisely, systematically, and completely as possible.

Lefrançois contends that insight is the cornerstone of Gestalt psychology (Lefrançois, 2000). Basically, it means the perception of relationships among elements of a problem situation. In essence, it is the solution of a problem as a result of perceiving relationships among all of the elements of a problem situation. Insightful thinking requires a mental reorganization of problem elements and a recognition of the correctness of the new organization.

Classroom Application

Some of the principles advocated by Gestalt psychology have reference for classroom application. The theory addresses the role of perception in learning. How students interpret information can accelerate or impede their learning. Specific educational interventions are needed to improve the perception of children. Some children may learn best from using the whole method. Children employ different methods in organizing and structuring learning. Teachers should be apprised of this method and organize appropriate learning activities.

SUMMARY

In this chapter, I summarized those theories, in my opinion, that have the greatest reference for classroom use. The work of Tolman provided us with valuable information concerning goal-directed behaviors. The impact of Piaget's work is evident in schools today. His stages of development provide detailed information relevant to how children learn at different stages and how the success of prior stages promotes the attainment of higher stages. Vygotsky's theory on the relationship between social skills and education achievement is supported through research findings. Gestalt psychology is most remembered for its stance on the importance of organizational processes in learning and problem solving.

Most of these theories have denounced behaviorism and emphasize mental processes in learning. They also believe that many aspects of learning may be unique to humans. Cognitive theorists believe that learning must be objectively studied and based on scientific research. The theories also have some common threads associated with them, such as information processing, constructivism, developmental aspects, and contextual information.

BIBLIOGRAPHY

Berk, L. E. 1991. *Child Development*. Boston: Allyn and Bacon.
Brunner, J. S. 1961a. "The Act of Discovery." *Harvard Educational Review* 31:21–32.

———. 1961b. *The Process of Education*. Cambridge, Mass.: Harvard University Press.

———. 1966. *Toward a Theory of Instruction*. New York: Norton.

Chomsky, N. 1957. *Syntactic Structures*. The Hague: Mouton.

Crain, W. C. 1985. *Theories of Development: Concepts and Applications*. Englewood Cliffs, N.J.: Prentice Hall.

Köhler, W. 1929. *Gestalt Psychology*. New York: Liveright.

Lefrançois, G. R. 2000. *Theories of Human Learning: What the Old Man Said*. 4th ed. Pacific Grove, Calif.: Brooks/Cole.

Moll, I. 1991. "The Material and the Social in Vygotsky's Theory of Cognitive Development." Clearinghouse on Teacher Education. ERIC. ED. 346988.

Murray, D. J. 1995. *Gestalt Psychology and the Cognitive Revolution*. New York: Harvester Wheatsheaf.

Ormrod, J. E. 1999. *Human Learning*. 3rd ed. Columbus, Ohio: Merrill.

Papert, S. 1999. "Jean Piaget: Child Psychologist." *Time* 100:105–107.

Piaget, J. 1959. *The Language and Thought of the Child*. 3rd ed. Trans. M. Gabain. New York: Humanities.

De Ribaupierre, A., and L. Rieben. 1995. "Individuals and Situational Variability in Cognitive Development." *Educational Psychologist* 30 (1): 5–14.

Tolman, E. C., and C. H. Hovzik. 1930. "Introduction and Removal of Reward and Maze Performance in Rats." *University of California Publications in Psychology* 4:257–275.

Tolman, E. C., B. F. Ritchie, and D. Kalish. 1946. "Studies in Spatial Learning: Orientation and the Short-Cut." *Journal of Experimental Psychology* 36:13–24.

Wertheimer, M. 1912. "Experimentelle Studien, Uber das sehen von Bewegung." *Zeitschrift fur Psychologie* 61:161–265.

CHAPTER 10

Theory of Multiple Intelligences

Gardner presents seven domains of abilities in his theory of multiple intelligences: linguistic, spatial, logical-mathematical, interpersonal, intrapersonal, bodily-kinesthetic, and music intelligence (Gardner, 1983). Recently, he added one-and-a-half intelligences to the above domains (Gardner, 1993). The eighth intelligence is the "naturalist" and the half intelligence is the "moralist." The naturalist intelligence is involved with one's intelligence that is sensitive to the ecological environment, while the moralist intelligence is concerned with ethical issues. The seven intelligences will be summarized at this point. For a detailed analysis, refer to Armstrong, who describes how to integrate the intelligences in the instructional process (Armstrong, 1994).

THE SEVEN INTELLIGENCES

The seven intelligences as described by Gardner are:

- Linguistic intelligence. The capacity to use words effectively, whether orally (e.g., as a story-teller, orator, or politician) or in writing (e.g., as a poet, playwright, editor, or journalist). This intelligence includes the ability to manipulate the syntax or structure of language, the phonology or sounds of language, the semantics or meanings of language, and the pragmatic dimensions or practical uses of language. Some of these uses include rhetoric (using language to convince others to take a specific course of action), mnemonics (using language to remember information), explanation (using language to inform), and metalanguage (using language to talk about itself).
- Logical-mathematical intelligence. The capacity to use numbers

effectively (e.g., as a mathematician, tax accountant, or statistician) and to reason well (e.g., as a scientist, computer programmer, or logician). This intelligence includes sensitivity to logical patterns and relationships, statements and propositions (if-then, cause-effect), functions, and other related abstractions. The kinds of processes used in the service of logical-mathematical intelligence include categorization, classification, inference, generalization, calculation, and hypothesis testing.

- Spatial intelligence. The ability to perceive the visual–spatial world accurately (e.g., as a hunter, scout, or guide) and to perform transformations on those perceptions (e.g., as an interior decorator, architect, artist, or inventor). This intelligence involves sensitivity to color, line, shape, form, and space and the relationships that exist between these elements. It includes the capacity to visualize, to graphically represent visual or spatial ideas, and to orient oneself appropriately in a spatial matrix.

- Bodily-kinesthetic intelligence. Expertise in using one's whole body to express ideas and feelings (e.g., as an actor, mime, athlete, or dancer) and facility in using one's hands to produce or transform things (e.g., as a craftsperson, sculptor, mechanic, or surgeon). This intelligence includes specific physical skills such as coordination, balance, dexterity, strength, flexibility, and speed, as well as proprioceptive, tactile, and haptic capacities.

- Musical intelligence. The capacity to perceive (e.g., as a music aficionado), discriminate (e.g., as a music critic), transform (e.g., as a composer), and express (e.g., as a performer) musical forms. This intelligence includes sensitivity to the rhythm, pitch or melody, and timbre or tone color of a musical piece. One can have a figural or top-down understanding of music (global, intuitive), a formal or bottom-up understanding (analytic, technical), or both.

- Interpersonal intelligence. The ability to perceive and make distinctions in the moods, intentions, motivations, and feelings of other people. This can include sensitivity to facial expressions, voices, and gestures; the capacity for discriminating among many different kinds of interpersonal cues; and the ability to respond effectively to those cues in some pragmatic way (e.g., to influence a group of people to follow a certain line of action).

- Intrapersonal intelligence. Self-knowledge and the ability to act adaptively on the basis of that knowledge. This intelligence includes having an accurate picture of oneself (one's strengths and limitations); awareness of inner moods, intentions, motivations, temperaments, and desires; and the capacity for self-discipline, self-understanding, and self-esteem (Gardner, 1993).

THE THEORETICAL BASIS FOR MULTIPLE INTELLIGENCE THEORY

Gardner develops eight factors that each intelligence has to meet to be considered valid (Gardner, 1993). They are:

1. Potential isolation by brain damage. Through research with brain-injured individuals, Gardner notes that all parts of the brain are not affected by the brain injury. Other parts of the brain not injured can perform other types of intelligences. He develops a system to show the brain structure for each intelligence and for ways these intelligences can be demonstrated for each damaged neurological system.
2. The existence of savants, prodigies, and other exceptional individuals. Individuals with exceptionalities may have deficits in one or more areas of functions. Most exceptional individuals can function at high levels with other types of intelligences.
3. A distinctive developmental history and a definable set of expert "end state" performances. Each intelligence-based activity has its own developmental pattern that originates in early childhood and has its own peak of growth and inclination. Specific developmental stages for the various intelligences are not within the scope of this text. The reader is referred to Armstrong (Armstrong, 1994).
4. An evolutionary history of evolutionary plausibility. Each of the seven intelligences must meet the test of having its roots deeply embedded in the evolution of human beings, and even earlier, in the evolution of other species.
5. Support from psychometric findings. Most theories of learning are based on standardized measures of human ability, which is denounced by Gardner. However, he suggests that we review existing standardized tests for support of multiple intelligences. He indicates further that many standardized tests include subtests similar to multiple intelligences. These subtests may assist in validating multiple intelligences.

6. Support from experimental psychological tasks. Psychological studies have shown the values of using specific skills to measure ability in various fields, but have failed to demonstrate how skills can be transferred to other areas. Certain individuals may be affluent readers but fail to transfer this knowledge in solving mathematical problems. Each of the cognitive skills listed are specific, which correlates with the principles of multiple intelligences; that is, individuals can demonstrate different levels of proficiency across the seven intelligences.

7. An identifiable core operation or set of operations. Each of the various types of intelligences has a set core of operations that derive the various activities under them. Refer to the description of the seven intelligences alluded to earlier in this chapter.

8. Susceptibility to encoding in a symbol system. According to Gardner, one of the best indicators of intelligent behavior is the capacity of human beings to use symbols (Gardner, 1993). He articulates that each of the seven intelligences meets the criterion of being able to be symbolized.

KEY POINTS IN MULTIPLE INTELLIGENCE THEORY

Gardner contends that there are four basic key points in his multiple intelligence theory:

1. Each person possesses all seven intelligences, however, they function differently from person to person depending on environmental, genetic, and cultural factors. Most individuals appear to fit one or more of these profiles; some are highly developed in some intelligences, some are moderately developed, and some are underdeveloped.

2. Most people can develop each intelligence to an adequate level of competency. In spite of disabilities, Gardner believes that all individuals have the capacity to develop all seven intelligences to acceptable levels if given the appropriate support (Gardner, 1993).

3. Intelligences usually work together in complex ways. Intelligences, according to Gardner, are always interacting with each other (Gardner, 1993). To complete a simple task will involve the integration of several types of intelligences. An example may be a child riding a

bike: The child will need bodily-kinesthetic intelligence to propel the bike, spatial intelligence to orient him/herself to the surroundings, and intrapersonal intelligence to believe that he/she can successfully control and guide the bike.

4. There are many ways to be intelligent with each category. A case and point presented was that a person may not be able to read, yet is highly linguistic because he/she can tell a story or has a large vocabulary. Most intelligences can be demonstrated in a variety of ways (Gardner, 1993).

Multiple intelligences theory is a cognitive model that seeks to describe how individuals use their intelligences to solve problems. Both learning styles and visual–auditory kinesthetic models have some similarities, but multiple intelligences are not specifically related to the senses. The multiple intelligences model is not regiment to one type of intelligence, it is multiple dimensionally and integratively.

Assessing Students' Multiple Intelligences

There is no one best way for assessing multiple intelligences of children. Standardized tests appear to be limited in assessing the multiple intelligences. Authentic measures of assessment that are criterion-referenced and that compare past performances of students, according to individuals competent in the field, probe students' understanding of material far more thoroughly than multiple choice or other standardized measures (Herman, Aschbacker, and Winters, 1992; Wolf, LeMahieu, and Fresh, 1992; Gardner, 1993).

Observations

There are many types of authentic measures, although the most common is observation. Teachers can observe and record children's behaviors in a variety of situations in the natural environment. These observations can serve as a source for documenting behaviors and comparing performances over a period of time.

Multiple Intelligences and Curriculum Development

Multiple intelligences can be easily infused throughout the curriculum if the teacher places emphasis on the seven intelligences. It provides a system where teachers can experiment with various strategies and methods and determine which methods work best for diverse or disabled learners. Multiple intelligence strategies such as promoting interpersonal skills may be introduced through cooperative learning, whole language instruction may promote linguistic intelligence, playing music may promote music intelligence, drawing may promote spatial intelligence, role-playing and dramatic activities may promote bodily-kinesthetic intelligence, and giving additional response time for students may promote intrapersonal intelligence.

Specific strategies for infusing multiple intelligences into curricula have been eloquently summarized by Armstrong (Armstrong, 1994). The reader is referred to his work for specific details and implementation of the strategies. Innovative ways may be used to infuse multiple intelligences into the curriculum by relating or transferring information and resources from one intelligence to another. Other strategies to promote multiple intelligences may include integrating curriculum, learning stations, self-directed learning activities, students' projects, assessments, and community apprenticeship programs (Campbell, 1997).

Multiple Intelligences and Teaching Strategies

Multiple intelligences provides a wide avenue for teachers to employ in their instructional programs. A variety of strategies must be developed to meet the diverse needs of children (Armstrong, 1994). There is a wide variety of strategies to promote multiple intelligences. Educators should feel free to experiment with other strategies.

1. Linguistic intelligence
   Some recommended strategies include:
   • Storytelling
   • Brainstorming
   • Tape recording
   • Journal writing
   • Publishing (forms may be ditto masters, photo copied, or keyed into a work processor and have multiple copies printed for distribution)
2. Logical-mathematical intelligence
   Some recommended strategies include:
   • Calculations and quantifications
   • Classification and categorization

- Socratic questioning (teacher participates in dialogues with students to assist them in arriving at the correct answer)
- Heuristics (finding analogies, separating, and proposing solutions to problems)
- Science thinking

3. Spatial intelligence

Some recommended strategies include:

- Visualization
- Color cues
- Picture metaphors (using one idea to refer to another, a picture metaphor expresses an idea in a visual image)
- Idea sketching (drawing the key point, main idea, or central theme being taught)
- Graphic symbols (drawing graphic symbols to depict the concept taught)

4. Bodily-kinesthetic intelligence

Some recommended strategies include:

- Body answers (children use their bodies as a medium of expression)
- The classroom theater (children dramatize or role-play problems or materials to be learned)
- Kinesthetic concepts (introducing children to concepts through physical illustrations or asking students to pantomime specific concepts)
- Hands-on thinking (making and constructing objects with hands)

5. Musical intelligence

Some recommended strategies include:

- Rhythms, songs, raps, and chants
- Discographies (music selections that illustrate the content to be conveyed)
- Super memory music (designed to improve memory in other subjects through music)
- Musical concepts (music tones can be used for expressing concepts in subject areas)
- Mood music (create an emotional atmosphere for a particular lesson)

6. Interpersonal intelligence

Some recommended strategies include:

- Peer sharing

- People sculptures (students are brought together to collectively represent in physical form an idea or some specific learning goal)
- Cooperative groups
- Board games
- Simulations (involves a group of people coming together to create a make-believe environment)

7. Intrapersonal intelligence
   Some recommended strategies include:
   - One-minute reflection periods (students have frequent time outs for deep thinking)
   - Personal connections (weave students' personal experiences into the instructional program)
   - Choice time
   - Feeling–tone moments (educators need to teach to the feelings and emotions of students)
   - Goal setting sessions (assisting students in setting realistic goals)

Educators may employ creative ways for infusing multiple intelligences in the classroom by examining their instructional program and classroom management techniques and changing instruction to meet the unique needs of the group. All of the multiple intelligences can be creatively used in the classroom by changing instructional procedures, structuring the classroom, arranging furniture, providing the opportunity for movement in the classroom, using music as an instructional medium, developing a sense of community, creating cooperative groups, and allowing time for independent work. These activities can be incorporated under many of the multiple intelligences. Teachers are encouraged to experiment and use various methods to include the seven intelligences.

INTEGRATING MULTIPLE INTELLIGENCES WITH LEARNING STYLES AND BRAIN-BASED RESEARCH

Silver, Strong, and Perini advocate a method for integrating multiple intelligences with learning styles (Silver, Strong, and Perini, 1997). Guild proposes the same strategy by integrating multiple intelligences with brain-based research (Guild, 1977). Both of these models have applications for improved human learning.

Silver, Strong and Perini have developed a model showing how the learning style of a child can be matched with his/her strongest intelligence (Silver, Strong, and Perini, 1997). They describe each of Gardner's intelligences with a set of learning styles. Samples of vocations and the particular intelligence associated with them are matched with a learning style profile.

Guild proposes that the multiple intelligences can be successfully overlapped with learning styles and brain-based research (Guild, 1977). She maintains that there are similarities and differences between multiple intelligences, learning styles, and brain-based learning. These fields are distinct and separate from one another in some ways, but practical in some instances in the classroom environment. It is further voiced that each of these theories projects a comprehensive approach to learning and teaching. Similarities in the three theories include the following:

1. Each theory is learning and learner centered
2. The teacher is a reflective practitioner and decision maker
3. The student is a reflective practitioner
4. The whole person is educated
5. The curriculum has substance, depth, and quality
6. Each of the theories promotes diversity

There are some cautions to be aware of, however:

1. No theory is a panacea for solving all of the problems in education
2. There is the potential of doing simplistic application of the theories
3. None of these theories offer a cookbook approach to teaching

The researchers conclude that multiple intelligences, learning styles, and brain-based research can be integrated to form a functional model of human intelligence. These models appear feasible, with additional studies and experimentations needed to validate the integration of multiple intelligences with learning styles and brain-based research.

The country of Bangladesh has made brain-based learning and multiple intelligences a national policy. A research team observed classrooms and trained teachers in multiple ways of learning and multiple intelligences theory. Teacher trainers were involved in a number of self-reflective strategies and cooperative group activities. This experimental project may well serve as a model in Bangladesh for using multiple intelligences strategies and brain-based research.

Most teachers cannot associate a theory of theories of learning with their instructional program. Generally, their teaching strategies are not grounded in a theory.

MULTIPLE INTELLIGENCES AND SPECIAL EDUCATION

The comprehensiveness of multiple intelligences theory makes it amenable to children with disabilities. The theory considers children with disabilities as having strength in many of the multiple intelligences. In order for children with disabilities to demonstrate their skills in multiple intelligences, educators must use accommodations and alternative strategies to assist them and to help them succeed in school.

Multiple intelligences theory does not subscribe to the deficit model used in special education; rather, it supports the elimination of labels. It does not endorse the use of standardized tests in assessment; rather, it supports the use of authentic assessment approaches. It does not support separation of children with disabilities from their normal peers; rather, it supports full inclusion. Finally, multiple intelligences theory does not support separate tracks and instructional staff for children with disabilities; rather, it advocates establishing collaborative models that enable instructional staff to work together. Additionally, it provides a growth paradigm for assisting children with disabilities without considering their disabilities as impediments to using their multiple intelligences. The theory has demonstrated how a child with a disability in one intelligence can frequently overcome the disability by using a more highly developed intelligence if appropriate alternatives are employed (Gardner, 1983).

SUMMARY

There is nothing new to multiple intelligences. Good teachers have employed the strategies for some time in their teaching. As indicated throughout the chapter, multiple intelligences theory has many implications for curriculum development, teaching strategies, assessment, cultural diversity, ecological factors, classroom management, integrations with other theories, and computer applications. The use of multiple intelligences theory has proven to be effective in promoting, motivating, and stimulating the many intelligences of learners. The schools have not accepted this concept wholeheartedly. Adequate research reported throughout this chapter proves the value of multiple intelligences theory. As with most research findings, the schools are usually decades behind implementation. The time is now for endorsing and using this theory.

In order to prepare students to use learning principles effectively, educators need to become knowledgeable about them. They need to be encouraged to study and learn how to transform learning theories into practice by infusing them in their instructional programs.

BIBLIOGRAPHY

Armstrong, T. 1994. *Multiple Intelligences in the Classroom.* Alexander, Va.: Association for Supervision and Curriculum Development.

Campbell, L. 1997. "How Teachers Interpret MI Theory." *Educational Leadership* 56 (1): 14–19.

Gardner, H. 1983. *Frames of Mind: The Theory of Multiple Intelligences.* New York: Basic.

———. 1993. *Multiple Intelligences: The Theory in Practice.* New York: Basic.

Guild, P. B. 1977. "Where Do the Learning Theories Overlap?" *Educational Leadership* 55 (1): 30–31.

Herman, J. L., P. R. Aschbacker, and L. Winters. 1992. *A Practical Guide to Alternative Assessment.* Alexandra, Va.: Association for Supervision and Curriculum Development.

Silver, H., R. Strong, and M. Perini. 1997. "Integrating Learning Styles and Multiple Intelligence." *Educational Leadership* 55 (1): 22–27.

Wolf, D. P., P. G. LeMahieu, and J. Fresh. 1992. "Good Measure: Assessment As a Tool for Educational Reform." *Educational Leadership* 49 (8): 8–13.

CHAPTER 11

Concept Learning

A concept can be defined to be a disjunction of a variety of conjunctions of attributes that share one of more similarities (Flavell, Miller, and Miller, 1993; Klaus-Meier, 1990). Some concepts are easily defined by observable characteristics and are easily recalled. Thus, the printed word "dog," the sound of a dog barking, and so on can all elicit the same concept representative. Similarly, the sight of a dog from various perspectives and the sight of dogs of different species with very different physical properties can all elicit the same general concept of a dog. It is hopeless to think that one can find some common set of physical attributes in all of the adequate cues for the concept "dog." Thus, it is erroneous to define concepts in a manner that require abstraction of common properties.

Understanding concepts improves the thinking process. Klein writes that instead of separately labeling and categorizing each new object or event we encounter, we simply incorporate them into existing concepts (Klein, 1996). Concepts enable individuals to group objects or events that have common characteristics.

COMPOSITIONS

Concepts are composed of attributes and rules. An attribute may be defined as any feature or an object or event that varies from one condition to another. Hair color, eye color, height, and weight are examples of attributes that deviate from individual to individual. Attributes also have fixed values, such as the classification of cold- and warm-blooded animals. Using this principle, animals are classified as either cold or warm blooded.

Concepts are generally classified as concrete and abstract (Wasserman,

DeVolder, and Coppage, 1992; Gagne, 1985). Concrete concepts are easily recognized by common characteristics or traits, such as the example of "dog" given earlier. Abstract concepts, however, are difficult to conceptualize using common characteristics or traits. They are best described in terms of a formal definition. Gagne uses the word "cousin" as an example (Gagne, 1985). There must be a formal definition of "cousin" in order to form a concept, because simply looking at and observing the word "cousin" does not provide enough information to form a concept.

THEORIES OF CONCEPT LEARNING

Various theories of conceptual learning are based on attributes and rules. It would probably be much too difficult by virtue of associative interference to associate one set of attributes to another without first chunking each set of attributes and defining a new internal representative to stand for the chunk. For this reason, it seems likely that one stage in human concept learning is to chunk each set of attributes that constitutes a set of sufficient cues for the elicitation of the concept. After two or more chunks have been defined, and if these chunks are sufficient cues for the elicitation of the same concept, then they are associated to each other. This association of chunking is the second stage of the concept learning (refer to chapter 16 for additional information concerning chunking).

PROTOTYPE OF A CONCEPT

The more attributes a specific object shares with a concept, the more the object exemplifies the concept. In support of this view, research by Rosch found that the five most typical members of the concept "furniture" had thirteen attributes in common, whereas the five least typical members had only two attributes in common (Rosch, 1978). This research defined the "prototype" of a concept as the object that has the greatest number of attributes in common with the other members of the concept. Likewise, once the prototype has been identified, and the more an object deviates from this prototype, the more different it will be to associate it as an example of the concept.

Rules and prototypes assist in defining the boundaries of concepts.

According to Klein, these rules determine whether differences between the prototype of a concept and another object mean that the other stimulus is less typical of the concept or that it is an example of another concept (Klein, 1996). Sometimes, boundaries of a concept are not clearly defined, such the difference between a river and a stream (Zazdeh, Fu, Tanak, and Shimura, 1975).

ROLES OF CONCEPTS

Concepts must have uniform rules that can be consistently applied to arrive at the same solution. Rules assist in this process by defining the objects and events that have particular characteristics of the concept (Bourne, 1967; Dodd and White, 1980; Klein, 1987). The following illustration will assist in clarifying this premise. The concept "dog" discussed earlier indicated the attributes employed to recognize a dog. Rules used to define concepts may range from very simple to complex. Only one attribute is needed to define a simple rule, while a complex rule requires two or more attributes to define.

According to this theory, individuals should learn very specific concepts at first, whereby "specific concepts" means concepts that are elicited by only one or a few sets of cues. Only gradually would an individual learn all of the different sets of cues that are considered sufficient by adults to elicit the concept. The contrary argument is often made that individuals learn "overgeneralized" concepts to the right specific instances. Examples are cited that an individual may call every man "father." Klein cites a number of examples that indicate that the overgeneralization position on concept learning is not correct and that individuals in fact learn much too specialized concepts at first (Klein, 1996).

However, the terms "specialized" and "overgeneralized" are usually not clearly defined, so it is difficult to evaluate the present hypothesis with the previous findings. Usually, these terms refer to logical generality, not psychological generality in the sense proposed here. Logical generality is a property of "dictionary definitions" of concepts. In this sense, the concept "dog" is more general than the concept "Saint Bernard" and less general than the concept "living thing." Clearly, the average individual learns the concept "dog" before he/she learns either of these other two concepts. It is doubtful that any important psychological principle can be formulated regarding the degree of logical generality of concepts learned initially by individuals. With the currently proposed psychological definition of concepts as disjunctions of chunks, it is quite plausible that concepts develop increasing generality in the sense of having more and more chunk representatives associated to them.

ASSOCIATIVE AND COGNITIVE PROCESSES

Other theoretical approaches to concept learning imply that it is both an associative and a cognitive process. According to Klein, associative theory has both relevant and irrelevant attributes (Klein, 1996). The theory proposes that individuals associate a characteristic or attribute with the concept name as demonstrated earlier with the "dog" example. Employing this theory, an individual should recognize that a stimulus is a member of a concept by determining whether or not it possesses those characteristics. Cognitive approaches in concept learning involve a different approach than associative processes.

In cognitive processes, individuals confirm concepts by testing hypotheses. On the one hand, if hypotheses testing supports the concept, the concept is deemed to be true. On the other hand, if hypotheses testing does not support the concept, other hypotheses should be generated until the concept is supported. It is assumed that the concept is true and can be tested using experimental conditions. Incorrect results may be attributed to individuals who are not fully employing appropriate experimental conditions or are not testing different hypotheses to confirm the concept. Levine's studies show that individuals can test more than one hypothesis at a time (Levine, 1996). Several researchers conclude that concept learning is a process of forming various hypotheses about the feature and rules that define a concept, and then employing methods and procedures to dispute or confirm the hypotheses (Bruner, Goodnow, and Austin, 1956). For specific examples of confirming or rejecting concepts through hypotheses testing, refer to Klein and Ormrod (Klein, 1996; Ormrod, 1999).

CLASSROOM APPLICATIONS

Concepts are learned by observations, experiences, and definitions. I alluded to this principle earlier in the chapter. The relationship between concept learning and transfer of learning has been well established providing that individuals are trained and taught the concepts (Phye, 1992;

Pressley and Yokoi, 1994; Price and Drisscoll, 1997). The researchers indicate that we cannot assume that this association is automatic. Concepts and skills must be taught if individuals are expected to transfer learning to life situations. Practical application of the concept taught and the learning to be transferred must have a positive relationship. In essence, what is taught in school should have transferability to living in society.

Children tend to understand some concepts better when those concepts are related to other concepts in which they have knowledge. Concepts are also better learned when many concrete examples are provided (Kinnick, 1990). Various amounts of abstraction can be infused once the concrete application is understood. Individuals also appear to understand concepts better when positive and negative examples are given simultaneously rather than sequentially (Bourne, Ekstrand, and Dominowski, 1997). In order to provide individuals with concepts they can understand, Kinnick states that individuals' understanding of a concept should be assessed by asking them to classify new examples of the concept (Kinnick, 1990). Another innovative approach that teachers may employ in developing individuals' understanding of concepts is to ask them to make up their own examples and applications of the concept under discussion.

Teaching concepts according to Tennyson and Park involves extensive and skillful use of examples (Tennyson and Park, 1980). They suggested that teachers follow the listed rules when presenting examples of concepts:

1. Order the example from easy to difficult
2. Select examples that differ from one another
3. Compare and contrast examples and nonexamples

Slavin writes that teachers can use conceptual models to assist students in organizing and integrating information (Slavin, 2000). His view is supported by research conducted by Hiebert, Wearne, and Taber, Mayer and Gallini, and Winn (Hiebert, Wearne, and Taber, 1991; Mayer and Wittrock, 1996; Winn, 1991). These researchers concluded that when models are part of the instructional sequence, not only do students learn more, but they are also better prepared to apply their learning to solve problems. Knowledge maps can be employed to teach a variety of content. A knowledge map can display the main concepts of an object and association between them. The values of using knowledge maps to teach concepts have proven to increase students' retention of content (Hall, Sidio-Hall, and Saling, 1995).

SUMMARY

Throughout this chapter, "concept" was defined as a group of objects that have common characteristics. The importance of rules, boundaries, and prototypes were articulated. Individuals can learn concepts by associating them with concrete objects initially and then being provided with more abstract forms. The importance of hypotheses testing was also addressed. I outlined specific strategies for hypotheses testing concerning attributes in concepts.

Concept learning is considered to be composed of two basic learning processes: chunking a set of attributes to define a new internal representative and associating one chunk to another. The first establishes a conjunction of attributes. The second establishes a disjunction of these conjunctions. This theory of concept learning and speculation regarding possible neural mechanisms to achieve it are presented in more detail by Wickelgren (Wickelgren, 1969).

It is possible that many individuals suffer to a large extent from an inability to form new concepts via deficits in the chunking process or deficits in the associative memory process. The simplest explanation might simply be that they have fewer free internal representatives available to become specified to stand for new concepts, but there are many alternative physiological difficulties that could impair concept learning. Whatever the reasons for this, the consequences for learning and for the memory of learning fewer concepts are that the encoding of anything one wishes to learn will be less distinctive from other materials coded into memory. This results in more retrieval and storage interference. For mentally retarded individuals, it may be very important to spend considerable time at the concept learning process, that is to say, learning the vocabulary in any area of knowledge, before proceeding to learn facts and principles involving those concepts. It could turn out that the learning of facts and principles would be almost normal in such an individual after sufficient time has been spent to teach him/her the basic concepts of the area.

Again, normal children learn many concepts that are later replaced by better concepts or are of no value to them in what they do later on. Although deciding in advance exactly what concepts individuals with disabilities should learn is more costly and limits their choices somewhat, this decision can greatly increase the efficiency of concept learning for them.

BIBLIOGRAPHY

Bourne, L. E., Jr. 1967. "Learning and Utilization of Conceptual Rules." In *Concepts and the Structures of Memory*, ed. B. Kleinmuntz. New York: Wiley.

Bourne, L. E., Jr., D. R. Ekstrand, and R. L. Dominowski. 1997. *The Psychology of Thinking*. Englewood Cliffs, N.J.: Prentice Hall.

Bruner, J. S., J. Goodnow, and G. Austin. 1956. *A Study of Thinking*. New York: Wiley.

Dodd, D. H., and R. M. White. 1980. *Cognition: Mental Structures and Processes*. Boston: Allyn and Bacon.

Flavell, J. H., P. H. Miller, and S. A. Miller. 1993. *Cognitive Development*. 3rd ed. Upper Saddle River, N.J.: Prentice Hall.

Gagne, E. D. 1985. *The Cognitive Psychology of School Learning*. Boston: Little, Brown.

Hall, R. H., M. A. Sidio-Hall, and C. B. Saling. 1995. "Spatially Directed Post Organization in Learning from Knowledge Maps." Paper presented at the annual meeting of the American Educational Research Association, San Francisco. March 1995.

Hiebert, J., D. Wearne, and S. Taber. 1991. "Fourth Graders' Gradual Construction of Decimal Fractions during Instruction Using Different Physical Representations." *Elementary School Journal* 91:321–341.

Kinnick, V. 1990. "The Effect of Concept Teaching in Preparing Nursing Students for Clinical Practice." *Journal of Nursing Education* 29:362–366.

Klaus-Meier, H. J. 1990. "Conceptualizing." In *Dimensions of Thinking and Cognitive Instruction*, ed. B. F. Jones and L. Idol. Hillsdale, N.J.: Erlbaum.

Klein, S. B. 1987. *Learning: Principles and Applications*. New York: McGraw-Hill.

———. 1996. *Learning: Principles and Applications*. 3rd ed. New York: McGraw-Hill.

Levine, M. 1996. "Hypothesis Behavior by Humand during Discrimination Learning." *Journal of Experimental Psychology* 71:331–338.

Mayer, R. E., and J. K. Gallini. 1990. "When Is an Illustration Worth Ten Thousand Words?" *Journal of Educational Psychology* 82:715–726.

Mayer, R. E., and M. C. Wittrock. 1996. "Problem-Solving Transfer." In *Handbook on Educational Psychology*, ed. D. C. Berlinear and R. C. Calfee. New York: Macmillan.

Ormrod, J. E. 1999. *Human Learning*. 3rd ed. Upper Saddle River, N.J.: Merrill.

Phye, G. D. 1992. "Strategic Transfer: A Tool for Academic Problem-Solving." *Educational Psychology Review* 4:393–421.

Pressley, M., and L. Yokoi. 1994. "Motion for a New Trial on Transfer." *Educational Researcher* 23 (5): 36–38.

Price, E. A., and M. P. Drisscoll. 1997. "An Inquiry into the Spontaneous Transfer of Problem-Solving Skills." *Contemporary Educational Psychology* 22 (4): 472–494.

Rosch, E. 1978. "Principles of Categorization." In *Cognition and Categorization*, ed. E. Rosch and B. Lloyd. Hillsdale, N.J.: Erlbaum.

Slavin, R. E. 2000. *Educational Psychology: Theory and Practice.* 6th ed. Boston: Allyn and Bacon.

Tennyson, R. D., and O. Park. 1980. "The Teaching of Concepts: A Review of Instructional Design Literature." *Review of Educational Research* 50:55–70.

Wasserman, E. A., C. L. DeVolder, and D. J. Coppage. 1992. "Non-similarity Based Conceptualization in Pigeons via Secondary or Mediated Generalization." *Psychological Science* 3:374–379.

Wickelgren, W. A. 1969. "Learned Specification of Concept Neurons." *Bulletin of Mathematical Biophysics* 31:123–142.

Winn, W. 1991. "Learning from Maps and Diagrams." *Educational Psychology Review* 3:211–247.

Zazdeh, L. A., K. S. Fu, K. M. Tanak, and M. Shimura. 1975. *Fuzzy Sets and Their Applications to Cognitive and Decision Processes.* New York: Academic.

CHAPTER 12

Critical Thinking and Problem Solving

Critical thinking is a complex intellectual skill that is consciously, deliberately, and consistently applied by a thinker when he/she is confronted by a body of data from which a conclusion or solution must be derived, or by an argument of a third party who wishes the thinker to accept a predetermined interpretation, point of view, or conclusion (Hudgins and Edelman, 1988). In this sense, critical thinking is regarded in the broadest terms rather than narrowly. To be more specific, it is an intellectual process that is a natural, if sometimes unrefined, outgrowth of normal educational efforts. Therefore, occasions for critical thinking occur frequently rather than rarely, and in a large number of situations, not in a few narrowly defined special cases.

Critical thinking consists of two levels of intellectual skills in attempting to resolve problems. One level of skill focuses on guidelines and directs the process of critical thinking. The other level of skill is used by thinkers to resolve immediate problems. Thus, critical thinking results when the two levels of intellectual skills are working in concert to resolve problems (French and Rhoder, 1992; Berk, 1991).

In the final analysis, critical thinking consists of the thinker deliberately and purposefully taking a series of actions to understand the nature of the difficulty before him/her, to conduct an exhaustive surveillance of the information available that can be brought to bear on the difficulty (including an awareness of what information that is not available), and to possess one or more criteria against which the available information can be appropriately assessed.

It was always believed that students would think if they could concentrate on developing skills and strategies in the basic skill areas of reading, writing, and arithmetic as well as on disseminating knowledge in the content areas. There was an assumption that there was little need for providing instruction on thinking. Therefore, schools placed little, if any, emphasis on enhancing thinking skills. As a result, over the past few decades, critical thinking among students has declined dramatically (Benderson, 1984). Declining test scores have been cited as evidence that students can perform well in dealing with note tasks but not with those demanding critical thought (Jones, 1990; Marzano, 1994). For example, Chipman and Segal suggest that the results from the National Assessment of Educational Progress test demonstrate that the problems in student writing lie in the thinking areas not the mechanics, the problems in reading in comprehension not decoding, and the problems in mathematics in solving problems not computing (Chipman and Segal, 1995). Generally, basic skills in reading, math, writing, and science have improved, but students' ability to interpret, evaluate, make judgments, and form supportive arguments continue to decline (Benderson, 1984). According to Nickerson, it is possible for a student to finish thirteen years of education without becoming a competent thinker (Nickerson, 1991). Thus, it appears schools are producing adult citizens who lack critical thinking skills.

However, over the past few years there has been an increasing interest in incorporating thinking instruction into elementary and secondary curriculum. This interest has been expressed by professional organizations associated with the various academic disciplines as well as by organizations with a broad perspective such as the College Board (Marzano, 1994). While some states have incorporated the teaching of thinking skills into the overall curriculum, many more states still have not. Basically, other concerns press for attention such as school safety, preparing for standardized tests, and negotiating teacher pay.

PRINCIPLES AND COMPONENTS OF CRITICAL THINKING AND PROBLEM SOLVING SKILLS

There are several components or strategies associated with critical thinking and problem solving skills. The major strategies associated with the processes include generic skills, content specific skills, and content knowledge.

A major difference between problem solving and critical thinking is that critical thinking does not seem to involve a series of sequential steps. In critical thinking, the skills and strategies are not seen as part of a sequence, but rather as a group of skills and strategies chosen and used as needed by the particular task (French and Rhoder, 1992). They can be used alone or in any combination.

In problem solving, students must employ a series of sequential steps. Strategies begin with a careful consideration of what problem needs to be solved, what resources and information are available, and how the problem can be graphically presented (Katayama and Robinson, 1998; Robin and Kiewra, 1995). The following steps systematically and sequentially require that some type of plan be developed. Developed by Bransford and Stein, IDEAL appears to provide such a plan. The five steps in their plan include the following:

I – Identify problems and opportunities
D – Define goals and represent the problem
E – Explore possible strategies
A – Anticipate outcomes and act
L – Look back and learn (Bransford and Stein, 1993)

Research findings by Bransford and Stein and Martinez agree that by employing systematic and sequential steps problem solving is a skill that can be taught and applied by children (Bransford and Stein, 1993; Martinez, 1998). Sternberg relates that most problems students face in school may require careful reading and some thought, but little creativity (Sternberg, 1995). This is a challenge to the schools to teach creative problem solving techniques. Creative problem solving techniques may be taught through incubation, suspension, judgment, appropriate climates, and analysis. Beyer and Frederiksen have adequately defined and provided examples for each of the strategies, so I will not attempt to repeat their findings; the reader, however, is referred to their research (Beyer, 1998; Frederiksen, 1984).

One set of generic skills, which is frequently included in a list of generic critical thinking skills, is that of reasoning (Benderson, 1984; Nickerson, 1996). The question of what is involved in reasoning has intrigued philosophers and psychologists for years. Nickerson claims that reasoning involves the production and evaluation of arguments, the making of inferences and the drawing of conclusions, and the generation and testing of hypotheses (Nickerson, 1991). It requires deduction and induction, analysis and synthesis, and criticality and creativity. Nickerson identifies language, logic, inventiveness, knowledge, and truth as concepts closely related to reasoning (Nickerson, 1991). Beyer articulates that reasoning is the "lubricant" in many critical thinking skills (Beyer, 1991).

Closely allied to reasoning is the role of logic in critical thinking. Whether logic is considered part of critical thinking directly or a component of reasoning, the skills associated with logical thinking are frequently included in a generic list of skills (Benderson, 1984; Cannon and Weinstein, 1985). Beyer gives ten mental operations that will aid critical thinking that is associated with logical principles (Beyer, 1991). The list includes determining the reliability of a source; the factual accuracy of a statement and the strength of an argument; distinguishing between verifiable facts and value claims, as well as between relevant and irrelevant information; and detecting bias, unstated assumptions, ambiguous arguments, and logical fallacies and inconsistencies in a line of reasoning.

While many approaches to critical thinking stress reasoning and/or a set of specific critical thinking skills, there is a growing recognition that critical thinking involves far more than reasoning and skills. There is increasing emphasis on the use of strategies in critical thinking. These strategies consist of cognitive, active, support, and metacognitive strategies.

Organization and reorganization of information and ideas is a critical cognitive strategy for thinking (Presseisen, 1988). The use of organizational strategies help thinkers identify and clarify relationships between information and ideas, as well as linking new information to prior knowledge and to even more new information.

There are two active study strategies that are useful in developing critical thinking: self-questioning and summarizing. By asking themselves questions, thinkers are able to make themselves active in the learning process (Wong, 1995). Wong indicates that self-questioning could have three major purposes (Wong, 1995). It enables thinkers to become active participants, to engage in metacognitive processes, and to activate prior knowledge and related new information to it. Self-questioning fosters a spirit of problem solving that is essential to developing critical thinking skills.

Another active study strategy that is effective in developing critical thinking skills is summarizing information. In addition to being able to organize and reorganize information and ask questions about the information, a thinker must be able to manage information in some usable manner. An effective way to manage information is to summarize information so that the information needed to suit the thinker's purpose is available.

Support strategies have been cited as particularly significant in the promotion of critical thinking skills (Ennis, 1985, 1986). Support strategies involve fostering a positive attitude and strong motivation toward critical thinking and problem solving. A disposition toward higher-order thinking is frequently cited as a characteristic of a good thinker (Nickerson, 1991; Halpern, 1987). Nickerson contends that a disposition toward thinking includes: fair-mindedness, open to evidence on any issue, respect for opinions that differ from one's own, inquisitiveness, a desire to be informed, and a tendency to reflect before acting (Nickerson, 1991).

Researchers and educators have found that critical thinkers use metacognitive knowledge and apply metacognitive strategies in a well-planned, purposeful method through the critical thinking process. "Metacognition" is knowledge about and awareness of one's own thinking (McCormick, 1997). It involves knowledge of one's own capacity to think and remember knowledge of task variables and strategies.

While there is substantial support for the generic nature of critical and problem solving thinking skills, there is growing support for the notion that critical thinking skills and problem solving strategies are content specific. In essence, it is widely believed that there is a body of critical thinking and problem solving skills that is applicable to every content area. However, there is some belief that how one thinks critically may be related to the specific material under consideration (Benderson, 1984). In this case, a thinker chooses the skills and problem solving strategies that are most appropriate for the task at hand. For example, in sorting through scientific data, there may be little need to distinguish between fact and opinion, but a great need to distinguish between relevant and irrelevant data. Basically, there is great controversy about whether critical thinking skills and problem solving strategies are generic or content-specific.

The need for appropriate and sufficient content knowledge is cited almost universally in relation to critical thinking (French and Rhoder, 1992). Nickerson implies that a thinker would not be able to reason effectively without some knowledge of the subject in question (Nickerson, 1996). In critically thinking and problem solving, however, thinkers must have more than a large storage of knowledge. They must also have the ability to evoke particular knowledge when needed and to integrate information from various sources (Perkins, Allen, and Hafner, 1993). In addition, thinkers need concepts and principles (Yinger, 1990). Basically, then, there is a kind of interdependency between critical thinking and problem solving. On the one hand, critical thinking is essential in solving problems and, on the other hand, problem solving is essential to critical thinking (Nickerson, Perkins, and Smith, 1995).

CRITICAL THINKING AND PIAGET'S THEORY OF COGNITIVE DEVELOPMENT

In his comprehensive theory of cognitive development, Jean Piaget viewed the development of thinking as a special case of biological growth in general. Piaget's theory postulates that all children progress through four stages and that they do so in the same order: first the sensorimotor period, then the preoperational period, then the concrete operational period, and finally the formal operational period. Since chapter 9 has provided detailed information on the four stages, I will not repeat the information. The reader is referred to that chapter for specific information.

CLASSROOM APPLICATIONS

Marzano sums up the value of developing critical thinking skills by stating that it is to enhance student's abilities to think critically and to make rational decisions about what to do or what to believe (Marzano, 1995). This view is supported by Halpern and Norris; they enumerate that learning to think critically requires practice (Halpern, 1995; Norris, 1985). Teachers must provide classrooms that encourage exploration, discovery, acceptance of divergent ideas, free discussions, and posing questions to refute or validate information.

Research findings by Beyer appear to be the strategies that teachers can employ in identifying critical thinking and problem solving skills that students should be exposed to and should recognize what strategies to use (Beyer, 1998). He lists the following strategies:

1. Distinguishing between verifiable facts and value claims
2. Distinguishing between relevant from irrelevant information, claims, or reasons
3. Determining the factual accuracy of a statement
4. Determining the credibility of a source
5. Identifying ambiguous claims or arguments
6. Identifying unstated assumptions

7. Detecting bias
8. Identifying logical fallacies
9. Recognizing logical inconsistencies in line or reasoning
10. Determining the strength of an argument or claim

Beyer further elaborates that these strategies cannot be introduced in sequential steps, rather, they should be based on the cognitive development of the students. Teachers should teach students how to use the scientific method to solve problems by observing information, formulating hypotheses, testing hypotheses, interpreting data, presenting findings, and drawing conclusions.

While there is considerable information about critical thinking in general, the available research on critical thinking skills among school-aged children is quite limited. Soloff and Houtz designed a method to measure the critical thinking ability in early elementary school students (Soloff and Houtz, 1991). In particular, they assessed the subjects' ability at detecting bias. The subjects consisted of 102 New York City elementary school students in approximately equal numbers of boys and girls ranging from kindergarten to grade four. The critical thinking test, developed by the researchers, contained short vignettes about two main characters. The tests were administered individually to each student. After hearing the story, the subject was asked a series of twenty questions that assessed the subject's ability, with differences becoming significant at grade four. No gender differences or interactions of gender by grade were found. The researchers concluded that critical thinking does begin to be seen at limited levels among the youngest age groups. However, in an earlier review of the literature, Norris concludes that critical thinking ability is not widespread among students (Norris, 1985). I was unable to find recent literature that neither confirms nor disconfirms this statement.

However, recent literature seems to suggest that instruction in critical thinking and problem solving skills can be beneficial. Hudgins and Edelman experiment on the effects of training students in the use of critical thinking skills (Hudgins and Edelman, 1988). Picking from three elementary schools in the same district, five experimental and two control groups consisting of a total of thirty-nine fourth and fifth grades were formed. A test on critical thinking ability was initially given to the subjects to ensure that the subjects in both groups matched for critical thinking ability. All subjects were given a problem to solve in an individual interview. The subjects in the experimental group subsequently participated in a series of small group discussions in which they learned and applied critical thinking skills. All the subjects were again interviewed and asked to resolve the two problems aloud. The researchers found that subjects in the experimental group were more likely to apply the critical thinking and problem solving skills that they learned, to use more available information, and to produce a better-quality answer.

Hudgins et al.'s research was designed to determined if teaching critical thinking skills to children would benefit children in resolving scientific problems (Hudgins et al., 1994). The sample consisted of two dissimilar experimental groups and one control group. One experimental group learned critical thinking skills and was taught a specific scientific concept (e.g., the effects of gravity). The other experimental group learned about gravity under the direct supervision of their regular science classroom teacher, but did not learn critical thinking skills. The control group studied neither science nor critical thinking skills. The subjects consisted of fifty St. Louis Catholic school students from grades four through six. All subjects were given a science information pre- and posttest. The researchers found that the two groups of experimental children did not differ significantly from each other on the science information test. In addition, the experimental groups scored higher on this test than the control group. The subjects were also interviewed separately and asked to solve a science problem involving the variables that affect the period of a pendulum and the motion of fallen bodies. As expected, the experimental group that was taught critical thinking skills outperformed both the control group and the experimental group that was not taught these skills.

Riesenmy et al. examined the degree to which children retain and transfer critical thinking skills after training (Riesenmy et al., 1991). The research was conducted with thirty-eight fourth- and fifth-grade students in a suburban St. Louis public school district, with another twenty-eight students serving as a control group. The thirty-eight subjects in the experimental group were randomly placed in small groups of four and trained in critical thinking skills through twelve discussion sessions. Each child in both the experimental and control groups was individually tested before and after the training sessions for his/her ability to solve critical thinking problems. Posttests were given either immediately after the conclusion of training sessions or four to eight weeks afterwards. The results showed that children the experimental group scored significantly better than the children in the control group in respect to retention of data. Specifically, the experimental group surpassed the control group in the use of critical thinking skills, in the amount of information used, and the quality of its answers. The results also showed that the experimental group did significantly better than the control group in respect to transfer problems.

There is a scarcity measure concerning critical thinking ability among students. The available research, however, seems to suggest that students do not perform extremely well on the kinds of tasks that are used to indicate competence in critical thinking ability as measured by the Cornell Critical Thinking Test (Ennis and Millman, 1985) and the Watson–Glaser Critical Thinking Appraisal (Watson and Glaser, 1980). In addition, there is evidence that students who are trained in critical thinking and problem solving skills do benefit from such training. Unfortunately, there are no studies available that provide evidence on the long-term impact of instruction in critical thinking. Moreover, there is little information available about what specifically makes students better thinkers and what specific ways they can still improve (Norris, 1985).

IMPLICATIONS FOR INDIVIDUALS WITH DISABILITIES

Some individuals with disabilities perform below expected levels in some academic areas, and some perform at or above expected levels of achievements for their age and grade. Disabilities may be specific to one or two or to a cluster of closely related competencies, such as reading and writing (McCormick, 1997). Fortunately, some disabled students are of normal intelligence or above. Thus, it is possible that critical thinking skills may be beneficial to many disabled students.

Unfortunately, while programs in critical thinking skills have been initiated in regular curriculum programs, less attention has been paid to special education classrooms. In fact, until recently, learning activities in special education classrooms have been heavily influenced by the view that students with disabilities must be taught basic skills before any instruction in critical thinking can be conducted. This tactic assumes that students with disabilities cannot benefit from instruction in reasoning until basic skills are mastered. However, research findings lend little support to this approach to instruction (Leshowitz et al., 1993). In the last few years, a new focus of special education research has emerged that seeks to develop and evaluate programs for teaching higher-order thinking to disabled students. Research findings support the values of teaching higher-order skills to children with disabilities. They profit significantly from such instruction (Means and Knapp, 1991).

Analysis of some of the new approaches to instruction in higher-order thinking with disabled students shows that these students can not only reason with higher-order skills, but also can outperform some of their nondisabled peers, depending on the degree of disability, after receiving brief intervention programs in higher-order thinking. Collins and Carmine note that students with disabilities in programs that emphasize higher-order reasoning significantly improved their performance in argument construction to levels that equaled that of students enrolled in logic courses (Collins and Carmine, 1998; Carmine, 1991).

Several of the current intervention programs for disabled students have relied on teaching the concept of "sameness" or "analogical reasoning" as a base for promoting higher-order thinking (Carmine, 1991; Grossen, 1991). Such programs operate on the assumption that the brain searches for similarities and categorizes things based on their common qualities. In this effort, Grossen finds that by using Euhler diagrams to facilitate understanding of the concept of "sameness," analyses of logic problems could be enhanced significantly (Grossen, 1991). The trained subjects with average or above intelligence not only were more proficient at reasoning when using Euhler diagrams than their untrained peers with disabilities, but also performed at levels equal to those of normal college students and sophomore honor class students.

Although a major emphasis of the literature in higher-order thinking for disabled students has been on teaching basic operations of critical thinking, some questions have been devoted to using normative rules of reasoning and logic to promote critical reading skills. Darch and Kameenui argue that critical reading is closely related to the notion of critical thinking (Darch and Kameenui, 1987). They propose that critical reading relies heavily on the application of the ability to detect faulty information, faulty causality, and false testimonial. By using direct instruction rather than discussion/working activity, they find that these teaching skills enhance the critical reading skills of some disabled students, thereby enabling them to distinguish between valid and invalid arguments.

Basically, some disabled students are less likely than normally achieving students to use strategies for performing academic tasks (Bauer, 1987a). However, when taught various strategies such as critical thinking skills, most disabled students are able to carry out strategies to perform adequately on academic tasks (Bauer, 1987b). Critical thinking skills instruction for disabled students should include providing content knowledge in the various academic areas, teaching the skills and strategies of critical thinking, and assisting these students in metacognitive processes (French and Rhoder, 1992). As disabled students are taught critical thinking skills, not only can task-related performances increase, but also these students can learn to attribute their performances to the use of the skills and strategies of critical thinking (Borkowski et al., 1990). The long-term commitment of disabled students to the use of these new skills is increased when they understand that their performances improve because of their use.

SUMMARY

For most people in education, it appears to be needless to ask why critical thinking is desirable. It is like asking why education is desirable. Philosophers of education argue that critical thinking is not just another educational option. Rather, it is an indispensable part of education because being able to think critically is a necessary condition for being educated and because teaching with the spirit of critical thinking is the only way to satisfy the moral injunction of respect for individuals (McPeck, 1991). Thus, critical thinking is an educational idea.

Yet, critical thinking among American students is not widespread. It was once believed that the mere fact of imparting factual knowledge would facilitate higher-order thinking among students. Unfortunately, research suggests that students do not posses the necessary skills that would indicate the ability to think critically. Students wind up graduating from high school and becoming adults who do not have the ability to think critically despite thirteen or more years of schooling.

As a result, critical thinking is among the most debated subjects in education. Investigation of critical thinking processes, integration of critical thinking instruction into the curriculum, and the evaluation of students as critical thinkers has become a major focus in education in recent years. Nevertheless, there has not been a widespread movement to incorporate critical thinking skill instruction into the curriculum despite increasing emphasis of the need for critical thinking among students.

There is research available that suggests that instruction in critical and problem solving thinking can beneficial not only in academic areas, but also in real life. However, research into this area is still quite limited

(Paul, Binker, Martin, Vetrano, and Kreklau, 1990). Moreover, such research has its own limitations. Thus, more studies are needed in the area of critical thinking skills, especially as it concerns disabled students.

BIBLIOGRAPHY

Bauer, R. H. 1987a. "Memory Processes in Children with Learning Disabilities." *Journal of Experimental Child Psychology* 34:415–430.

———. 1987b. "Short-Term Memory in Learning Disabled and Nondisabled Children." *Bulletin of the Psychonomic Society* 20:128–130.

Benderson, A. 1984. *Critical Thinking Focus*. Princeton, N.J.: Educational Testing Service.

Berk, L. E. 1991. *Child Development*. Boston: Allyn and Bacon.

Beyer, B. K. 1991. *Practical Strategies for the Teaching of Thinking*. Boston: Allyn and Bacon.

———. 1997. *Improving Student Thinking: A Comprehensive Approach*. Boston: Allyn and Bacon.

———. 1998. *Developing a Thinking Skills Program*. Boston: Allyn and Bacon.

Borkowski, J. G., M. Carr, E. A. Rellinger, and M. Pressley. 1990. *Dimensions of Thinking: Review of Research*. Hillsdale, N.J.: Erlbaum.

Bransford, J. D., and B. S. Stein. 1993. *The Ideal Problem Solver*. 2nd ed. New York: Freeman.

Cannon, D., and M. Weinstein. 1985. "Reasoning Skills: An Overview." *Journal of Philosophy for Children* 6:29–33.

Carmine, D. 1991. "Curricular Interventions for Teaching Higher Order Thinking to All Students: Introduction to the Special Series." *Journal of Learning Disabilities* 24:261–269.

Chipman, S. F., and J. W. Segal. 1995. *Higher Cognitive Goals for Education: An Introduction*. Hillsdale, N.J.: Erlbaum.

Collins, M., and D. Carmine. 1998. "Evaluating the Field Test Revision Process by Comparing Two Versions of a Reasoning Skills CAI Program." *Journal of Learning Disabilities* 21:375–379.

Darch, C., and E. Kameenui. 1987. "Teaching LD Students Critical Reasoning Skills: A Systematic Replication." *Learning Disabilities Quarterly* 10:82–91.

Ennis, R. H. 1985. *Developed Minds: A Resource Book for Teaching Thinking*. Alexander, Va.: Association for Supervision and Curriculum Development.

———. 1986. "A Logical Basis for Measuring Critical Thinking Skills." *Educational Leadership* 44:44–48.

Ennis, R. H., and J. Millman. 1985. *Cornell Critical Thinking Tests: Levels X and Z*. Pacific Grove, Calif.: Midwest.

Frederiksen, N. 1984a. "Implications of Cognitive Theory for Instruction in Problem Solving." *Review of Educational Research* 54:363–407.

French, J. N., and C. Rhoder. 1992. *Teaching Thinking Skills.* New York: Garland.

Grossen, B. 1991. "The Fundamental Skills of Higher Order Thinking." *Journal of Learning Disabilities* 24:343–353.

Halpern, D. F. 1987. *Thinking Skills Instruction: Concepts and Techniques.* Washington, D.C.: National Education Association.

———. 1995. *Thought and Knowledge: An Introduction to Critical Thinking.* 3rd ed. Hillsdale, N.J.: Erlbaum.

Hudgins, B. B., and S. Edelman. 1988. "Children's Self-Directed Critical Thinking." *Journal of Educational Research* 81:262–273.

Hudgins, B. B., M. R. Riesenmy, S. Mitchell, C. Klein, and V. Navarro. 1994. "Teaching Self-Direction to Enhance Children's Thinking in Physical Science." *Journal of Educational Research* 88:15–26.

Jones, B. F. 1990. "Quality and Equality through Cognitive Instruction." *Educational Leadership* 47:204–211.

Katayama, A. D., and D. H. Robinson. 1998. "Study Effectiveness of Outlines and Graphic Organizer: How Much Information Should Be Provided for Students to Be Successful on Transfer Test?" Paper presented at the annual meeting of the American Educational Research Association, San Diego. April 1998.

Leshowitz, B., K. Jenkens, S. Heaton, and T. L. Bough. 1993. "Fostering Critical Thinking Skills in Students with Learning Disabilities: An Instructional Program." *Journal of Learning Disabilities* 26:483–490.

Martinez, M. E. 1998. "What Is Problem Solving?" *Phi Delta Kappan* 70 (8): 605–609.

Marzano, R. J. 1994. *The Theoretical Framework for an Instructional Model of Higher Order Thinking Skills.* Denver, Colo.: Mid-Continent Regional Educational Lab.

———. 1995. "Critical Thinking." In *School Improvement Programs*, ed. J. H. Block, S. T. Everson, and T. R. Guskey. New York: Scholastic.

McCormick, C. R. 1997. *Educational Psychology: Learning, Instruction, Assessment.* New York: Longman.

McPeck, J. 1991. *Critical Thinking and Education.* Oxford: Martin Robertson.

Means, B., and M. Knapp. 1991. "Cognitive Approaches to Teaching Advanced Skills to Educationally Disadvantaged Students." *Phi Delta Kappan* 72:282–289.

Nickerson, R. S. 1991. *Review of Research in Education.* Washington, D.C: American Educational Research Association.

———. 1996. *Reflections on Reasoning.* Hillsdale, N.J.: Erlbaum.

Nickerson, R. S., D. N. Perkins, and E. E. Smith. 1995. *The Teaching of Thinking.* Hillsdale, N.J.: Erlbaum.

Norris, S. P. 1985. "Synthesis of Research on Critical Thinking." *Educational Leadership* 42:40–45.

Paul, R., A. J. Binker, D. Martin, C. Vetrano, and H. Kreklau. 1990. *Critical Thinking Handbook*. Rohnert Park, Calif.: Center for Critical Thinking and Moral Critique.

Perkins, D. N., R. Allen, and J. Hafner. 1993. *Thinking: The Expanding Frontier*. Philadelphia, Pa.: Franklin Institute Press.

Presseisen, B. Z. 1988. "Avoiding Battle at Curriculum Gulch: Teaching Thinking and Content." *Educational Leadership* 45:7–8.

Riesenmy, M. R., S. Mitchell, B. B. Hudgins, and D. Ebel. 1991. "Retention and Transfer of Children's Self-Directed Critical Thinking Skills." *Journal of Educational Research* 85:14–25.

Robin, D. H., and K. A. Kiewra. 1995. "Visual Argument: Graphic Organizers Are Superior to Outlines in Improving Learning from Text." *Journal of Educational Psychology* 87:455–467.

Soloff, S. B., and J. C. Houtz. 1991. "Development of Critical Thinking among Students in Kindergarten through Grade 4." *Perceptual and Motor Skills* 73:476–478.

Sternberg, R. L. 1995. "Investing in Creativity: Many Happy Returns." *Educational Leadership* 53 (4): 80–84.

Watson, G., and E. M. Glaser. 1980. *Watson–Glaser Critical Thinking Appraisal, Forms A and B*. Cleveland, Ohio: Psychological Corporation.

Wong, B. L. 1995. "Self-Questioning Instructional Research: A Review." *Review of Educational Research* 65:227–268.

Yinger, R. J. 1990. *New Directions for Teaching and Learning: Fostering Critical Thinking*. San Francisco, Calif.: Jossey-Bass.

CHAPTER 13

Holistic Learning and Education

The origin of holistic learning and education stems from a philosophy called "holism." The credit for this term goes to General Jan Christian Smuts, the former prime minister of South Africa: "Smuts coined the term 'holism' from the Greek 'Olos' (which means whole) in his epic book 'Holism in Evolution' published in 1926" (Kun, 1995). Smuts is said to be before his time. He believed in an increasingly conscious universe that is leading to more of a wholeness among various entities through interactions and interconnections (Holdstock, 1987). These entities included spiritual, organic, and material wholes that should not be viewed in isolation of one another. The principles of holism direct these entities toward a higher sense of order. "Every facet of life is engaged in a lawful evolutionary pilgrimage toward greater unity and wholeness" (Holdstock, 1987).

Although the term "holism" originated in 1926, A.S. Neill started Summerhill, an English school based on the philosophy of holism, in 1921. Neill believed that children had more potential for learning when they had less adult influence. He believed that their individuality, uniqueness, and learning potential would emerge from being in an environment of love and freedom. Treating all students the same would be like producing robots (Holdstock, 1987). Meier supports Neill's philosophy by stating: "Look at children. They learn holistically. That's why they are such accelerated learners . . . to children, the world is geodesic—they plunge right into the whole of it" (Meier, 1985). Even further support of this philosophy is given by Tarver, who states, "The holists contend that learning, if it is to be meaningful, must be a product of the learners' constructions or discoveries; meaningful learning cannot be programmed in advance by either teachers or curriculum developers" (Tarver, 1986).

HOLISTIC LEARNING

There are numerous definitions of holistic learning and education. I define those terms that have relevance for classroom application. Holdstock writes that defining holistic education is like trying to harness the full extent of education. He further states that holistic education is multimodal (Holdstock, 1987). It attempts to define everything about an individual in relation to environmental aspects associated with learning. Even our relatedness to inanimate matter and time is considered. It strives to complete that which is incomplete, to pay attention to those aspects of our humanness that have not received their proper or fair share of attention.

A similar view of holistic education is expressed by Miller, who believes that the essence of holistic learning is conveyed in the following poem "There Was a Child Went Forth" by Walt Whitman.

> There was a child went forth every day.
> And the first object he looked upon, that object he became, and that object
>   became part of him for the day or a certain part of the day.
> Or for many years or stretching cycles of years (Miller, 1998)

In this poem, the child connects with his/her environment so that learning is deeply integrated. Holistic education goes beyond the existing curricula. It surpasses the three Rs (reading, writing, and arithmetic) and the three Ls (logic, language, and linearity) by asking previously unasked questions and making sure the inner self is not suffering from neglect (Holdstock, 1987).

HOLISTIC LEARNING AND EDUCATION

A better understanding of holistic education can be achieved by a description of its theoretical framework and its origin. The theoretical framework for holistic education is that all aspects of a child's education must be connected in order for learning to be meaningful. If education is broken up into segments, which are then taught independently of one another, then concepts become disconnected and disjointed. According to this theory, which was developed several decades ago, the material universe is seen as a dynamic web of interrelated events. None of the properties of any part of the web is fundamental; they all follow from the properties of the other parts, and the overall consistency of their interrelatedness determines the structure of the entire web (Holdstock, 1987).

RELATIONSHIP TO THEORIES OF LEARNING

One does not have to research the topic of holistic learning very long before coming across the name Jean Piaget. Many aspects of holistic learning are based on Piagetian theory. Piaget believed that a child and his/her environment were interactive and that the mind was unable to separate itself from the social and physical world (Grobecker, 1996). He believed that error and failure promoted understanding by transforming previously misunderstood concepts and that if this process were interrupted, it could totally disrupt the learning process (Macinnis, 1995). He envisioned unstructured education (Tarver, 1986).

Lev Vygotsky is another name that appears in research involving holistic education. "Vygotsky thought that social interaction with others provided the necessary scaffolding for construction of meaning" (Macinnis, 1995). He supported Piaget's view that development could not be separated from social and cultural activities (Santrock, 1999). This supports the holistic approaches of integration, cooperative learning, and interactive teaching.

Friedrich Froebel is another individual who deserves mention. In the 1840s, his philosophy of education for young children led to the founding of kindergarten, which literally meant a garden for children (Santrock, 1999). He advocated a nurturing child-centered approach to early childhood education, with emphasis on achievement and success. The process of learning, rather than what is learned, is emphasized (Santrock, 1999). This is one of the core values of holistic education.

Based on Piagetian theory, constructivism has recently become a trend in education. A theory of learning that describes the central role that learners' ever-transforming mental schemes play in their cognitive growth, constructivism powerfully informs educational practice. Advocates of constructivism believe that equating lasting student learning with test results is folly (Brooks and Brooks, 1999). By being so concerned with test outcomes, schools have begun to downsize their curricula to include test material, almost solely. This limits students' learning as well as teacher creativity. Students are programmed to memorize information and spit it out on a test so that their levels of knowledge can be assessed.

These authors contend that the complexity of the curriculum, instructional methodology, student motivation, and student developmental readiness cannot be captured on a paper-and-pencil test.

Constructivism, like holism, focuses not so much on what students learn, but on how they learn. It involves helping students internalize what they learn. By constructing mental structures, experiences are organized and further understanding is possible (Holloway, 1999). Since teachers have no way of knowing what mental structures exist within the mind of a particular child, it is important to vary teaching methods. Five principles of constructivism, as identified by Brooks and Brooks, are as follows:

1. Seek and value students' points of view
2. Structure lessons to challenge students' suppositions
3. Recognize that students must attach relevance to the curriculum
4. Structure lessons around big ideas, not small bits of information
5. Assess student learning in the context of daily classroom investigations, not as separate events (Brooks and Brooks, 1999)

Even though constructivism is a recent trend in education, it has its criticisms: that it is too permissive and that it lacks vigor.

COMPONENTS OF HOLISTIC LEARNING

According to Miller, three components that assist in holistic learning are balance, inclusion, and connection (Miller, 1998). Miller believes that a balance must exist between learning and assessment so that one is not given more emphasis than the other. Focusing too much on test results distracts teachers from fostering the learning process, and vice versa. By inclusion, Miller means having students of different races and abilities working together, as well as balancing different types of learning, such as transmission, transaction, and transformational. Teachers who know how to balance a variety of teaching strategies will keep their students' interest as well as promote their development.

Educators must find a balance between the various types of learning and learning styles that children bring to the classroom, such as individualized and group instruction, analytic thinking, intuitive thinking, content and process learning, assessment, abstract learning, and concrete learning.

To achieve holistic learning in the classroom, educators need to balance instruction and assessment with learning (Wagner and Sternberg, 1984).

Holistic education, in its truest sense, implies that all children are included in all activities in the classroom. To accommodate the diverse needs of children, teachers must employ various types of learning strategies. Miller advocates four kinds of learning:

1. Transmission—one-way flow of information from the teacher or the textbook to the student. The focus is on accumulating factual information relevant to basic skills.
2. Transaction—is characterized by greater interaction between the student and teacher. Problem solving and developing cognitive skills are emphasized.
3. Transformational—the focus is on the total intellectual, physical, emotional, aesthetic, moral, and spiritual development of the child. Activities are designed to nurture all aspects of the student's development, such as storytelling and the arts.
4. Connection—the child connects with his/her environment so that learning is deeply integrated. Connections may be among school subjects by integrating topics around a major theme. Connection learning also implies a degree of cooperation and collaboration with others by participating in cooperative groups (Miller, 1998).

Holistic learning, to be effective, must include the integration of several theories of learning to promote learning. Educators should abstract from the major theories of learning discussed in previous chapters in the text and choose those aspects that will promote their instructional plans and the needs and interest of the learners under their supervision.

ADVOCATES FOR HOLISTIC LEARNING EDUCATION

Holistic education has arisen out of a belief that traditional education does not work. The reason why it does not work is because our approach is based on Newtonian principles—that is, knowledge is constructed by stacking building blocks on a solid foundation (Holdstock, 1987). This means that our knowledge is constructed piecemeal with the idea that the whole cannot be understood without first understanding each individual part. Advocates of holistic education believe that education should not be broken into pieces, with each piece being taught individually, because education is more than the sum of its parts.

Holistic thinkers believe that traditional education dulls the conscious, leads everyone down the same path, takes the meaning out of learning by teaching concepts in a disjointed way, forces people to conform, and robs people of their innovation, creativity, productivity, uniqueness, and potential (Meier, 1985). According to Kun, conventional education "fills minds rather opens them, kills creativity and confuses knowledge with knowing, and learning with studying." Kun states it is clear that traditional Western educational policies and practices function at a level of efficiency and effectiveness that is far inferior to our biological, organizational, and technological systems (Kun, 1995).

Additionally, Meier writes that we are leaving the linear age of assembly line thinking and learning (Meier, 1985). Education's simulation of a factory where there is uniformity of both process and output is on its way out. Meier believes that we have entered a new age of learning known as the geodesic age. It's an age that takes as its symbol the geodesic sphere—an interlocking network that suggests integration, interrelationship, and a sense of the whole. Geodesic relationships are mutual and do not involve hierarchies. Everything is equal and everything exists and occurs simultaneously—just one whole, interdependent flow of energy (Meier, 1985). Nobel Prize–winner Ilya Prigogine supports this by stating that educational institutions are open systems that are self-organizing and maintained by a continuous dynamic flow (Holdstock, 1987).

The theory of the geodesic age falls under the umbrella of new age learning, which seems to be a synonym for holistic learning. The philosophy of new age learning deals with becoming whole. This is identical to holistic thinking, which emphasizes contexts, relationships, and wholes (Kun, 1995). Instead of studying parts that lead up to a whole, new age learning involves beginning with the whole and branching out into parts. Some of the techniques involved in new age learning are mind–body relaxation, mind-setting exercises, mental imagery, special music, embedded stimuli, and positive paraconscious suggestion (Meier, 1985). One of the reasons why these techniques are thought to be effective is because of Prigogine's theory that learning occurs more efficiently when the brain's fluctuations are augmented (Holdstock, 1987).

A current leader in holistic education is Bruce Copley, a South African–based writer and motivational speaker who used to be a university professor. After twenty years of teaching, Copley so believed that a holistic approach was needed in education that he helped develop "Cogmotics," which is said to be a revolutionary approach to learning, teaching, and training. The essence of this unique approach is to consciously stimulate and integrate the mental, physical, spiritual, social, and emotional faculties within a safe, nurturing environment (Holloway, 1999). According to Kun, Cogmotics is widely considered to be the "missing link" in education. He uses the following quote by Eric Butterworth to capture the essence of Cogmotics: "When the ties of learning that bind the human mind again and again and again are lost, and a person is introduced finally to himself, the real self that has no limitation, then the bells of heaven ring for joy and we are thrust forward into a grand rendezvous with life" (Kun, 1995). In support of the holistic philosophy, Hilliard and Myers articulate that learning at the middle school level has focused too much on parts rather than wholes (Hilliard and Myers, 1997). That is why they support the approaches of cooperative learning, literature-based reading, and holistic literacy. These approaches, which involve identifying with the real-life needs of the students, will lead us to a current trend in education: whole language. "Whole language" is a holistic perspective on how language operates (Hilliard and Myers, 1997). Instead of breaking up the components of language (reading, writing, speaking, and listening) into separate parts, they are taught together as a whole. The connections used in holistic learning involve those between school subjects, school members, the earth, and one's self. These connections lead to links, integrations, discoveries, collaborations, cooperation, respect, responsibilities, and relationships (Miller, 1998). The learning environment for whole language is student-centered with the teacher acting as a facilitator. According to Schurr, Thompson, and Thompson, there are three guidelines for creating this environment.

1. Immerse students in reading, writing, speaking, and listening. Working on all these skills at once is more like real-world experiences involving language.
2. Create an environment that encourages students to take risks. Encouraging the interaction of ideas among students helps to make them feel secure.
3. Focus on meaning. Emphasize clarity in all facets of language (Schurr, Thompson, and Thompson, 1995).

Watson and Crowley summarize nine holistic approaches that they consider helpful when implementing a whole language environment:

1. Find out what interests students and use that information to structure the curriculum—enthusiasm + motivation = accomplishment
2. Read to students every day and/or tell them stories since all literature comes from oral tradition and children learn to love literature by experiencing it
3. Provide young adolescents with the opportunities to write every day by using topics of interest and various activities
4. Encourage students to read "real" literature by finding books that appeal to their interests and by minimizing the use of the "skills-focused" textbook
5. Take advantage of the social nature of reading and writing to promote paired and other cooperative learning activities since integrating several skills at once promotes learning of all skills involved
6. In addition to encouraging integrated reading, writing, speaking, and listening activities, encourage students to discuss the processes of reading, writing, speaking, and listening as well since discussion promotes clarity and reduces anxiety
7. Set the example where reading and writing are concerned by letting students know that you read for pleasure and variety
8. To promote the home-school connection, encourage parents to involve themselves in their children's education, particularly by setting an example for family literacy
9. Use what works—be eclectic and use various, innovative approaches (Watson and Crowley, 1988)

Holistic approaches can also be applied to mathematics instruction. Instead of dividing math into its parts (numbers, problems, and concepts), and performing drills and exercises from workbooks, all of these skills can be taught interactively (Archambeault, 1993). The teacher is once again a facilitator, guiding students through problem solving activities. Learners develop complete understandings of the math concepts as they become proficient in the language of mathematics through verbal communication, paragraph answers, and written problems based on real-life situations. According to Archambeault, there exists a phobia of math in our society (Archambeault, 1993). Individuals who may be intelligent in other areas of education exhibit deficits in the area of mathematics. One study of the National Research Council (1989) reported that math anxiety is rooted in the belief that success in mathematics is dependent on some sort of special ability, which most students do not have (Archambeault, 1993).

It is believed that a holistic approach to teaching mathematics will reduce both math anxiety and the belief that math is such a foreign subject. This concept, similar to whole language, is called whole math and involves real-life, hands-on, interactive, problem solving learning experiences.

Archambeault writes that there are a host of activities that can be included in a whole mathematics unit (Archambeault, 1993). Some of these include:

1. Shopping for groceries—using newspaper ads, preparing lists, calculating costs, comparing costs of different items, and converting pounds to ounces
2. Eating in a restaurant—ordering from menus, totaling bills, comparing costs of meals, and writing menus
3. Buying gasoline—using maps, estimating miles per gallon, calculating costs of gas, comparing costs of car to bus, and recording speedometer readings and gas purchases
4. Introducing fractions—using folded strips of paper to demonstrate halves, fourths, eighths, and so on, comparing fractions to wholes, and reducing, adding, and subtracting fractions
5. Shopping by catalog—filling out order forms, calculating costs of items, and discussing pros and cons of shopping by catalogs
6. Taking medicine—discussing ways of measuring medicines, comparing differences between tableware and measuring spoons, preparing charts showing when to take medicines, and calculating numbers of doses and pills to be taken over a period of time

This is not even the complete list of ideas for whole math activities, which proves that there are many creative, nonthreatening ways to teach math so that it is relevant, interesting, and useful to learners. It is also interesting to note that most of the aspects of whole language are incorporated into whole math since it involves reading, writing, speaking, and listening. This supports the holistic viewpoint that learning is integrated and cannot be separated into parts. Everything is connected to everything else.

Although whole language is currently a widespread trend in schools around the country, it is not always welcomed by teachers with open arms. Ridley identifies four factors that appear to constrain teachers' acceptance of whole language: an orientation toward activities versus philosophy, resistance to change, a lack of resources, and concerns about accountability (Ridley, 1990; Au and Scheu, 1996; Weaver, Stevens, and Vance, 1984).

Another reason why some teachers avoid holistic instruction is because it is often ambiguous and vague (Au and Scheu, 1996). It has been said that holistic education has not been, and perhaps cannot be, the subject of formal evaluation. The pure holists contend that truly meaningful learning is too elusive to be measured; if that is the case, then there is no scientifically acceptable way to evaluate the approach (Tarver, 1986). Therein lies the problem with holistic education. If we do away with standardized tests because they reduce education to a listen-memorize-regurgitate mind-set (Kun, 1995), how will we discover what our students know? Education cannot exist without some way of assessing student achievement. This view is in direct contrast to an article by Keefe that states "[o]nly from a holistic perspective can assessment approach accuracy and validity" (Keefe, 1992). She believes that assessment in holistic education is possible but that it takes time and that it should come from a variety of sources.

TEACHING CHILDREN WITH DISABILITIES

Aside from regular education, there has been a long-time debate between the reductionist and constructivist (holistic) approaches in the field of special education. Reductionists believe that learning can be taught in parts that will eventually equal a whole. Learning is sequential, observable, and verifiable. The constructivists believe that learning is created by the learner. Learning is made meaningful through the application of new information to previous experiences. Practices in special education such as task analysis, specific skill training, and even the individualized education program (Macinnis, 1995) are based on the reductionist approach to education.

The constructivists believe that the reductionist approach keeps students from learning because the elements being taught are not made into a whole that they can relate to. They believe that error is an important element of learning because it provides the teacher with some insight as to the students' thought processes. A rich-learning environment should be provided that caters to the students' needs and interests, and skills should be taught when necessary to perform meaningful tasks (Macinnis, 1995). Students should also have lots of opportunities to interact with others because social interaction helps to construct their knowledge. Students should have a say in what is taught and in developing rules, expectations, and procedures.

Macinnis states that there is some common ground between the reductionist and constructivist approaches in special education (Macinnis, 1995). Some examples from the book *Understanding Whole Language: From Principle to Practice* (Weaver, Stevens, and Vance, 1984) are direct teaching in the forms of teacher/student demonstrations, seizing "teachable moments," "authentic literacy events," and minilessons that take place during the holistic activity of whole language. Also, according to Macinnis a number of cognitive strategy theorists are moving away from the more reductionist approach to focus more on the work of Vygotsky's and Piaget's constructivist concepts (Macinnis, 1995).

In an article by Tarver, three approaches to the education of learning disabled students are compared: Cognitive Behavior Modification (CBM), Direct Instruction (DI), and holism (Tarver, 1986). According to Tarver's research, the holistic approach receives little or no support in comparison to the CBM and DI approaches. Several models based on Piagetian theory of education that were studied in Head Start and Follow through Projects produced little or no gains in areas such as basic skills, cognitive problem solving, and affective measures. According to Wagner and Sternberg, Piagetian theory lacks sufficient empirical support to serve, at present, as a basis for educational interventions, and successively larger chunks of the theory are being undermined by new data (Wagner and Sternberg, 1984; Tarver, 1986).

Grobecker finds that skill generalization in children with learning disabilities persists because too much emphasis is placed on skill development and the information learned is not meaningful to the students (Grobecker, 1996). Generalizing is an abstract process of which many learning disability students are not capable. She states that there are a number of adaptive strategies that can be used as students are learning. Also, research conducted by Grobecker indicates the active, strategic, learning behavior is advanced by honoring students' thinking processes, making contact with their unique thought structures, and encouraging self-reflection (Grobecker, 1996). Furthermore, children need to be engaged in meaningful problems within relevant learning contexts. Her article "Reconstructing the Paradigm of Learning Disabilities: A Holistic/Constructivist Implementation" is in support of a holistic approach to teaching learning disabled students.

SUMMARY

It is evident from the research that a holistic approach to education is a controversial and much debated topic. The supporters of holistic education believe it is the only way to go with the future of education, and those in opposition feel it is too vague and unstructured. Still others believe that success can be achieved through a combination of approaches used simultaneously, which in my opinion seems to make the most sense since the idea of reaching every student through the same technique is unrealistic.

To summarize holistic learning, I believe that Miller captures its essence: "In a way, holistic learning is a return to basics. It asks us to focus on what is ultimately important in life. It asks that we see our work as more than just preparing students to compete with one another. Although we still must teach skills to ready students for the workplace, we need broader vision of education that fosters the development of whole human beings" (Miller, 1998).

BIBLIOGRAPHY

Archambeault, B. 1993. "Holistic Mathematics Instruction: Interactive Problem Solving and Real Life Situations Help Learners Understand Math Concepts." *Adult Learning* 5:21–23.

Au, K. H., and J. A. Scheu. 1996. "Journey toward Holistic Instruction: Supporting Teachers' Growth." *The Reading Teacher* 49 (6): 468–477.

Brooks, J. G., and M. G. Brooks. 1999. "The Courage to Be Constructivist." *Educational Leadership* (November): 18–24.

Grobecker, B. 1996. "Reconstructing the Paradigm of Learning Disabilities: A Holistic/Constructivist Implementation." *Learning Disability Quarterly* 19:179–200.

Hilliard, R. D., and J. W. Myers. 1997. "Holistic Language Learning at the Middle Level: Our Last, Best Chance." *Childhood Education* 73:286–289.

Holdstock, L. 1987. Excerpts from "Education for a New Nation." Africa Transpersonal Association. Reprinted with the permission of the author. <http://www.icon.co.za/-cogmotics/articles/newnation.htm> [last accessed: March 15, 2001].

Holloway, J. H. 1999. "Caution: Constructivism Ahead." *Educational Leadership* (November): 85–86, <http://www.icon.co.za/-cogmotics/drbruce.htm> [last accessed: August 20, 2001].

Keefe, C. H. 1992. "Developing Responsive IEPs through Holistic Assessment." *Intervention in School and Clinic* 28 (1): 34–40.

Kun, B. 1995. "Stop Studying and Start Learning." *IT Review* 2 (6) <http://www.icon.co.za/-cogmotics/articles/stopstudying.htm> [last accessed: May 21, 2001]

Macinnis, C. 1995. "Holistic and Reductionist Approaches in Special Education: Conflicts and Common Ground." *McGill Journal of Education* 30 (1): 7–20.

Meier, D. 1985. "New Age Learning: From Linear to Geodesic." *Training and Development Journal* <http://www.icon.co.za/-cogmotics/articles/newagelearning.htm> [last accessed: October 15, 2001].

Miller J. J. 1998. "Making Connections through Holistic Learning." *Educational Leadership* 56 (4) (December–January): 46–48.

Ridley, L. 1990. "Enacting Change in Elementary School Programs: Implementing a Whole Language Perspective." *The Reading Teacher* 43:640–646.

Santrock, J. W. 1999. *Life-Span Development.* 7th ed. New York: McGraw-Hill.

Schurr, S., J. Thompson, and M. Thompson. 1995. *Teaching at the Middle Level: A Professional's Handbook.* Lexington, Mass.: D. C. Health.

Tarver, S. 1986. "Cognitive Behavior Modification, Direct Instruction and Holistic Approaches to the Education of Students with Learning Disabilities." *Journal of Learning Disabilities* 19 (6): 368–375.

Wagner, R. K., and R. J. Sternberg. 1984. "Alternative Conceptions of Intelligence and Their Implications for Education." *Review of Educational Research* 54 (2): 179–223.

Watson, D., and P. Crowley. 1988. "How Can We Implement a Whole Language Approach?" In *Reading Process and Practice*, ed. C. Weaver. Portsmouth, N.H.: Heinemann Educational.

Weaver, C., D. Stevens, and J. Vance. 1984. "Understanding Whole Language: From Principle to Practice." *Review of Educational Research* 54 (2): 179–223.

CHAPTER 14

Reciprocal Teaching

Reciprocal teaching is a method that applies cognitive science to reading instruction. It is an instructional approach developed from research conducted by Palincsar and Klenk at the University of Michigan and Brown at the University of Illinois at Urbana–Champaign. According to Palincsar and Klenk, "reciprocal teaching" is an instructional procedure in which teachers and students take turns leading discussions about shared texts (Palincsar and Klenk, 1991). The purpose of these discussions is to achieve joint understanding of the text through the flexible application of four comprehension strategies: prediction, clarification, summarization, and questions generation. These strategies are modeled by the teacher in the context of instruction, and students practice the comprehension strategies in cooperative groups.

According to the developers, by using students' prior knowledge and experiences in order to make predictions, the text becomes more meaningful and important to them (Englert and Palincsar, 1991; Lysynchuk, Pressley, and Vye, 1990; Palincsar and Brown, 1986). By seeking clarification, students identify information important to understanding the text and rely on other members of the group to help them understand the key points. They also learn to reread the text to find evidence for their understandings (Lysynchuk, Pressley, and Vye, 1990). By generating questions, students establish ownership in the reading process. As students summarize, inaccuracies that cause misunderstandings become apparent and students are given explicit instructions in developing critical thinking skills. Teachers monitor the discussion and provide cognitive scaffolding (guided instruction). Brown, Palincsar, and Purcell conclude that the strength of reciprocal teaching is that it focuses on reading to learn rather than learning to read (Brown, Palincsar, and Purcell, 1986).

KEY STRATEGIES

- Reciprocal teaching—is an instructional approach in which teachers and students take turns leading discussions about shared texts. It is an interactive dialogue between the teacher and the students about content/materials that helps students to learn how to become effective readers (Brown and Palincsar, 1987; Campione, Shapiro, and Brown, 1995; Rosenshine and Meister, 1994).

  The teacher first models the technique, providing practice time for students to take turns being the teacher, while the teacher monitors progress and provides feedback. When students are proficient at using the technique, it can be incorporated into cooperative learning activities. There are four steps involved in implementing the reciprocal teaching strategy: summarizing, questioning, clarifying, and predicting (Palincsar and Brown, 1984). Each of these strategies helps students to construct meaning from shared texts and to monitor their reading to ensure that they understand what they have read.

- Summarizing—this strategy provides students the opportunity to restate what they have read in their own words. They work to find the most important information in the text. Initially, their summaries may be of sentences or paragraphs, but should later focus on larger units of text.

- Generating questions—when students generate questions, they must first identify the kind of information that is significant enough that it can provide the substance for a question. In order to do this, they must identify significant information, pose questions related to this information, and check to make sure they can answer their own question.

- Clarifying—when teaching students to clarify, their attention is called to the many reasons why the text is difficult to understand; for example, new vocabulary, unclear reference words, and unfamiliar or difficult concepts. Recognizing these blocks to understanding, students may clarify or ask for clarification in order to make sense of the text.

- Predicting—this strategy requires the students to hypothesize about what the author might discuss next. This provides a purpose for the students: to confirm or disapprove their hypotheses. An opportunity has been created for the students to link the new knowledge they will encounter in the text with the knowledge they already possess. It also facilitates the use of the text structure as students learn that headings, subheadings, and questions imbedded in the text are useful means of anticipating what might occur next.

The four strategies are used in a session when the discussion leader generates a question to which the group has to respond. The leader then summarizes the text and asks other members if they would like to elaborate on or revise the summary. Clarifications are discussed. Then, in preparation for moving on to the next portion of the text, the groups generate predictions. The goal is flexible use of the strategies.

INTRODUCING RECIPROCAL THINKING STRATEGIES

When introducing the strategies to the students, in the initial stage the teacher assumes primary responsibility for leading the dialogues and implementing the strategies. Through modeling, the teacher demonstrates how to use the strategies while reading the text. During guided practice, the teacher supports students by adjusting the demands of the task based on each student's level of proficiency. Eventually, the students learn to conduct the dialogues with little or no teacher assistance. The teacher assumes the role of a coach/facilitator by providing students with evaluative information regarding their performance and prompting them to higher levels of participation (Slavin, 2000; Ormrod, 1999).

Students should be taught in small heterogeneous groups to ensure that each student has ample opportunity to practice using the strategies while receiving feedback from other group members. The optimal group size is between six and eight students. Frequent guided practice is essential in helping students become more proficient in their use of the strategies.

The instructional materials selected should be appropriate based on certain criteria. The teacher should select material that is based on the student's reading/listening comprehension level. The material used should be sufficiently challenging, however. Incorporate text that is representative of the kinds of materials students are expected to read in school and on their level. Generally, students are taught the reciprocal teaching procedure using expository informational texts. The story structure in narrative texts lends itself quite well. Also, students are taught to use the four strategies incorporating the elements of story grammar (character, plot, problem, and solution).

There are no specific guidelines for a time frame. The first day of instruction is spent introducing the students to the four strategies. The length of each session will depend on the age and the attention of the students, but will usually fall within the range of twenty to forty minutes per session. It is recommended that the initial instruction take place on consecutive days. After this point, instruction can be provided on alternate days if needed.

INSTRUCTIONAL USES OF RECIPROCAL TEACHING

The primary goal of reciprocal teaching is to improve the reading comprehension skills for students who have not benefited from traditional reading instructional methods. This is achieved through an established collaborative discourse in order to help students acquire strategies useful for constructing meaning from texts (Palincsar and Klenk, 1992).

Content area texts have been found useful, especially at the middle school level. Palincsar and Klenk explain that "shared texts contribute to the development of a learning community in which groups explore principles, ideas, themes, and concepts over time" (Palincsar and Klenk, 1992). They report improved results of reciprocal teaching when using texts related by themes and/or concepts; for example, science concepts related to animal survival themes such as adaptations, extinctions, and the use of camouflage and mimicry. They also explain that shared texts contribute to the development of a learning community in which groups explore principles, ideas, themes, and concepts over time.

The participants of reciprocal teaching vary according to reading ability. Reciprocal teaching is most compatible with classrooms that are social, interactive, and holistic in nature. Since reciprocal teaching places emphasis on helping students to connect their personal background experiences with the text, it can be used in diverse classrooms and communities. Research conducted by Palincsar and Klenk illustrates that small groups of six to eight students work best using reciprocal teaching dialogue, although teachers at the middle school level have used reciprocal teaching dialogue with as many as seventeen students (Palincsar and Klenk, 1992). Teachers have also trained students as tutors and have successfully monitored several groups led by the tutors. Reciprocal teaching has been used with students ranging in age from seven to adulthood. Reading levels and grade levels of students also varied (Rosenshine and Meister, 1994). Palincsar and Klenk report that since the beginning of the research program in reciprocal teaching in 1981, "nearly 300 middle school students and 400 first to third graders have participated" (Palincsar and Klenk, 1992). The early studies focused on students who were successful at decoding but scored poorly on tests of comprehension. The program was designed primarily for students considered at-risk for academic failure. Many of the participating students in the reciprocal teaching research program had been identified as remedial or special education students. Later, studies tested the success of reciprocal teaching for students who were only learning to decode (Brown and Palincsar, 1987). Studies have also considered the success of reciprocal teaching in content areas such as social studies and science. Many research replications have been conducted at the high school and junior college level (Brown and Campione, 1992).

Teachers begin reciprocal teaching by reflecting on their current instructional strategies and activities that teach students' reading comprehension. Next, theory supporting reciprocal teaching is introduced. Key theoretical elements include teachers' modeling the strategies by thinking aloud and consciously striving to have students control the dialogue. All students are expected to participate and to develop skills at using the strategies and critical thinking. Variation exists in the amount of scaffolding the teacher must provide. Next, teachers watch tapes, examine transcript of reciprocal teaching dialogues, and role-play. Teachers and researchers coteach a lesson. After the formal instruction, coaching is provided to teachers as they begin implementing reciprocal teaching (Palincsar and Klenk, 1992).

RESEARCH FINDINGS

Palincsar and Klenk report that the criterion for success was the attainment of an independent score of 75 percent to 85 percent correct on four out of five consecutively administered measures of comprehension, assessing recall of text, ability to draw inferences, ability to state the gist of material read, and application of knowledge acquired from the text to a novel situation (Palincsar and Klenk, 1992). Using this criterion, approximately 80 percent of both the primary and middle school students using reciprocal teaching strategies were judged successful following three months of instruction. Furthermore, these gains were maintained for up to six months to a year following instruction.

Palincsar and Brown report that "quantitative and qualitative analyses of transcripts showed substantial changes in the dialogue during the 20 instructional days" (Palincsar and Brown, 1986). In addition, they showed that "students improved criterion-referenced test scores over a five-day period of reciprocal teaching while control students made no gains. Students improved in the writing of summaries, generating text-related questions, and identifying discrepancies in texts." Students who had been at the twentieth percentile or below in social studies and science increased their scores in these subjects areas to or above the fiftieth percentile.

Reciprocal teaching, according to Rosenshine and Meister, is dependent on the quality of dialogue among participants (Rosenshine and Meister, 1994). The quality of the dialogue can be determined through observation and by assessing the students' questions and summaries during the discussion. Students' reading comprehension is also measured by standardized tests or experimenter-made tests can be multiple choice, short-answer, or summarizing essays.

Palincsar and Brown attribute success of reciprocal teaching to its interactive nature (Palincsar and Brown, 1986). Understanding the text and providing scaffolding while the students acquire the skills are important to the success of reciprocal teaching. Palincsar, Ransom, and Derber cite the alignment of instructional strategies with assessment criteria as a major contributor to the success of reciprocal teaching (Palincsar, Ransom, and Derber, 1989).

Soto attributes the success of reciprocal teaching to the social construction of knowledge (Soto, 1989). Students collaborate to construct meaning of texts. This allows them to focus on information in texts that is meaningful to them and to use their diverse backgrounds and experiences to introduce multiple perspectives. In addition, through reciprocal teaching dialogues teachers are better able to assess students' understandings of text and nonmainstream students' perspectives are given merit in discussions, while status differentiation based on ethnicity and home language is reduced.

KEY TERMS AND VOCABULARY LIST

Palincsar and Brown compile an excellent list for terms and vocabulary in reciprocal teaching that can be easily applied in the classroom (Palincsar and Brown, 1984, 1989):

1. Inert knowledge: encapsulated information rarely accessed again unless you need it for an exam.
2. Theory change: paradigm shift, conceptual upheaval.
3. Restructuring: modifying the knowledge base.
4. Self-directed learning: conceptual development is inner directed and inner motivated.
5. Social learning: conceptual development is other directed and has an intrinsically social genesis.
6. Cooperative learning: an environment of group explanation and discussion, often with tasks or responsibilities divided up.
7. Participant structures: interactive environments with agreed on rules for speaking, listening, and turn taking.
8. Thinking roles:
   - Executive: designs plans for action and suggests solutions.
   - Skeptic: questions premises and plans.
   - Instructor: takes on tasks of explanation and summarization for less-able group members.
   - Record keeper: keeps track of events that have passed.
   - Conciliator: resolves conflicts.
9. Epistemic consideration: organizing knowledge by defining the problem, isolating variables, referring to previous knowing, and evaluating the process.
10. Jigsaw method: children are divided into groups of five or six. Each group is held responsible for a large body of knowledge, on which each member will be tested individually. Each member is assigned a topic area. In the same topic area from different groups share information, then return to their groups and share that information with their group.
11. Elaboration: an explanation; a new proposition formed by linking old ones.
12. Preoperational thought: below five years old, children cannot comprehend concepts such as conservation of volume, conservation of spatial extent, perspective, and so on.
13. Concrete operational thought: nonabstract thinking for kids seven and up.
14. Intrapersonal function of language: language turned inward; the person checks and demonstrates his/her ideas to a hypothetical opponent (internalized socialization); silent verbalization.
15. Zone of proximal development: the difference between potential

and actual learning, and between what a novice can do unaided and in a supportive cooperative environment with an expert.

16. Proleptic teaching: group apprenticeship; novices participate in group activity before they are able to perform the task unaided.

17. Expert scaffolding: the expert provides support as needed, commensurate with the novice's expertise and the difficulty of the task, then removes it as the novice progresses.

18. Scaffolding structure: (usually individual) apprenticeship or mother–child relationship; aid decreases as the learner's skill increases; activity is shaped by the expert; scaffolding is internalized; and the expert does not verbalize.

19. Socratic dialogue: discovery learning; teacher probes for novel inferences and applications of knowledge by the student.

20. Tripartite teaching goals: facts, rules, and methods for deriving rules.

21. Knowledge-worrying activities: testing hypotheses.

22. Reciprocal teaching: an expert-led cooperative learning procedure involving the activities of questioning, clarifying, summarizing, and predicting.

23. Heuristics: general rules that evolve from experience.

24. Self-testing mechanisms: assess your own level of expertise by trying to paraphrase some text; if you fail, you need to work on it.

25. Emergent skill: a skill that is partly learned.

SUMMARY

The unique feature of reciprocal teaching is that the teacher and students take turns leading a discussion that focuses on application of the four reading strategies. It also focuses on several different techniques such as teaching, modeling, scaffolding, direct instruction, and guided practice. Teachers should purposefully model their use of strategies so that students can emulate them. "Think alouds" allow teachers to verbalize all their thoughts for students as they demonstrate skills or processes. Some key points to include in the think alouds are making predictions or showing students how to develop hypotheses; describing visual images; sharing an analogy that links prior knowledge with new information; verbalizing confusing points; and demonstrating fix-up strategies. These points should be identified by teachers so that students will realize how and when to use them. After several modeling experiences, students should practice using the strategy in pairs. Ultimately, students should work independently with the strategy, using a checklist to monitor usage of the critical points for think alouds.

"Scaffolding" is the process of providing strong teacher support and gradually removing it until students are working independently (Pearson, 1985; Collins, Brown, and Newman, 1987). This instructional strategy is effective in helping students accelerate their learning. Scaffolding can be applied by sequence texts and through teacher modeling that gradually leads to students' independence.

Palincsar, Ransom, and Derber outline strategies for mastering reciprocal teaching skills:

1. Make sure the strategies are overt, explicit, and concrete through modeling.
2. Link the strategies to the contexts in which they are to be used and teach the strategies as a functioning group, not in isolation.
3. Instruction must inform students. Students should be aware of what strategies work and where they should use particular strategies.
4. Have students realize that strategies work no matter what their current level of performance.
5. Comprehension must be transferred from the teacher to the pupil. The teach should slowly raise the demands made on the students and then fade into the background. Students gradually take charge of their learning (Palincsar, Ransom, and Derber, 1989).

Teachers in Highland Park, Michigan, decided to implement reciprocal teaching as part of their reading instruction program at the elementary through high school levels, and they were very well rewarded for their efforts (Carter, 1997). At the school level, dramatic improvements were observed in the Michigan assessment reading comprehension test. At the faculty level, teachers themselves used reciprocal teaching on each other to enhance their proficiency in acquiring a second language (a goal for their staff development).

Generally, research on using reciprocal teaching with children at-risk and children with disabilities shows that it increases their achievement (Alfassi, 1998; Carter, 1997; Lysynchuk, Pressley, and Vye, 1990; Palincsar and Brown, 1984).

BIBLIOGRAPHY

Alfassi, M. 1998. "Reading for Meaning: The Efficacy of Reciprocal Teaching in Fostering Reading Comprehension in High School Students in Remedial Reading Classes." *American Educational Research Journal* 35 (2): 309–332.

Brown, A. L., and J. C. Campione. 1992. "Students As Researchers and Teachers." In *Teaching for Thinking*, ed. J. W. Keefe and H. J. Walberg. Reston, Va.: National Association of Secondary School Principals.

Brown, A. L., and A. S. Palincsar. 1987. "Reciprocal Teaching Comprehension Strategies: A National History of One Program for Enhancing Learning." In *Cognition in Special Education Comparative Approaches to Retardation, Learning Disabilities, and Giftedness*, ed. J. Borkowsky and J. D. Day. Norwood, N.J.: Ablex.

Brown A. L., A. S. Palincsar, and L. Purcell. 1986. *Poor Readers: Teach, Don't Label. The School Achievement of Minority Children: New Perspectives*. Hillsdale, N.J.: Erlbaum.

Campione, J. C., A. M. Shapiro, and A. L. Brown. 1995. "Forms of Transfer in a Community of Learners: Flexible Learning and Understanding." In *Teaching for Transfer: Fostering Generalization in Learning*, ed. A. McKeough, J. Lupant, and A. Marini. Mahwah, N.J.: Erlbaum.

Carter, C. 1997. "Why Reciprocal Teaching?" *Educational Leadership* 54 (6): 64–68.

Collins, A., J. S. Brown, and S. E. Newman. 1987. "Cognitive Apprenticeship: Teaching the Craft of Reading, Writing, and Mathematics." Tech. Rep. No. 403. Champaign: Center for the Study of Reading, University of Illinois at Urbana–Champaign.

Englert, C. S., and A. S. Palincsar. 1991. "Reconsidering Instructional Research in Literacy from a Sociocultural Perspective." *Learning Disabilities Research and Practice* 6:225–229.

Lysynchuk, L. M., M. Pressley, and N. J. Vye. 1990. "Reciprocal Teaching Improves Standardized Reading-Comprehension Performance in Poor Comprehenders." *The Elementary School Journal* 90 (5): 469–484.

Ormrod, J. E. 1999. *Human Learning*. 3rd ed. Columbus, Ohio: Merrill.

Palincsar, A. S., and A. L. Brown. 1984. "Peer Interaction in Reading Comprehension Instruction." *Educational Psychologists* 22:231–253.

———. 1986. "Interactive Teaching to Promote Independent Learning from Text." *The Reading Teacher* 39 (8): 771–777.

———. 1989. "Classroom Dialogues to Promote Self-Regulated Comprehension." In *Advances in Research on Teaching*, vol. 1, ed. J. Brophy. Greenwich, Conn.: JAI Press.

Palincsar, A. S., and L. Klenk. 1991. "Dialogues Promoting Reading Comprehension." In *Teaching Advanced Skills to At-Risk Students*, ed. B. Means, C. Chelemer, and M. S. Knapp. San Francisco, Calif.: Jossey-Bass.

————. 1992. "Fostering Literacy Learning in Supportive Contexts." *Journal of Learning Disabilities* 25 (4): 211–225, 229.

Palincsar, A. S., K. Ransom, and S. Derber. 1989. "Collaborative Research and Development of Reciprocal Teaching." *Educational Leadership* 46 (4): 37–40.

Pearson, P. D. 1985. "Changing the Face of Reading Comprehension Instruction." *The Reading Teacher* 38:724–728.

Rosenshine, B., and C. Meister. 1994. "Reciprocal Teaching: A Review of the Research." *Review of Educational Research* 64 (4): 479–530.

Slavin, R. E. 2000. *Educational Psychology: Theory and Practice.* Boston: Allyn and Bacon.

Soto, L. D. 1989. "Enhancing the Written Medium for Culturally Diverse Learners via Reciprocal Interaction." *Urban Review* 21 (3): 145.

CHAPTER 15

Brain-Based Learning

The brain is a fascinating organ that is composed of billions of cells. The cells involved in learning are neurons and glial cells. A complete discussion of the anatomy of the brain is not within the scope of this book; however, Sprenger provides detailed information on the anatomy and functions of the brain (Sprenger, 1999). A brief summary on the structure of the brain is provided for the reader's information.

The brain accounts for only about 2 percent to 3 percent of body weight, but uses 20 percent to 25 percent of the body's energy. It is encased in the skull and protected by cerebrospinal fluid. The largest part of the brain is called the cerebrum, which consists of two deeply wrinkled hemispheres of nerve tissue located in each hemisphere of the brain. Its major function is to control all conscious activities, such as memory, perception, problem solving, and understanding meanings. At the back of the skull are the two hemispheres of the cerebellum, which automatically controls and coordinates the muscles involved in such activities like riding a bicycle. The medulla—located in the brain stem, it channels information between the cerebral hemispheres and the spinal cord—controls involuntary muscle activity such as the beating of the heart, voluntary muscle activity in the body, the rate of breathing, stomach activities, swallowing, and other vital body activities. The spinal cord extends downward from the medulla through the bony rings of the spinal column. Nerves that extend upward from the spinal cord to the brain pass through the medulla where they cross. The left side of the brain controls the right side of the body, and the right side controls the left side of the body.

The human brain weighs less than six pounds. It can store more information than all the libraries of the world. It communicates with itself through billions of neurons and their connections. All functions of the nervous system depend on the coordinated activities of individual neurons. The cells have a cell membrane, a nucleus, and other structures within the cell body. They differ significantly in size and shape. Research on learning and memory shows that the brain uses discrete systems for different types of learning. The basal ganglia and cerebellum, according to Damasio, are critical for the acquisition of skills such as learning to ride a bicycle or to play a musical instrument; and the hippocampus is integral to the learning of facts pertaining to such entities as people, places, or events (Damasio, 1999). The left hemisphere of the brain seems to be specialized for the representation of verbal material and the right for a variety of nonverbal information processing (especially visual–spatial material). At the present time, it is not clear how many different nonverbal modalities one ought to distinguish, nor is it clear how many verbal modalities or levels of a verbal modality one ought to distinguish. However, it is clear that many individuals who suffer moderate to severe deficits in a particular modality, without showing any deficits, often times show partially compensating superiority in other modalities of functioning. Once facts are learned, the long-term memory of those facts relies on multicomponent brain systems, whose key parts are located in the vast brain expanse known as the cerebral cortex. The role of memory in learning will be highlighted in chapter 16.

PRINCIPLES OF NEUROSCIENCE RESEARCH

Caine and Caine have conducted extensive research in brain-based learning (Caine and Caine, 1977). They articulate that every human being has a virtually unlimited set of memory systems that are designed for programming and for the memorization of meaningless information. Individuals also have the need to place memories and experiences into wholes. Both memorization and integration are essential in the learning process. Caine and Caine also indicate that there are several principles associated with brain-based learning:

1. The brain is a complex adaptive system that functions as both independent and interdependent and that is self-organized (Kelso, 1995). If a certain part of the brain that controls a function is damaged, with training the other parts of the brain can perform the function.
2. The brain is a social brain. It is capable of early interpersonal and

social relationships with others that greatly advance or impede learning.

3. The search for meaning is innate, which implies that the brain is attempting to make sense of our experiences. Many of these experiences are necessary for survival and the development of relationships.

4. The search for meaning occurs through "patterning." Patterns may be innate or developed through interactions with individuals and their environments. The brain gives meaning and understanding to these patterns.

5. Emotions are critical to patterning and significantly influence learning, therefore emotions and learning are inseparable. Social interactions are influenced by one's emotional tone.

6. The brain simultaneously perceives and creates parts and wholes. It is interdependent, in that both hemispheres actively interact and reduce information to both parts and wholes.

7. Learning involves both focused attention and peripheral perception. The brain absorbs information regardless if the individual is paying or not paying attention to a task. Peripheral signals are also recorded and have significant importance on learning as well.

8. Learning always involves conscious and unconscious processes. Educators should be aware that the brain is constantly at work with conscious as well as unconscious experiences. Consequently, some learning may not occur immediately because the experiences have not been internalized.

9. We have at least two ways of organizing memory. O'Keefe and Nadel indicate that we have two sets of memories, one for recalling meaningless information and the other for meaningful information (O'Keefe and Nadel, 1978). Information from these two sources is stored differently, in that less meaningful experiences are motivated by reward and punishment, where meaningful experiences do not need rehearsal and allow for instant recall of experiences. The brain uses and integrates both approaches in learning (Cowley and Underwood, 1998).

10. Learning is developmental. The brain is constantly developing throughout childhood. Most of the development is shaped and molded by environmental influences. Children should be exposed to multiple experiences early in life to facilitate all aspects of learning.

11. Complex learning is enhanced by challenge and inhibited by threat. Teachers who employ strategies, which promotes a relaxed environment, provide challenges rather than threats to students. Learning is expedited in a challenging and relaxed environment where students are safe to try, think, speculate, and make mistakes (Kohn, 1993).
12. Every brain is uniquely organized. Genetic makeup and environmental influences determine to a significant degree how the brain is organized. The organization determines the various learning styles, talents, and intelligence of individuals.

Educators should provide experiences that promote all of the various principles outlined. This assessment is supported by Duff and Jonassen (Duffy and Jonassen, 1992). They indicate that learning is an active process in which meaning is developed on the basis of experiences. Similarly, Benson and Hunter state that humans do not passively encounter knowledge in the world, rather, they generate meaning based on what they choose to pay attention to (Benson and Hunter, 1992). Attention is related to the meaning and purpose of the learning act.

The brain is constructed to adapt to changing elements in society. Educators must capture how the brain learns and program this knowledge into instructional programs to promote self-directed learning activities for children.

Brain principles state that every human being has a virtually unlimited set of memory systems that are designed for programming and for the memorization of meaningless information, as well as placing memories and experiences into wholes. Both memorization and integration are critical in learning. Research by Caine and Caine shows that teaching for memorization of meaningless facts usually induces downshifting, which is defined as a response to a threat associated with fatigue, helplessness, or both (Caine and Caine, 1991, 1994). Critical and higher-order thinking are impeded by downshifting.

The theory of brain-based learning projects children as active participants in the learning process. The teacher becomes the facilitator in guiding the learning activities of children. The instructional approach is changed from rote and information to one that is receptive, flexible, creative, and student-centered. This theory advocates that students should be engaged in tasks that are meaningful to them and that facilitate their interests (Sprenger, 1999).

IMPLICATION OF NEUROSCIENCE RESEARCH IN
THE CURRICULUM

Correlation between brain research and pedagogy has not been well established. According to Wolfe and Brandt, much experimentation has to be conducted before brain research information can be taken into the classroom (Wolfe and Brandt, 1998). Nevertheless, educators can use research findings from neuroscience to infuse into the instructional program. Neuroscientific research validates the following:

1. The brain changes physiologically as a result of experience. The environment in which a brain operates determines to a large degree the functioning ability of that brain (Kotulak, 1996; Green, 1992). Appropriate development of the brain requires interaction between an individual's genetic inheritance and environmental influences (Diamond and Hopson, 1998). As such, educators need to provide an enriched environment to promote and stimulate intellectual growth.
2. Intelligence is not fixed at birth. Damasio demonstrates that an intervention program based on needs of impoverished children may improve intelligence (Damasio, 1999). His research findings indicate that the earlier the intervention the greater an improvement in intelligence can be noted.
3. Some abilities are acquired more easily during certain sensitive or critical periods. Chugani reports that during the early years, the brain overdevelops and has the ability to adapt, reorganize, and develop some capacities at this stage more readily than in the years after puberty (Chugani, 1996). If certain sensorimotor functions are not stimulated at birth, the brain cells designed to interpret these functions will fail to develop. The cells controlling these functions are "lost" because they are diverted to other tasks during certain critical periods of brain development. During critical periods, factors such as preterm birth; maternal smoking, alcohol, and/or drug use; maternal and infant malnutrition; postbirth lead poisoning; or child abuse may make a significant impact on brain development (Newman and Buka, 1997). The results pinpoint that there is an urgent need to develop early intervention programs that are adequately funded and peopled by competent staff for at-risk parents and children.

4. Learning is strongly influenced by emotions as reported by Goleman and LeDoux, summarize the importance of emotions in learning (Goleman, 1995; LeDoux, 1996). Chemicals in the brain send negative and positive information—which may be perceived as threatening or satisfying—to that part of the brain controlling the information. If perceived as threatening, learning may be impeded, and if positive, learning may be accelerated.

5. Attention is a prime factor in learning. Students must be exposed to strategies to promote attention. Educators should be aware of the factors that may impede or promote attention, such as diet, emotions, and hormones. Students should be taught the value of eating plenty of proteins, drinking an abundance of fluids, and limiting carbohydrates in large amounts (Jensen, 1998). Proteins will assist the brain in staying alert by providing the needed amino acids to produce dopamine and norepinephrine, the alternate neurotransmitters. Wurtman articulates that the brain consists of about 80 percent water (Wurtman, 1986). Fluids are necessary to keep neuron connections strong. Excessive carbohydrates are calming. Limiting the intake of them assists in producing an alert state of the brain.

6. Semantic memory is associated with the memory of words. Sprenger articulates that each learning experience should be organized to present a short chunk of information (Sprenger, 1999). The brain must process the information in some way after receiving it. Specific strategies such as graphic organizers, peer teaching, questioning strategies, summarizing, role-play, debates, outlines, time lines, practice tests, paraphrasing, and mnemonic devices may be used to assist students in building their semantic memories (refer to chapter 16 for specific strategies).

The brain can only receive data and information through the sensory perceptions. The brain categorizes nonlanguage sensory perceptions in various sections of the brain. Lowery writes that human knowledge is stored in clusters and organized within the brain into systems that people use to interpret familiar situations and to reason about new ones (Lowery, 1999). Construction in the brain depends on factors such as interest, prior knowledge, and positive environmental influences. Learning is best facilitated through the introduction of concrete and manipulative objectives, the use of prior experiences, and a gradual introduction of abstract symbols. New learning is basically a rearrangement of prior knowledge into new connections (Lowery, 1999). Curriculum innovation permits learners to construct their own patterns of learning through experimenting with various ideas and through the use of prior knowledge. Experimentation and practice reinforms the storage areas within the brain. If connections are not strengthened, they will dissipate (Diamond and Hopson, 1998).

Curriculum innovations must include strategies suited to the age range and development sequence, consider the interests and emotional states, and determine the learning styles of the learners. Brain research can assist educators in understanding what promotes learning and in determining which teaching techniques can be integrated into the instructional program.

BRAIN-BASED MODELS

Human behavior and learning are too complex to be regulated to one theory of learning. The behavioral–rational model that principally dominates our thinking in education is too limited. Brown and Moffett remark that this paradigm suggests that learning is neat, controllable, and programmable (Brown and Moffett, 1999). It is grounded in empirical, behavioral notions of human learning, especially in the idea that there is a discrete cause-and-effect linkage between teacher input and student output. Teaching is a one-size-fits-all process, in which students are passive recipients of information. Brain-based models contrast the behavioral–rational model. They support the notion that learning is open-ended, uncontrollable, greatly influenced by the learners' cognitive makeup, and dependent on the teachers' ability to assist diverse students to construct and draw meaning from learning experiences. The models recognize that learning is a complex and diverse process.

The importance of emotions, feelings, relationships, and human interaction combine to influence learning. The schools have failed to promote what Goleman calls the "emotional intelligence" of students and teachers (Goleman, 1995). He summarizes that emotional intelligence actually adds values to students' classroom learning and teachers' professional learning. Educational change needs more depth. Brain-base models appear to provide education with strategies to make the learner the center of the instructional process by promoting the whole child in the learning process.

PRINCIPLES OF LEARNING USING BRAIN-BASED RESEARCH

In promoting brain-base models, several researchers have advanced principles of learning, which educators can employ in promoting learning using brain-based research.

Principle 1. Brown and Moffett assert that true learning comes from a fusion of head, heart, and body (Brown and Moffett, 1999). The body reacts as a unified whole to promote learning; individuals are intellectually connected, emotionally engaged, and physically involved.

Principle 2. Wheatley's research indicates that learning occurs in environments in which motivation is largely intrinsic rather than extrinsic (Wheatley, 1992). Learning cannot be confined into narrow roles, learning activities must involve the whole child, and the integration of intellectual, emotional and physical factors must be infused in the learning process.

Principle 3. Innovative schools provide brain compatible learning environments (Caine and Caine, 1991). These schools plan curriculum, instruction, and assessment that are integrated and stimulate students' diverse ways of learning. They also recognize the importance of emotions in learning and develop strategies to enhance them.

Principle 4. Innovative schools attend to the new findings in cognitive psychology and constructivist education Brown and Moffett relate that innovated schools structure the learning process on the principle that knowledge is constructed and that learning is a process of creating personal meaning from new information by relating it to prior knowledge and experience (Brown and Moffett, 1999). Educators provide experiences for students to transfer information from one context to another. This transfer will not occur unless promoted by the teacher.

Principe 5. Above all, learning is strategic. Herman, Aschbacker, and Winters and Marzano agree that learning is goal directed and involves the learner's assimilation of strategies associated with knowing when to adapt, modify, and use knowledge to manage one's learning process (Herman, Aschbacker, and Winters, 1992; Marzano, 1992).

Principle 6. Recognizing the role of learning styles. The brain is a closed system, in which information can only enter through the five senses. A multisensory experience will provide a better opportunity for attention. Different brains favor different sensory stimuli. Kinesthetic learners need more movement, auditory learners need to talk about the material, and visual learners need to see something concrete. Appropriate teaching styles will allow each of these kinds of learners to lock in on their learning (Rose and Nicholl, 1997).

Teachers frequently find it difficult to assess an individual's learning style preference. Pupils learn through a variety of sensory channels and demonstrate individual patterns of sensory strengths and weaknesses. Educators should capitalize on students' learning styles. When the preferences of learning styles are not considered, classroom performance may be affected (Taylor, 1998).

Recognizing and understanding student learning styles in the classroom is one critical factor associated with student outcomes. Indeed, in reality it may be more important for instructors to have an understanding of the learning process and skill in facilitating individual and group learning than subject matter skill. For a brief summary of the various types of learning styles and their classroom implications, refer to Taylor (Taylor, 1997).

SUMMARY

Brain research is not new. Neuroscientists have been experimenting with brain research for well over two decades. Ways of implementing these research findings into the classroom have been demonstrated to be effective in promoting learning. The brain is inseparable in the learning process. The more educators understand how to implement brain-based research strategies, the better they will meet the learning needs of pupils.

BIBLIOGRAPHY

Benson, G. D., and W. J. Hunter. 1992. "Chaos Theory: No Strange Attraction in Teacher Education." *Action in Teacher Education* 14 (4): 61–67.

Brown, J. L., and C. A. Moffett. 1999. *The Hero's Journey*. Alexandria, Va.: Association for Supervision and Curriculum Development.

Caine, R. N., and G. Caine. 1977. *Education on the Edge of Possibility*. Alexandria, Va: Association for Supervision and Curriculum Development.

———. 1991. *Making Connections: Teaching and the Human Brain*. Alexandria, Va.: Association for Supervision and Curriculum Development.

———. 1994. *Making Connections: Teaching and the Human Brain (Revised)*. Menlo Park, Calif.: Addison Wesley.

Chugani, H. T. 1996. "Functional Maturation of the Brain." Paper presented at the Third Annual Brain Symposium, Berkeley, Calif.

Cowley, G., and A. Underwood. 1998. "Memory." *Newsweek* 131 (24): 48–49, 51–54.

Damasio, A. R. 1999. "How the Brain Creates the Mind." *Scientific American* 6 (281): 112–117.

Diamond, M., and J. Hopson. 1998. *Magic Trees of the Mind: How to Nurture Your Child's Intelligence, Creativity, and Healthy Emotions from Birth through Adolescence*. New York: Penguin Putnam.

Duffy, T. M., and A. D. Jonassen. 1992. *Constructivism and the Technology of Instruction: A Conversation*. Hillsdale, N.J.: Erlbaum.

Goleman, D. 1995. *Emotional Intelligence*. New York: Bantam.

Green, W. T. 1992. "Experience-Dependent Sunaptogenesis As a Plausible Memory Mechanism." In *Learning and Memory: The Behavioral Biological Substrates*, ed. I. Gormezano and E. A. Wasserman. Hillsdale, N.J.: Erlbaum.

Herman, J. L., P. R. Aschbacker, and L. Winters. 1992. *A Practical Guide to Alternative Assessment*. Alexandria, Va.: Association for Supervision and Curriculum Development.

Jensen, E. 1998. *Teaching with the Brain in Mind*. Alexandria, Va.: Association for Supervision and Curriculum Development.

Kelso, J. A. 1995. *Dynamic Patterns: The Self-Organization of Brain and Behavior*. Cambridge: MIT Press.

Kohn, A. 1993. *Punished by Rewards: The Trouble with Gold Stars Incentive Plans, A's, Praises and Other Bribes*. New York: Houghton Mifflin.

Kotulak, R. 1996. *Inside the Brain: Revolutionary Discoveries of How the Mind Work*. Kansas City, Miss.: Andrews McMeel.

LeDoux, J. 1996. *The Emotional Brain: The Mysterious Underpinning of Emotional Life*. New York: Simon and Schuster.

Lowery, L. 1999. "How New Science Curriculums Reflect Brain Research." *Educational Leadership* 55 (3): 26–30.

Marzano, R. 1992. *A Different Kind of Classroom*. Alexandria, Va.: Association for Supervision and Curriculum Development.

Newman, L., and S. L. Buka. 1997. *Every Child a Learner: Reducing Risks of Learning Impairment during Pregnancy and Infancy*. Denver, Colo.: Education Commission of the States.

O'Keefe, J., and L. Nadel. 1978. *The Hippocampus As a Cognitive Map*. Oxford: Clarendon.

Rose, C. P., and M. Nicholl. 1997. *Accelerated Learning for the 21st Century.* New York: Delacourt.

Sprenger, M. 1999. *Learning and Memory: The Brain in Action.* Alexandria, Va.: Association for Supervision and Curriculum Development.

Taylor, G. R. 1997. *Curriculum Strategies: Social Skills Intervention for Young African-American Males.* Westport, Conn.: Greenwood.

————. 1998. *Curriculum Strategies for Teaching Social Skills to the Disabled: Dealing with Inappropriate Behaviors.* Springfield, Ill.: Thomas.

Wheatley, M. C. 1992. *Leadership and the New Science: Learning about Organization from an Orderly Universe.* San Francisco, Calif.: Berrett-Koehler.

Wolfe, P., and R. Brandt. 1998. "What Do We Know from Brain Research?" *Educational Leadership* 56 (3): 8–13.

Wurtman, J. J. 1986. *Managing Your Mind and Mood through Food.* New York: Perennial Library.

CHAPTER 16

Strategies for Improving Memory

The study of memory can be traced to the pioneer work of Hermann Ebbinghaus, who used more than 600 nonsense syllables (Ebbinghaus, 1885/1964). Using himself as the subject, he recognized in early experiments that associations made with words assisted him in learning new words. He designed a study to control the effects of associations by using nonsense syllables.

The results were plotted on learning curves that indicated the amount of information retained as well as forgotten over time. Almost half of the initial list of nonsense syllables were forgotten after twenty-four hours, and six days later he recalled only one fourth of the initial list of nonsense syllables. Ebbinghaus's experiments have assisted psychologists in verifying that: (1) items are more quickly learned when they are meaningful (Cofer, 1971); (2) items that can be pronounced are easier to learn (Underwood and Schulz, 1960); (3) concrete items are easier to learn than abstract ones (Gorman, 1961); and (4) visual images appear to improve the ease in which items can be learned. Ebbinghaus's experiments laid the foundation for future research and experimentations in memory research.

MEMORY DEFINED

There are many definitions of memory; however, for the purpose of this text, "memory" is the ability of an individual to retrieve previously learned information or skills. This definition correlates with one advanced by Hintzman, who states that "one assumption of an intuitive understanding of memory is that if a memory is to influence behavior, it has to be retrievable" (Hintzman, 1990). The three types of memory to be discussed in this chapter are: sensory, short-term, and long-term. A detailed discussion of memory is outside the scope of this chapter. Refer to Klein for specific details concerning memory (Klein, 1996).

SENSORY MEMORY

For a while, some people thought that memory might be in a modality of its own, separate from the various sensory, motor, and cognitive modalities. Lesion studies have completely failed to discover an area of the brain that is the repository of memories that are not also intimately concerned with perceptual, motor, or cognitive aspects of functioning. There is, however, one exception to this general statement; namely, a few human neurological patients have a rather specific loss of the ability to consolidate new long-term memories, while their old long-term memories remain relatively intact with other aspects of sensory, motor, and cognitive functioning (Scoville and Milner, 1957; Milner, 1966). Thus, there may be a special area of the brain concerned largely or exclusively with a consolidation process. However, the actual shortage of both long-term and short-term memories must be considered to be distributed throughout the various sensory, motor, and cognitive modalities of the brain.

Memory begins at the sensory organs, which receive and transform energy such as light, heat, and sound into electrical nerve impulses. The encoded information is filed and stored for later use; when we have need of it, we can search the complex filing system (memory) and retrieve specific information. Memory is generally described in terms of its age— short-term memory is for recent events, and long-term memory for remote events. The memory process is divided into two phases, a reverberating circuit for short-term memory, and some form of permanent change in the synaptic connections for long-term memory.

Research conducted by Paivio and Csapo provides evidence that the verbal memory modality is specialized to learn and remember sequentially ordered material, while the visual–spatial memory modality is specialized to learn and remember nonsequential material (Paivio and Csapo, 1969). Visual sensory input is surely primary for the visual–spatial modality, and auditory sensory input is at least developmentally primary in establishing traces in the verbal modality. Conrad contends that even in short-term memory for visually presented verbal materials there is often storage in a verbal phonetic modality, instead of, or in addition to, storage in visual memory (Conrad, 1964). In the second place, auditory sensory input apparently can lead to storage in the visual–spatial memory modality. Paivio and Okovita have repeatedly shown that the establishment of long-term memory traces in paired-associate and other learning tasks is facilitated by using words with high visual imagery (Paivio and Okovita, 1971).

SHORT-TERM MEMORY

Lefrançois writes that another way of looking at sensory memory is that it precedes attention; when an individual attends to stimulus, it passes into short-term memory (Lefrançois, 2000). Sensory memory refers to a phenomenon that lasts milliseconds; short-term memory is a phenomenon that lasts seconds—not hours or even minutes. Specifically, short-term memory refers to the awareness and recall of items that will no longer be available as soon as the individual stops rehearsing them.

Short-term memory, according to Baddeley, Barkley, and Cowan, is a component of memory in which the active processing of information occurs (Baddeley, 1996; Barkley, 1996; Cowan, 1995). It determines what information will be attended to the sensory mechanisms, and then saves the information to be processed later.

Short-term memory makes information available for a short period of time, approximately five to twenty seconds if information is not rehearsed. Short-term memory is frequently referred to as working memory (Calfee, 1981). Chunking has been proven to assist short-term memory.

Chunking

According to Miller (1956), the effect on the number of alternatives on short-term memory are extremely small. Memory span appears to be limited to a certain number of events or chunks. Chunking is an organization process where two or more pieces of information are combined. Information in the chunks appears to be independent of the amount of information present. Information can be organized in a variety of ways to give meaning (Ormrod, 1999). An individual can improve his/her memory by recoding a sequence of events into a sequence of fewer chunks, with each chunk covering information concerning the occurrence of several events. Miller cites an experiment that showed that students could greatly increase their memory span for binary digits (i.e., sequences of ones, and zeros) by learning to recode binary digits into octal digits according to the following rules: $000 = 0$; $001 = 1$; $010 = 2$; $011 = 3$; $100 = 4$; $101 = 5$; $110 = 6$; $111 = 7$. This recoding scheme maps three events into one event, thereby, reducing the number of chunks while preserving all of the information in the original sequence. Memory span almost triples using such a recording procedure.

The chunking process allows one to achieve as great a difference in representation of highly similar concepts as is desired. Phenomena consistent with a chunking process abound in the area of human memory. First, there are the sometimes dramatic improvements in memorizing efficiency that can be achieved by learning a recoding scheme to reduce the number of chunks that must be learned.

Research findings show that sentences are easier to remember in both short- and long-term memory than comparably long lists of random words (Coleman, 1963; Marks and Jack, 1952). Indeed, these studies show a gradual increase in the ease of memorizing material as one increases the degree of approximation of a random sequence of words to a grammatical sentence.

Coding

"Coding" refers to the internal representation in memory of our knowledge of the world and to the processes by which representation is achieved. Coding is concerned with what is learned and how this is represented in memory. The capacity aspects of coding are concerned with the logical structure of memory, what its components are, and how they are organized into a system (Clark and Paivio, 1991).

Let us assume for the moment that all human beings possess certain basic associative-memory and concept-learning processes. Even if the parameters for these basic memory processes are the same for two individuals the degree to which one uses these processes and the types of associations or concepts formed depend critically on the strategy the individual chooses to adopt (Klein, 1996). In the investigation of the memory capacity, it is desirable to attempt to control these coding strategies, but one can only control them if he or she has some idea of what they are. Coding strategies include such mechanisms as selective attention, relating current materials to previously learned materials, verbal mnemonics, visual-image mnemonics, representing order information by group and serial position labeling (Clark and Paivio, 1991; Mayer and Moreno, 1998).

Levels of Processing

Craik and Lockhart (1972) implied that loss from short-term memory involves several levels of processing information. They indicated that the main difference between short- and long-term memory involves how information is processed. The following is an example of processing, a word may be processed in terms of its physical appearance, which is a low level of processing, or processed in terms of its sound, a deeper level of processing. According to Lefrançois (2000) there are several theories to explain why short-term memory is limited to only a few items and why forgetting occurs. Decay theory holds that memory traces vanish quickly with the passage of time if rehearsal does not take place. Displacement theory, according to Miller, indicates that there are a limited number of slots to be filled in short-term memory and that incoming information displaces old information (Miller, 1956). Interference theory advances the notion that previous learning might somehow interfere with short-term memory. None of the listed theories, however, are completely accepted by researchers. Also, researchers still need to research sufficiently the impact of and the relationship of forgetting in reference to short-term memory.

LONG-TERM MEMORY

Several researchers have stated that long-term memory is that part of the memory system that retains information for a long period of time. Most information stored in long-term memory can be easily retrieved, while some may not be brought to the conscious level due to physical, mental, or developmental problems (Tulving, 1991, 1993; Ellis, 1994; Graf and Mason, 1993; Schacter, 1993).

Characteristics of Long-Term Memory

Since the early 1950s, researchers have attempted to characterize long-term memory. Inhelder and Piaget's research supported the notion that long-term memory is influenced by understanding (Inhelder and Piaget,

1958). Young children were instructed to draw lines indicating the level of water in tilted jars. Since the children could not transfer the concept of water in tilted jars, they could not correctly draw the level of water in the jars until the tilted jars were horizontal. Bower states that some things are more easily remembered than others (Bower, 1981). Concrete information that is of interest and meaningful is retained longer.

Smith and Graesser, and Schacter, Norman, and Koutstaal concur that long-term memory is generative rather than simply reproductive (Smith and Graesser, 1981; Schacter, Norman, and Koutstaal, 1998). Long-term memory is not always error-free from distortions, because it is significantly influenced by preconceived beliefs about some phenomenon. Goldman and Seamon's experiment demonstrated that long-term memory is highly stable, unlike short-term memory (Goldman and Seamon, 1992).

THEORETICAL PHASES OF MEMORY

Many investigators of human memory assume that there are three theoretical phases of memory—acquisition, storage, and retrieval—corresponding to the three operationally distinguishable phases of a memory experiment—learning, retention, and usage. In the case of short-term memory, these three theoretical phases may indeed be sufficient to describe the dynamics of memory. However, in the case of long-term memory, there is some evidence favoring a consolidation phase of the memory process, in addition and interpolated between, the acquisition and storage phases (Squire, Knowlton, and Musen, 1993).

Acquisition

Acquisition refers to the phase of memory in which an individual is actively studying the material to be learning and laying down potential short-term and long-term memory traces. In the case of short-term memory, these traces are presumed to be consolidated almost immediately, and there may be no necessity to assume that consolidation is a separate phase from acquisition. In the case of long-term memory, however, these potential memory traces may have to be converted by the consolidation process into retrievable memory traces. All of the coding and recoding aspects of learning and memory are assumed to take place during the acquisition process. It is here, when an individual is consciously considering the material, that he/she can think of a mnemonic or visual image to aid in the memory or chunk the separate elements of a list into a single element or meaningful phrase (Groeger, 1997).

Consolidation

The consolidation phase of the memory process is assumed to be an unconscious process in which the potential long-term memory traces, established during acquisition, are converted into a stable usable form. Note that consolidation is not being thought of as a logical recoding type of change in the memory trace. Any and all recoding is assumed to take place during acquisitions and is assumed to be a conscious process. Consolidation is assumed to be a relatively automatic, unconscious process that may be affected by arousal, certain drugs, and so on in its speed or extent of operation, but nothing during the consolidation process is assumed to change the qualitative nature of the established memory trace.

Consolidation of long-term memory appears to take place during the first minute after learning, primarily the first ten to thirty seconds after learning. There are a number of different studies that indicate approximately the same time course for consolidation of long-term memory (Keane, et al., 1997; Monti, Gabrieli, Wilson, and Beckett, 1997).

Storage

During acquisition and consolidation, the memory trace is assumed to be protected to some extent from various degradative forces. At the end of the acquisition and consolidation phases, the memory trace enters the storage phase in which it becomes subject to these degradative forces. "Storage interference" refers to a reduction in the strength of previously established memory traces as a result of intervening activity. By contrast, "retrieval interference" refers to a reduction in the probability of correct recall as a result of establishing competing memory traces during the retention interval, but not necessarily weakening previously established memory traces (Hinrichs, 1970).

In the case of long-term memory, the degree of storage interference caused by interpolated activity is greater for interpolated activity that involves material that is similar to the previously learned or processed memory in the retention interval and the difficulty of such learning or processing (Wickelgren, 1970b).

The storage interference properties of short-term and long-term memory are different, but both types of memory do show storage inference effects and cannot be explained by a passive temporal decay process. Wickelgren shows that this theory of storage in long-term memory accounts for the form and relative decay rates of a large variety of different long-term retention functions obtained for delays from one minute to two years for a variety of different subjects and a variety of different types of verbal materials learned under a variety of different conditions (Wickelgren, 1971).

Retrieval

Retrieval is the process by which an individual finds information he/she has previously stored in memory so that he/she can use it again (Ormrod, 1999). Sternberg writes that retrieval of information from working memory depends to a large degree on how much information is stored and organized in the working memory (Sternberg, 1996). He further articulates that retrieval of information from working memory involves a process of successively scanning all the information of working memory until the desired information is located. Retrieval is easier when one is relaxed rather than anxious about receiving information.

Much of our everyday retrieval of memory traces involves a complex sequence of recognition, recall, and recency judgments. Thus, for example, in attempting to recall someone's name, we try to go directly from a visual image of the person to his/her name. If that fails, we may attempt to generate alternative names, testing each one via recognition memory. A common scheme is to go through the alphabet trying to use the first letter in conjunction with various information about the individual.

Factors that affect retrieval include distractions. To keep from remembering unpleasant events, people have the ability to prevent recall by way of distraction. Repression also can influence retrieval of information. Some individuals with emotional problems may be capable of preventing recall of unpleasant memories. There are many reasons why individuals may not be able to retrieve information at a particular time, due to a variety of physical, mental, social, and emotional disabilities. Specific treatments and techniques are available to assist these individuals. The reader is referred to books that discuss the psychology of exceptional individuals.

Rehearsal

Through rehearsal, information can be stored in long-term memory for a considerable length of time (Atkinson and Shiffrin, 1971). Several research studies show that individuals remember rehearsed information better than unrehearsed information (Nelson, 1977; Rundus and Atkinson, 1971; Shaffer and Shiffrin, 1972).

Rehearsal is another mechanism by which goals can influence learning and memory. Rehearsal aids both short-term and long-term retention by increasing the degree of learning of the material being rehearsed (Craik and Watkins, 1973; Klazky, 1975; Craik and Tulving, 1975). In addition, rehearsal aids short-term memory by periodically renewing the short-term trace, thereby effectively preventing decay for small amounts of material that are rehearsed.

Intuitively, imaging has usually been considered less effective in trace maintenance than rehearsal, but there is really little definite evidence on this matter. Findings by Conrad indicate that visually presented sequential material may be translated into a verbal short-term trace (Conrad, 1964). This suggests that the visual rehearsal process is used by most people, but, of course, it does not rule out the possibility of some beneficial visual rehearsal process. However, Shaffer and Shiffrin increased exposure time in their experiment to improve the degree of learning for pictures, since blank time for visual rehearsal following a picture has no effect on recognition memory for the picture. Their results provide rather strong evidence against the possibility of a visual analogue to verbal rehearsal. Thus, rehearsal may be a unique property of the verbal memory modality. Regardless, rehearsal is apparently not a property of the visual–spatial memory modality. This lends some support to the notion that rehearsal is in some way a consequence of a special correspondence between auditory and articulatory speech representatives.

ASSOCIATIVE VERSUS NONASSOCIATIVE MEMORY

Two basic types of memory structures have been proposed as models for human memory: associative and nonassociative. In an associative memory, each event or concept has a unique or relatively unique internal representative, and internal representatives have different degrees of association to each other depending on how frequently they have been contiguously activated in the past. An associative memory uses a single element or a small group of elements in the system to represent any concept or set of concepts.

Thus, an important defining property of an associative memory is parsimony of representation of concepts. The parsimony comes in because time is largely irrelevant to defining the internal representative of an event. No matter what time that event occurs, there are relatively unique internal representatives for the concepts cued by the event. In an associative memory, the representation of order is accomplished by having connections between the internal representatives whose strengths are incremented every time two representatives are activated close to each other in time.

By contrast, in a nonassociative memory there is an ordered set of locations (cells, registers, boxes, and so on) into which the internal representative of any event or concept is stored in order. A tape recorder is a good example of a nonassociative memory. As each successive sound occurs, a pattern representing that sound is impressed on a successive portion of the magnetic recording tape.

In a nonassociative memory, the representation of an event is by a particular pattern that stands for the event being impressed on any location in memory. Thus, there can be numerous representations of a single event or concept occurring at different times in the individual's life.

The representation of the order of events in a nonassociative memory is usually assumed to occur by virtue of having a fixed order in which one fills the locations in memory. Thus, a tape recorder fills successive sections of the magnetic tape in a single, linear order preserving the information concerning the order of the events. The representation of events in a nonassociative memory is said to be location-addressable, because one can go directly to a particular location, but cannot know what he/she will find in that location. This applies to both the initial acquisition and the retrieval of a memory trace. Most human conceptual memory is probably associative. At least one type of human sensory memory, namely, visual, is known to have very short-term sensory memory and is probably nonassociative (Wickelgren, 1970b).

LONG-TERM IS ASSOCIATIVE MEMORY

Existing evidence overwhelmingly favors the hypothesis that long-term memory is associative rather than nonassociative (Holyoak and Spellman,

1993; Wickelgren, 1971). First, long-term memory has an enormously large capacity. There must be hundreds of thousands, perhaps millions, of associations between events or concepts stored with reasonable strength in long-term memory. These associationistic models are basically cognitive models. A nonassociative memory with a serial search process would, on average, have to search half of all the locations in the storage system looking for the cue word in order to come up with the correct response word.

Second, the major advantage of a nonassociative memory is that it could be extremely precise in its temporal resolution of events. A nonassociative memory might tell you the exact time at which different events occurred, and surely would store the exact order, frequency, spacing, and so on of events. A number of studies indicate that human beings do have some ability to judge the recency, temporal ordering, spacing, and frequency of events (Klein, 1996; Lefrançois, 2000; Ormrod, 1999).

It is not at all obvious why a nonassociative memory should have recorded perfectly the existence of the events, but somehow scrambled or otherwise lost the memory for the order of the events, when this seems to be the primary advantage of using a nonassociative storage system in the first place.

MEMORY IN CHILDREN

A number of additional considerations are applicable to the study of memory in young children who have and do not have disabilities. In the first place, the sessions must be relatively short, which means that the amount that can be learned in one session is correspondingly reduced. In paired-associate learning, the list of pairs must be short, perhaps on the order of four or five pairs for a six-year-old child. The total length of session for a six-year-old should probably not exceed twenty or thirty minutes, and the shorter the session the better. In addition to the desirability of short total sessions, only relatively short periods of sustained attention can be demanded of a young child. Thus, a continuous learning task longer than thirty minutes may be unreasonable for even normal children below the ages of eight to ten.

Children often require special procedures to maintain the proper level of motivation. A child may have a high degree of motivation to interact with the experimenter, but not in the manner required by the experiment. The child may have high motivation, but his/her motivation is inappropriate for the task. It may be necessary to satisfy the child's curiosity and desire to get to know the experimenter for a short period of time prior to beginning the experiment. The courses of action in this include changing the experimental procedure to make it more interesting, make it less difficult, or introducing social or other types of reinforcement.

The material to be learned must be carefully analyzed for its degree of familiarity to the child. A child has a vastly smaller vocabulary than an adult, so if one is to use familiar words, the experimenter must limit him/herself to a much smaller total vocabulary of items. In general, for young children concrete objects tend to be good materials for memory experiments, followed by pictures, and then familiar words. In some cases, a child may have a word in his/her spoken repertoire but not yet to be able to read the word, even though he/she can read simple books (Craik and Lockhart, 1972).

Many of the differences found in learning or memory as a function of age can be attributed to differences in reading, recoding, rehearsal, or learning strategy capability, each of which varies sharply as a function of age. Once these factors have been eliminated from a memory experiment, it remains to be seen what, if any, differences remain in the acquisition, consolidation, or decay of either short- or long-term memory. Research findings have found that a fast rate of presentation will minimize the difference in short-term memory span as a function of age (Murray and Roberts, 1968). Fast rates of presentation presumably minimize the differences between children and adults because they provide less opportunity for rehearsal and recoding at which adults are greatly superior to children.

THEORIES OF FORGETTING

Major theories of forgetting support the notion that forgetting is simply not being able to bring information to the conscious level when needed. The concept does not imply a complete loss of memory. Wixted and Ebbesen imply that over time, people remember less and less about the events they have experienced and the information they have acquired. Individuals tend to retain information that has utility and meaning to them (Wixted and Ebbesen, 1991). According to Anderson and Schooler and Reisberg, many of the things we learn have little use to us later, and we rarely need to remember things exactly as we originally experienced them (Anderson and Schooler, 1991; Reisberg, 1997). Major theories of forgetting have been adequately covered in Klein and Ormrod, so they will not be elaborated in this chapter. The reader is referred to these two sources for specific information relevant to the theories (Klein, 1996; Ormrod, 1999).

REMEMBERING

Lefrançois states that psychology has identified three main strategies for promoting remembering: rehearsal (which has been discussed earlier in the chapter), elaboration, and organization (Lefrançois, 2000). These cognitive processes are necessary in remembering information.

Elaboration

Elaboration involves adding details to information received by adding minute details. The collaborateness of memory encoding refers to the extent to which events are related or organized with other events. An excellent example to the concept of elaboration was advanced in a study conducted by Bradshaw and Anderson (Bradshaw and Anderson, 1982). They gave subjects a sentence to remember: "The fat man read the sign." Subjects who elaborated on the sentence by adding, "The fat man read the sign warning of thin ice," recalled the information more effectively than the subjects who did not elaborate.

Organization

Individuals must organize information to facilitate learning. Earlier in the chapter, I addressed the role of chunking in organizing information. I mentioned that chunking places or organizes learned information into related categories or units. An example of chunking is using letters from the alphabet to form words.

Coding is another way of organizing information. Coding involves transforming information into new forms. The example given by Klein supports our understanding of coding (Klein, 1996). He states that persons using Morse code change letters into dots and dashes to transmit a message.

Another essential strategy for organizing information is the formation of associations. Associations imply that a relationship exists between information or events. Individuals can form associations on similar or different events. Associations can assist individuals in organizing, classifying, recalling, and memorizing events and information when relationships exist.

RECONSTRUCTING THE PAST

Long-term memory retains information for a considerable length of time. While the bulk of stored information can be easily retrieved, not all of it is retrievable. Environmental, physical, and social factors may affect the retrievable process. Generally, long-term memory is stable, recallable, generative, and associationistic. Characteristics of long-term memory contain the same factors as short-term memory. The major difference is that long-term memory is longer in all of the characteristics.

SUMMARY

Memory problems of all kinds tend to increase with age. Mild deficits can start in the forties and fifties, and become more obvious in the sixties and seventies (Schacter, Norman, and Koutstaal, 1998; Monti et al., 1997). Researchers alluded that people do not simply learn information: they either remember or forget it. No part of the brain is responsible for creating, starting, and retrieving memories. Ebbinghaus discovered that different parts of the brain hold on to selective types of experiences. These experiences are coordinated by a special memory system in the brain.

Not all stored information can be retrieved, as Ebbinghaus's experiments proved. The memory of some experiences is not always accurate. The role of forgetting can influence the accuracy of information. Environmental, social, and physical factors during retrieval can affect short- and long-term memory and can lead to a change in the memory of past experiences.

The most important and difficult consideration when studying memory in young children is to provide instructions regarding a memory task that a child can understand. In general, it has been found that recognition memory instructions are harder for young children to understand than recall memory instructions. Thus, a memory span test that, from a theoretical viewpoint, is far more complex than a recognition memory task, is vastly easier for a child to understand than a three-phase recognition memory task. This is extremely annoying, but it is a fact that one must live with. Telling children to repeat what you say is something that, for one reason or another, they understand at a very early age. By contrast, a delayed matching task, which is in essence what "yes-no" recognition memory is, is a higher-level concept that children attain only somewhat later in life.

Memory and learning can be improved by practice, repetition, rehearsal, elaboration, and organization. Strategies for improving memory include games, rhymes, using concrete objects, counting objects, using letters of the alphabet, rote memory activities, and posing questions. Memory is short in duration, unless there is practice. Short-term memory is frequently called working or active memory. Characteristics of short-term memory include sensory register (stimuli received through the five senses), capacity (this is very limited for storing information), form of storage (which is mostly stored in the auditory channel), and duration (which is very short recall).

BIBLIOGRAPHY

Anderson, J. R., and L. J. Schooler. 1991. "Reflections of the Environment in Memory." *Psychological Science* 2:396–408.

Atkinson, R. C., and R. M. Shiffrin. 1971. "The Control of Short-Term Memory." *Scientific American* 225 (2): 82–90.

Baddeley, A. D. 1986. *Working Memory.* Oxford: Clarendon.

Barkley, R. A. 1996. "Linkages between Attention and Executive Functions." In *Attention, Memory and Executive Function*, ed. G. R. Lyon and N. A. Krasnegor. Baltimore, Md.: Brookes.

Bower, G. H. 1981. "Mood and Memory." *American Psychologist* 36:129–148.

Bradshaw, G. L., and J. R. Anderson. 1982. "Elaborative Encoding As an Explanation of Levels of Processing." *Journal of Verbal Learning and Verbal Behavior* 21:65–74.

Calfee, R. 1981. "Cognitive Psychology and Educational Practice." In *Review of Research in Education*, vol. 9, ed. D. C. Berliner. Washington, D.C.: American Educational Research Association.

Clark, J. M., and A. Paivio. 1991. "Dual Coding Theory and Education." *Educational Psychology Review* 3 (3): 149–210.

Cofer, C. 1971. "Properties of Verbal Materials and Verbal Learning." In *Woodworth and Schlosberg's Experimental Psychology*, ed. J. Kling and L. Riggs. New York: Holt, Rinehart, and Winston.

Coleman, E. B. 1963. "Approximations to English." *American Journal of Psychology* 76:239–247.

Conrad, R. 1964. "Acoustic Confusions in Immediate Memory." *British Journal of Psychology* 55:75–84.

Cowan, N. 1995. *Attention and Memory: An Integrated Framework.* New York: Oxford University Press.

Craik, F. M., and R. S. Lockhart. 1972. "Levels of Processing: A Framework for Memory Research." *Journal of Verbal Learning and Verbal Behavior* 11:671–684.

Craik, F. M., and E. Tulving. 1975. "Dept. of Processing and the Retention of Words in Episodic Memory." *Journal of Experimental Psychology: General* 104:268–294.

Craik, F. M., and M. J. Watkins. 1973. "The Role of Rehearsal in Short-Term Memory." *Journal of Verbal Learning and Verbal Behavior* 12:598–607.

Ebbinghaus, H. 1885. Memory: A Contribution to the Experimental Psychology. H. A. Ruger and C. E. Bussenius, trans. New York: Dover.

Ellis, N. C., ed. 1994. *Implicit and Explicit Learning of Language.* London: Academic.

Goldman, W. P., and J. G. Seamon. 1992. "Very Long-Term Memory for Odors: Retention of Odor-Name Associations." *American Journal of Psychology* 105:549–563.

Gorman, A. M. 1961. "Recognition Memory for Nouns As a Function of Abstractness and Frequency." *Journal of Experimental Psychology* 61:23–29.

Graf, P., and M. E. Mason, eds. 1993. *Implicit Memory: New Directions in Cognition, Development, and Neuro-psychology.* Hillsdale, N.J.: Erlbaum.

Groeger, J. A. 1997. *Memory and Remembering: Everyday Memory in Context.* New York: Addison Wesley.

Hinrichs, J. A. 1970. "Memory-Strength Theory for Judgement of Recency." *Psychological Review* 72:223–233.

Hintzman, D. L. 1990. "Human Learning and Memory: Connections and Dissociations." *Annual Review of Psychology* 41:109–139.

Hintzman, D. L., and R. A. Block. 1970. "Memory Judgments and the Effects of Spacing." *Journal of Verbal Learning and Verbal Behavior* 9:561–566.

———. 1971. "Repetition and Memory: Evidence for a Multiple-Trace Hypothesis." *Journal of Experimental Psychology* 88:297–306.

Holyoak, K. J., and B. A. Spellman. 1993. "Thinking." *Annual Review of Psychology* 44:265–315.

Inhelder, B., and J. Piaget. 1958. *The Growth of Logical Thinking from Childhood to Adolescence.* New York: Basic.

Keane, M. M., J. D. Gabrieli, L. Monti, and D. A. Fleischman. 1997. "Intact and Impaired Conceptual Memory Processes in Amnesia." *Neuropsychology* 11:59–69.

Klazky, R. L. 1975. *Human Memory.* San Francisco, Calif.: Freeman.

Klein, S. B. 1996. *Learning: Principles and Applications.* 3rd ed. New York: McGraw-Hill.

Lefrançois, G. R. 2000. *Theories of Human Learning: What the Old Man Said.* 4th ed. Pacific Grove, Calif.: Brooks/Cole.

Marks, M. R., and O. Jack. 1952. "Verbal Context and Memory Span for Meaningful Material." *American Journal of Psychology* 65:298–300.

Mayer, R. E., and R. Moreno. 1998. "A Split-Attention Effect and Multimedia Learning: Evidence for Dual Processing Systems in Working Memory." *Journal of Educational Psychology* 90 (2): 312–320.

Miller, G. A. 1956. "The Magical Number Seven, Plus or Minus Two: Some Limits on Our Capacity for Processing Information." *Psychology Review* 63:81–97.

Milner, B. 1966. "Amnesia Following Operation on the Temporal Lobes." In *Amnesia,* ed. C. W. M. Whitty and O. L. Zangwill. London: Butterworths.

Monti, L. A., J. D. Gabrieli, R. S. Wilson, and L. A. Beckett. 1997. "Sources of Priming in Text Reading: Intact Implicit Memory for New Associations in Older Adults and in Patients with Alzheimer's Disease." *Psychology and Aging* 12:536–547.

Murray, D. J., and B. Roberts. 1968. "Visual and Auditory Presentation, Presentation Rate, and Short-Term Memory in Children." *British Journal of Psychology* 59:119–125.

Nelson, T. O. (1977). "Repetition and Depth of Processing." *Journal of Verbal Learning and Verbal Behavior* 16:151–171.

Ormrod, J. E. (1999). *Human Learning.* 3rd ed. Columbus, Ohio: Merrill.

Paivio, A., and K. Csapo. 1969. "Concrete Image and Verbal Memory Codes." *Journal of Experimental Psychology* 80:279–285.

Paivio, A., and H. W. Okovita. 1971. "Word Imagery Modalities and Associative Learning in Blind and Sighted Subjects." *Journal of Verbal Learning and Verbal Behavior* 10:506–510.

Reisberg, D. 1997. *Cognition: Exploring the Science of the Mind.* New York: Norton.

Rundus, D. 1971. "Analysis of Rehearsal Processes in Force Recall." *Journal of Experimental Psychology* 89:63–77.

Rundus, D., and R. C. Atkinson. 1971. "Rehearsal Processes in Free Recall: A Procedure for Direct Observation." *Journal of Verbal Learning and Verbal Behavior* 9:99–105.

Schacter, D. L. 1993. "Understanding Implicit Memory: A Cognitive Neuroscience Approach." In *Theories of Memory,* ed. A. F. Collins, S. E. Gathercole, M. A. Conway, and P. E. Morris. Hove, UK: Erlbaum.

Schacter, D. L., K. A. Norman, and W. Koutstaal. 1998. "The Cognitive Neuroscience of Constructive Memory." *Annual Review of Psychology* 49:289–318.

Scoville, W. B., and B. Milner. 1957. "Loss of Recent Memory after Bilateral Hippocampal Lesions." *Journal of Neurosurgery and Psychiatry* 12:60–65.

Shaffer, W. O., and R. M. Shiffrin. 1972. "Rehearsal and Storage of Visual Information." *Journal of Experimental Psychology* 22:292–296.

Smith, D. A., and A. C. Graesser. 1981. "Memory for Actions in Scripted Activities As a Function of Typicality, Retention Interval, and Retrieval Task." *Memory and Cognition* 9:550–559.

Squire, L. R., B. Knowlton, and G. Musen. 1993. "The Structure and Organization of Memory." *Annual Review of Psychology* 44:453–495.

Sternberg, S. 1996. "High-Speed Scanning in Human Memory." *Science* 153:652–654.

Tulving, E. 1991. "Concepts in Human Memory." In *Memory: Organization and Locus of Change*, ed. L. R. Squire, N. M. Weinberger, G. Lynch, and J. L. McGaugh. New York: Oxford University Press.

———. 1993. "What Is Episodic Memory?" *Current Directions in Psychological Science* 2:67–70.

Underwood, B. J., and R. W. Schulz. 1960. *Meaningful and Verbal Learning*. Philadelphia, Pa.: Lippincott.

Wickelgren, W. A. 1970a. "Multitrace Strength Theory." In *Models of Human Memory*, ed. D. A. Norman. New York: Academic.

———. 1970b. "Time, Interference, and Rate of Presentation in Short-Term Recognition Memory for Items." *Journal of Mathematical Psychology* 7:219–235.

———. 1971. "Trace Resistance and the Decay of Long-Term Memory." Invited address, Division 3, American Psychological Association Convention. May 1971.

———. 1991. "Human Learning and Memory." *Annual Review of Psychology* 32:21–52.

Wixted, J. T., and E. B. Ebbesen. 1991. "On the Form of Forgetting." *Psychological Science* 2:409–405.

CHAPTER 17

Some Concluding Remarks

The psychology of human learning and behavior is basically concerned with how learners learn under different situations. I clarified this concept in chapter 1 by indicating that learning is a change in performance through conditions of activity, practice, and experience. Many factors affect the learning process such as physical disability, biochemical factors, habits, attitudes, interests, and social and emotional adjustments to name but a few. Frequently, these factors must be modified in order to improve learning. Learning is a life-long process and the permanent effects of it may not be immediately apparent; sometimes, the effects of learning are latent. Many psychologists have contributed to the study of learning since the later part of the nineteenth century. Wilhelm Wundt is considered by many to be the father of psychology. Other psychologists such as Ivan P. Pavlov, Edward L. Thorndike, John B. Watson, Edward C. Tolman, Burrhus F. Skinner, and Albert Bandura made their impact on the field of learning theory during this time frame. The major impact of their works with the exception of Tolman are addressed in chapters 3, 4, and 5.

CONTRASTING VIEWS IN LEARNING THEORY

The two major views of learning are expressed by behavioristic and cognitive psychologists. Views expressed by these psychologists are diametrically opposite to each other.

According to behavioristic psychologists, learning theory is based on observable behaviors reinforced with rewards. In their view, the mind has limited applications in human behavior and learning. Behaviorists believe that their principles can be applied to all organisms. Cognitive psychologists refer to these views of learning. Chiefly among them are Tolman,

Jean Piaget, Lev Vygotsky, and several other Gestalt psychologists. An overview of these theorists may be found in chapter 9. According to these theories, learning is too complex to be relegated to stimulus–response behavior. They advocate that human behavior involves processes such as problem solving, decision making, perceptions, information processing, attitudes, emotions, judgment, memory, and motivation. Cognitive models emphasize these unobservable mental processes in assessing how individuals learn (Amsel, 1989; Newell, 1990; Thomas, 1992, 1996).

Both of the major theories of learning support the role of memory and motivation in learning. On the one hand, cognitive models tend to emphasize these traits more than behavioral models. Behavioral models tend to limit memory in learning. On the other hand, cognitive models tend to minimize the notion that students learn only because they are rewarded, reinforced, or punished. Memory models reflect the cognitive view of learning more than behavioristic models. Both major theories have strategies that educators may employ (refer to chapters 2, 3, 4, 9, 11, 12, 13, and 14).

The major two learning theories remained separated until the mid-twentieth century. It was the work of Bandura that combined them (Bandura, 1977). He integrated the models by combining environmental and cognitive factors into studying human behavior through observation and modeling techniques (refer to chapter 5 for details on Bandura's social learning theory).

IMPORTANCE OF LEARNING THEORIES TO EDUCATIONAL PRACTICES

Theories reviewed in this text have covered several decades of experimentation. It should be readily concluded from this text that no one learning theory is comprehensive enough to cover all aspects of human learning and behavior. Theories can bias our understanding of learning by producing research findings in conflict with our beliefs. Individually, each theory has made its contribution to learning. Collectively, the importance of theories in educational practices may be summed up by the following.

1. Theories provide us with information relevant to the learning process by reporting research studies that can be applied to instructional procedures in the classroom.

2. Theories assist educators in determining areas of the curriculum that should be investigated. Since the introduction of new and innovative strategies is usually based on some theoretical concept, educators should test these concepts and discover practical ways of applying them in the classroom through action research methods.

3. Educators can apply information from learning theories to design learning environments to facilitate learning. This is particularly important for arranging learning environments for children with specific types of disabilities and behaviors.

COMMONALITIES AMONG LEARNING THEORIES

Most learning activities proceed from the simple to the complex, from the known to the unknown, from the concrete to the abstract. Some of the learning theories outlined and discussed in this text follow the aforementioned principles. Real and concrete experiences, which have practical application to the real world, should be the foundation for developing educational units. A preponderance of theories in both behavioristic and cognitive learning theories supports this view. Learning experiences should move from the concrete to various levels of abstractions.

Motivation, which is viewed as important by most learning theories, is important in the learning process. Without motivation, learning will not precede in an orderly and systematic manner. Students who are motivated appear to perform better academically. They generally have higher activity levels, are goal directed, and are persistent in completing assigned or designated tests. Educators should be aware of the values of motivation in learning. Ormrod, Baddeley and Hitch, and Hergenhahn and Olson outline strategies that educators can apply in improving extrinsic and intrinsic motivation in students (Ormrod, 1999; Baddeley and Hitch, 1974; Hergenhahn and Olson, 1997).

Sprenger writes that brain research is not new but the application to instruction use in the classroom is (Sprenger, 1999). She further states that there are hundreds of theories on brain research, but they are not applicable to practical application in the classroom. Presently, neuroscientists are exploring ways to apply brain research to the classroom. I discussed some of this research in chapter 15.

Learning, brain research, and memory are integral components linked together. The various types of memories explained in chapter 16 work in conjunction with the brain. Neuroscientists have discovered that there are storage areas in the brain that control the various memory functions. According to Sprenger, research shows that memory lanes begin in specific brain areas (Sprenger, 1999). These lanes contain the file in which memory is stored. Educators may employ memory strategies outlined in chapter 16 to assist students in the learning and memory process.

REQUIREMENTS OF AN ADEQUATE THEORY OF LEARNING FOR TEACHERS

According to Lindgren, if a theory of learning is to aid educators in becoming effective teachers, it must accomplish the following:

1. It must help us understand all the processes of human learning. It also applies to the entire range of skills, concepts, attitudes, habits, and personality traits that may be acquired by the human organism. It is our view that no one learning theory is comprehensive enough to cover all of the aforementioned processes. Consequently, educators must abstract from several learning theories those processes that best fit the individual needs for their classes.
2. It must extend our understanding of the conditions or forces that stimulate, inhibit, or affect learning in any way. Not only must the learner's attitudes be considered, but also parental attitudes, social class, and emotional climate of the school and classroom should be considered important by behavioristic theories. Educators must infuse cognitive factors in their instructional programs in order to facilitate learning.
3. It must enable us to make reasonably accurate predictions about the outcome of learning activity. A learning theory is useful only to the extent that it enables us to make accurate predictions about learning. Most learning theories are concerned with success; few consider factors associated with failure. Both factors must be considered in the classroom. Educators need to know the factors associated with success as well as with failure so that effective instruction strategies can be conducted.
4. It must be a source of hypotheses, clues, and concepts that we can use to become more effective teachers. An adequate theory of learning should be dependable with ideas and insight that provide the

basis for a variety of approaches to the solution of the teaching–learning process. Learning theories should provide educators with a variety of approaches to promote learning in students.

5. It must be a source of hypotheses or informed hunches about learning that can be tested through classroom experimentation and research, thus extending our understanding of the teaching–learning process. Classroom experimentation and other kinds of research offer the means where ideas about learning and new techniques can be tested for their validity and practicality. Educators should consider the classroom as a learning laboratory where experiments with various strategies, methods, theoretical constructs, and theories are conducted to validate effective teaching and classroom management techniques (Lindgren, 1967).

SOME PREDICTIONS

Cognitive strategies outlined in chapters 11 to 14 were considered by behaviorists to be subjective and outside of the scope of empirical research. Today, theories and hypotheses testing show that these strategies have deepened our understanding of human learning and behavior. Cognitive theories and strategies have stood the test of time, and it is projective that empirical research will continue to validate the importance of these processes.

Traditional theories used to differentiate and define human behavior will become more marginalized and unified and will provide ways in which human behavior will be described as flexible and interactive, rather than remain as separate theories. The field of neuroscience will have a significant impact on unifying theories of learning by providing new research and information about the mind and learning.

BIBLIOGRAPHY

Amsel, A. 1989. *Behaviorism, Neobehaviorism, and Cognitivism in Learning Theory: Historical and Contemporary Perspectives*. Hillsdale, N.J.: Erlbaum.

Baddeley, A. D., and G. J. Hitch. 1974. "Working Memory." In *The Psychology of Learning and Motivation*, ed. G. Bower. New York: Academic.

Bandura, A. 1977. *Social Learning Theory*. Englewood Cliffs, N.J.: Prentice Hall.

Hergenhahn, B. R., and M. H. Olson. 1997. *An Introduction to Theories of Learning*. Upper Saddle River, N.J.: Prentice Hall.

Lindgren, H. S. 1967. *Educational Psychology in the Classroom*. New York: Wiley.

Newell, A. 1990. *Unified Theories of Cognition*. Cambridge, Mass.: Harvard University Press.

Ormrod, J. E. 1999. *Human Learning*. 3rd ed. Columbus, Ohio: Merrill.

Sprenger, M. 1999. *Learning and Memory: The Brain in Action*. Alexandria, Va.: Association for Supervision and Curriculum Development.

Thomas, L. M. 1992. *Comparing Theories of Child Development*. 3rd ed. Belmont, Calif.: Wadsworth.

———. 1996. *Comparing Theories of Child Development*. 4th ed. Belmont, Calif.: Wadsworth.

Glossary

Accommodation—Modification of an activity or ability in the face of environmental demands. In Jean Piaget's description of development, assimilation and accommodation are the means by which individuals interact with and adapt to their world.

Acquisition—In conditioning theories, "acquisition" is sometimes used interchangeably with the term "learning." It might be used to signify the formation of associations among stimuli or between responses and their consequences.

Adaptation—Changes in an organism in response to the environment. Such changes are assumed to facilitate interaction with that environment. Adaptation plays a central role in Jean Piaget's theory.

Amino acids—Fast-action neurotransmitters that include gamma-aminobutyric acid (**GABA**) and glutamate.

Assimilation—The act of incorporating objects or aspects of objects into previously learned activities. To assimilate is, in a sense, to ingest or to use for something that is previously learned.

Behaviorism—The school of psychology founded by John B. Watson. The behaviorist believed that the proper subject matter is behavior, not mental events.

Behavior management—The deliberate and systematic application of psychological principles in an attempt to change behavior. Behavior management programs are most often based largely on behavioristic principles.

Behavior modification—The deliberate application of operant conditioning principles in an effort to change behavior.

Behavior therapy—The systematic application of Pavlovian procedures and ideas in an effort to change behavior.

Chaining—A Skinnerean explanation for the linking of sequence of responses through the action of discriminative stimuli that act as secondary reinforcers.

Chunking—A memory process whereby related items are grouped together into more easily remembered "chunks" (e.g., a prefix and four digits for a phone number, rather than seven unrelated numbers).

Classical conditioning—Involves the repeated pairing of two stimuli so that a previously neutral (conditioned) stimulus eventually elicits a response (conditioned response) similar to that originally elicited by a nonneutral (unconditioned) stimulus. Originally described by Ivan P. Pavlov.

Clinical method—An open-ended form of questions in which the researcher's questions are guided by the child's answers to previous questions.

Closure—A Gestalt principle referring to our tendency to perceive incomplete patterns as complete.

Cognitive strategies—The processes involved in learning and remembering. Cognitive strategies include procedures for identifying problems, selecting approaches to their solution, monitoring progress in solving problems, selecting approaches to their solution, monitoring progress in solving problems, and using feedback.

Cognitivism—A general term for approaches to theories of learning concerned with such intellectual events as problem solving, information processing, thinking, and imagining.

Combined schedule—A combination of various types of schedules of reinforcement.

Concept—An abstraction or representation of the common properties of events, objects, or experiences; an idea or notion.

Concrete operations—The third of Jean Piaget's four major stages, lasting from age seven or eight to approximately age eleven or twelve and characterized largely by the child's ability to deal with concrete problems and objects, or objects and problems easily imagined.

Conditioned response—A response elicited by a conditioned stimulus. In some obvious ways, a conditioned response resembles, but is not identical to, its corresponding unconditioned response.

Conditioned stimulus—A stimulus that initially does not elicit any response (or that elicits a global, orienting response) but that, as a function of being paired with an unconditioned stimulus and its response, acquires the capability of eliciting that same response.

Conditioning—A type of learning describable in terms of changing relationships between stimuli, responses, or both stimuli and responses.

Connectionism—Edward L. Thorndike's term for his theory of learning, based on the notion that learning is the formation of neural connections between stimuli and responses.

Conservation—A Piagetian term for the realization that certain quantitative attributes of objects remain unchanged unless something is added to or taken away from them. Such characteristics of objects as mass, number, area, and volume are capable of being conserved.

Continuous reinforcement—A reinforcement schedule in which every correct response is followed by a reinforcer.

Control group—In an experiment, a group comprising individuals as similar to those in the experimental group as possible except that they are not exposed to an experimental treatment.

Counterconditioning—A behavior modification technique in which stimuli associated with an undesirable response are presented below threshold or at times when the undesirable response is unlikely to occur. The object is to condition a desirable response to replace the undesirable one.

Decay theory—An explanation for loss of information in short-term memory based on the notion that the physiological effects of stimulation fade. Similar to fading in connection with forgetting in long-term memory.

Dependent variable—The variable that reflects the assumed effects of manipulations of the independent variable(s) in an experiment.

Discriminative stimulus—Burrhus F. Skinner's term for the features of a situation that an organism can discriminate to distinguish between occasions that might or might not be reinforced.

Elaboration—A memory strategy involving forming new associations. To elaborate is to link with other ideas or images.

Elicited response—A response brought about by a stimulus. The expression is synonymous with the term "respondent."

Episodic memory—A type of declarative, autobiographical (conscious, long-term) memory consisting of knowledge about personal experiences that are tied to specific times and places.

Equilibration—A Piagetian term for the process by which people maintain a balance with assimilation (changing behavior; learning new things). Equilibration is essential for adaptation and cognitive growth.

Experimental group—In an experiment, the group of participants who are exposed to a treatment (see **control group**).

Explicit memory—Type of memory associated with the hippocampus that involves memories of words, facts, and places.

Extinction—In classical conditioning, the cessation of a response following repeated presentations of the conditioned response without the unconditioned response. In operant conditioning, the cessation of a response follows the withdrawal of reinforcement.

Fading—A conditioning technique in which certain characteristics of stimuli are gradually faded out, eventually resulting in discriminations that did not originally exist.

Fading Theory—The belief that inability to recall in long-term memory increases with the passage of time as memory "traces" fade.

Fixed schedule—A type of intermittent schedule of reinforcement in which the reinforcement occurs at fixed intervals of time (an interval schedule) or after a specified number of trials (a ratio schedule) (see **continuous reinforcement**).

Forgetting loss from memory—May involve inability to retrieve, or might involve actual loss of whatever traces or changes define storage.

Formal operations—The last of Jean Piaget's four major stages. It begins around age eleven or twelve and lasts until age fourteen or fifteen. It is characterized by the child's increasing ability to use logical thought processes.

GABA (Gamma-aminobutyric acid)—A very prevalent inhibitory neurotransmitter.

Gestalt—A German word meaning "whole" or "configuration." Describes an approach to psychology concerned with the perception of wholes, insight and awareness. Gestalt psychology is a forerunner of contemporary cognitive psychology.

Higher mental processes—A general phrase to indicate unobservable processes that occur in the "mind."

Hippocampus—Structure located in the forebrain that catalogs long-term factual memories.

Hypothesis—An educated guess, often based on theory, that can be tested. A prediction based on partial evidence of some effect, process, or phenomenon, which must then be verified experimentally.

Implicit learning—Unconscious learning, not represented in symbols or analyzable with rules. Roughly equivalent to procedural or unconscious learning.

Implicit memory—Involuntary memory, such as the procedural, emotional, and automatic memories.

Independent variable—The variable that is manipulated in an experiment to see if it causes changes in the dependent variable. The "if" part of the if-then equation implicit in an experiment (see **dependent variable**).

Information processing—Relates to how information is modified (or processed), resulting in knowledge, perception, or behavior. A dominant model of the cognitive approaches, it makes extensive use of computer metaphors.

Insight—The perception of relationships among elements of a problem situation. A problem solving method that contracts strongly with trial and error. The cornerstone of Gestalt psychology.

Intermittent reinforcement—A schedule of renforcement that does not present a reinforcer for all correct responses (see **interval schedule, ratio schedule**).

Internalization—A Piagetian concept referring to the processes by which activities, objects, and events in the real world become represented mentally.

Interval schedule—An intermittent schedule of reinforcement based on the passage of time (see **fixed schedule**).

Law of Effect—A Thorndikean law of learning stating that the effect of a response leads to its being learned (stamped in) or not learned (stamped out).

Law of Exercise—One of Thorndike's laws of learning, basic to his pre-1930s system but essentially repudiated later. It maintained that the more frequently, recently, and vigorously a connection was exercised, the stronger it would be.

Law of Multiple Responses—Law based on Thorndike's observation that learning involves the emission of a variety of responses. Often referred to as a theory of trial-and-error learning.

Law of Prepotency of Elements—A Thorndikean law of learning stating that people tend to respond to the most striking of the various elements that make up a stimulus situation.

Law of Readiness—A Thorndikean law of learning that takes into account the fact that certain types of learning are impossible or difficult unless the learner is ready. In this context, readiness refers to maturational level, previous learning, motivational factors, and other characteristics of the individual that relate to learning.

Learning—All relatively permanent changes in behavior that result from experience, but that are not due to fatigue, maturation, drugs, injury, or disease.

Learning Theory—A systematic attempt to explain and understand how behavior changes. The phrase "behavior theory" is used synonymously.

Long-term memory—Process by which the brain stores information for a long period of time.

Memory—The physiological effects of experience, reflected in changes that define learning. Includes both storage and retrieval. Nothing can be retrieved from memory that has not been stored, but not all that is stored can be retrieved.

Motivation—The causes of behavior. The conscious or unconscious forces that lead to certain acts.

Negative reinforcement—An increase in the probability that a response will recur following the elimination or removal of a condition as a consequences(s) of the behavior. Negative reinforcement ordinarily takes the form of an unpleasant or noxious stimulus that is removed as a result of a specific response.

Nervous system—The part of the body that is made up of neurons. Its major components are the brain and the spinal cord (the central nervous system), receptor systems associated with major senses, and effector systems associated with functioning of muscles and glands.

Neural network—A connectionist model of brain functioning premised on the functioning of the parallel distributed processing computer. Neural networks are complex arrangements of units that activate each other, thereby modifying patterns of connections. In this model, meaning resides in patterns within the network, and responses are also determined by patterns.

Neuron—A single nerve cell, the basic building block of the human nervous system. Neurons consist of four main parts: cell body, nucleus, dendrite, and axon.

Neurotransmitter—Chemical produced in a neuron that carries information in the brain.

Norepinephrine—Neurotransmitter associated with alertness.

Operant—Skinnerean term for a response not elicited by any known or obvious stimulus. Most significant human behaviors appear to be operants.

Operant conditioning—The process of changing behavior by manipulating its consequences. Most of Burrhus F. Skinner's work investigates the principles of operant conditioning.

Parsimonious—Avoiding excessive and confusing detail and complexity. Parsimonious theories explain all important relationships in the simplest, briefest manner possible.

Population—Collections of individuals (or objects or situations) with similar characteristics. For example, the population of all first-grade children in North America (see **sample**).

Positive reinforcement—An increase in the probability that a response will recur as a result of a positive consequence(s) resulting from that behavior (i.e., as a result of the addition of something). Usually takes the form of a pleasant stimulus (reward) that results from a specific response.

Positive reinforcer—An event added to a situation immediately after a response has occurred that increases the probability that the response will recur. Usually takes the form of a pleasant stimulus (reward) that results from a specific response.

Pragnanz—A German word meaning "good form." An overriding Gestalt principle that maintains that what we perceive (and think) tends to take the best possible form where "best" usually refers to a principle such as closure.

Preconceptual thinking—The first substage in the period of preoperational thought, beginning around age two and lasting until age four. It is so called because the child has not yet developed the ability to classify.

Premack Principle—The recognition that behaviors that are chosen frequently by an individual (and that are therefore favored) may be used to reinforce other, less frequently chosen behaviors.

Preoperational thinking—The second of Jean Piaget's four major stages, lasting from around age two to age seven, characterized by certain weaknesses in the child's logic. It consists of two substages: intuitive thinking and preconceptual thinking.

Primary reinforcer—An event that is reinforcing in the absence of any learning. Stimuli such as food and drink are primary reinforcers because, presumably, an organism does not have to learn that they are pleasant.

Ratio schedule—An intermittent schedule of reinforcement that is based on a proportion of correct responses (see **fixed schedule**).

Reflex—A simple, unlearned stimulus–response link, such as salivating in response to food in one's mouth or blinking in response to air blowing into one's eye.

Refractory period—A brief period after firing during which a neuron is "discharged" and is incapable of firing again.

Rehearsal—A memory strategy involving simple repetition. The principal means of maintaining items in short-term memory.

Reinforcement—The effect of a reinforcer; specifically, to increase the probability that a response will occur.

Respondent—Skinnerean term for a response that (unlike an operant) is elicited by a known, specific stimulus. Unconditioned responses are examples of respondents (see **unconditioned response**).

Sample—A subset of a population. A representative selection of individuals with similar characteristics drawn from a larger group. For example, a sample comprising 1 percent of all first-grade children in North America (see **population**).

Schedule of reinforcement—The timing and frequency of a presentation of reinforcement to organisms (see **continuous reinforcement**).

Schema—The label used by Jean Piaget to describe a unit in cognitive structure. A schema is, in one sense, an activity together with whatever biology or neurology that might underlie that activity. In another sense, a schema may be thought of as an idea or a concept.

Science—An approach and an attitude toward knowledge that emphasize objectivity, precision, and replicability. Also, one of several related bodies of knowledge.

Secondary reinforcer—An event that becomes reinforcing as a result of being paired with other reinforcers.

Sensorimotor intelligence—The first stage of development in Jean Piaget's classification. It lasts from birth to approximately age two and is so called because children understand their world during this period primarily in terms of their activities in it and sensations of it.

Sensory memory—The simple sensory recognition of such stimuli as a sound, a taste, or a sight. Also called short-term sensory storage.

Shaping—A technique for training animals and people to perform behaviors not previously in their repertoires. It involves reinforcing responses that are progressively closer approximations to the desired behavior.

Short-term memory—Also called primary or working memory; a type of memory in which material is available for recall for a matter of seconds. Short-term memory primarily involves rehearsal, rather than more in-depth processing. It defines our immediate consciousness.

Significant—In research, refers to findings that would not be expected to occur by chance alone by more than a small percentage (e.g., 5 percent or 1 percent) of the time.

Skinnerean Box—One of various experimental environments used by Burrhus F. Skinner in his investigations of operant conditioning. The typical Skinnerean Box is a cage-like structure equipped with a lever and a food tray attached to a food-delivering mechanism.

Social learning—The acquisition of patterns of behavior that conform to social expectations; learning what is and is not acceptable in a given culture.

Structure—A term used by Jean Piaget in reference to cognitive structure in effect, the individual's mental representations that include knowledge of things as well as knowledge of how to do things.

Theory—A body of information pertaining to a specific topic that makes sense out of a large number of observations and indicates to the researcher other factors to explore.

Token—Something indicative of something else. In behavior management programs, token reinforcement systems consist of objects like disks or point tallies that are themselves worthless but later can be exchanged for more meaningful reinforcement.

Trial and error—Thorndikean explanation for learning based on the idea that when placed in a problem situation, an individual will emit a number of responses but will eventually learn the correct one as a result of reinforcement.

Unconditioned response—A response that is elicited by an unconditioned stimulus.

Unconditioned stimulus—A stimulus that elicits a response prior to learning. All stimuli that are capable of eliciting reflexive behaviors are examples of unconditioned stimuli. For example, food is an unconditioned stimulus for the response to salivation.

Variable—A property, measurement, or characteristic that can vary from one situation to another. In psychological investigations, qualities such as intelligence, sex, personality, age, and so on can be important variables.

About the Author

George R. Taylor is a professor and the head of the Department of Special Education at Coppin State College and Core Faculty at the Union Institute. He received a bachelor's degree in elementary education in 1959 from Fayetteville State University, and master's and doctoral degrees in educational psychology and special education in 1967 and 1969 from the Catholic University of America. Dr. Taylor taught and chaired the Department of Special Education for thirty years. He has written numerous articles for professional journals and is author of the following books: *Basic Guides for Administrators* (1972), *Educational Strategies and Services for Exceptional Children* (1976), *Curriculum Strategies for Teaching Social Skills to the Disabled: Dealing with Inappropriate Behaviors* (1998), *Curriculum Models and Strategies for Educating Individuals with Disabilities in Inclusive Classrooms* (1999), and *Parental Involvement: A Model for Collaboration and Teamwork* (2000), all from Charles C Thomas.

Books published by other companies: *Curriculum Strategies: Social Skills Intervention for Young African-American Males* (Greenwood, 1997), *Integrating Quantitative and Qualitative Research Methods* (University Press, 2000), *Developing Individualized Programs: Strategies and Perspectives* (Mellon Press [forthcoming]).

DATE DUE

MR 31 '04			
OC 28 '04			
JA 04 '06			
OC 25 '06			
AG 07 '07			
JUN 1 ~ 2000			